To Enrol or not to Enrol in Community Health Insurance

Challenges in Public Health

Editor: Prof. Dr. Oliver Razum, Bielefeld

Formerly/früher: Medizin in Entwicklungsländern
Herausgegeben von
Prof. Dr. Hans Jochen Diesfeld, Heidelberg

Band 52

PETER LANG
Frankfurt am Main · Berlin · Bern · Bruxelles · New York · Oxford · Wien

Manuela De Allegri

To Enrol or not to Enrol in Community Health Insurance

Case Study from Burkina Faso

PETER LANG
Internationaler Verlag der Wissenschaften

Bibliographic Information published by the Deutsche Nationalbibliothek
The Deutsche Nationalbibliothek lists this publication in the Deutsche Nationalbibliografie; detailed bibliographic data is available in the internet at <http://www.d-nb.de>.

Zugl.: Heidelberg, Univ., Diss., 2006

Cover design: Atelier Platen

D 16
ISSN 1863-768X
ISBN 978-3-631-56460-8

www.peterlang.de

To my parents,
For sending me to study in Africa
When I was only seventeen

and

To the people of Nouna
For opening their homes and their hearts to me

Preface of Prof. Oliver Razum

The Challenge of Equitable and Inclusive Health Insurance in Africa

Every year, 10.6 million children are dying before their 5th birthday. Of the 20 countries with the highest under-5 mortality rates, 19 are located in sub-Saharan Africa (Black et al. 2003). World-wide, under-5 mortality declined from 147/1000 life births in 1970 to about 80/1000 in 2002. This decline, however, was least pronounced in Africa. Worse still, in 16 countries, under-5 mortality started to increase again after 1990 – of these, 14 are African countries, among them Angola, South Africa, Central African Republic and Zimbabwe (Prüss-Üstün et al. 2006).

Newborns in sub-Saharan Africa have 29 times the risk of dying before their 5th birthday compared to newborns in industrialised countries. It is estimated that at least 60 % of the deaths among African children can be avoided by relatively simple interventions that could – in principle – be made available everywhere (Reitmaier et al. 2006). There are few other examples of inequities in our world that are more dramatic and, at the same time, are affecting more individuals.

What can be done to amend this situation? Many of the interventions that are available do not reach those most in need – the part of the population with the lowest income and living in the farthest-off regions (WHO 2005; Wagstaff et al. 2004). An example for such an intervention is the Integrated Management of Childhood Illness (IMCI) strategy. It does, in theory, address the needs of the poor. However, actual coverage is far from universal. IMCI is often implemented first in the easier-to-reach, better-off-districts and then not scaled up, not the least because basic financial infrastructure and trained staff are lacking (Gwatkin 2006).

Universal coverage requires not only increasing the supply of services and the development of human resources (which includes decent remuneration of health care providers). An equally important step is to eliminate financial barriers to access and to provide financial protection against household catastrophic health expenditure (WHO 2005; Wagstaff et al. 2004).

User fees turned out to create substantial financial barriers towards uptake of health care interventions, while contributing little towards improving service quality. By now, there is ample evidence that priority should be given towards making health services less expensive (Wagstaff et al. 2004). A promising step to achieve this goal is to set up pre-payment or pooling schemes. Such financial protection systems need to be inclusive for all population groups, including the poor. A prerequisite for setting up an inclusive system is to understand why people choose to enrol, or not to enrol, in prepayment or pooling schemes.

Manuela De Allegri took up this challenge as her research topic. She investigated the decision to enrol in community health insurance (CHI) in rural Burkina Faso, a low-income region even by the standards of sub-Saharan Africa. Her findings show that people are willing to consider the concept of health insurance. The decision to enrol is, however, not entirely that of an individual household but mediated by community circumstances. Thus, health insurance schemes need to be flexible in order to meet community preferences. Previous negative experiences, be it with insurance schemes or with the availability and quality of health care provided, discourage uptake. This observation confirms that merely setting up a CHI scheme will not suffice: in parallel, the health system needs to be developed.

What else can we do to reduce childhood mortality? As WHO sums it up in the Word Health Report 2005, it boils down to providing more money (WHO 2005). To improve child health care, "First, increased funding is required to pay for building up the services toward universal access. Second, financial protection systems have to be built at the same time as access improves". Thus, besides pooling/prepayment schemes, new mechanisms to add to global health financing have to be developed. These could include e.g. taxing currency transactions (the so-called Tobin Tax) and airline tickets (Kickbusch & Lister 2006).

Manuela De Allegri has made a substantial addition to the body of knowledge supporting the introduction of equitable and inclusive health insurance in sub-Saharan Africa. Her work will be of interest not only to the people of Nouna/Burkina Faso, but also to many other communities of the continent. If applied well, her findings will contribute to improving the health of many children and their families.

Prof. Oliver Razum

Series Editor, Challenges in Public Health

Dept. of Epidemiology & International Public Health
Bielefeld School of Public Health
Bielefeld University
Germany

References

Black RE, Morris SS & Bryce J (2003) Where and why are 10 million children dying every year? The Lancet 361, 2226-2234.

Gwatkin DR (2006) IMCI: what can we learn from an innovation that didn't reach the poor? Bulletin of the World Health Organization 84, 768.

Kickbusch I & Lister G (2006) European Perspectives on Global Health. A Policy Glossary. Brussels, European Foundation Centre.

Prüss-Üstün A, Stein C & Zeeb H (2006) Globale Krankheitslast: Daten, Trends und Methoden. In: Globalisierung – Gerechtigkeit – Gesundheit. Einführung in International Public Health. Eds. Razum O, Zeeb H & Laaser U. Huber, Bern, pp. 27-42.

Reitmaier P, Ziehm D & Razum O (2006) Kindersterblichkeit. In: Globalisierung – Gerechtigkeit – Gesundheit. Einführung in International Public Health. Eds. Razum O, Zeeb H & Laaser U. Huber, Bern, pp.223-231.

Wagstaff A, Bustreo F, Bryce J & Claeson M (2004) Child health: reaching the poor. American Journal of Public Health 94, 726-736.

WHO (2005) The World Health Report 2005: Make every mother and child count. Eds. Van Lerberghe W, Manuel A, Matthews Z & Wolfheim C. Geneva, WHO.

Preface of Prof. Rainer Sauerborn

This book shows a remarkable example of how health systems research can and should be carried out in developing countries. There are four requirements for excellent health systems research. Manuela de Allegri succeeded in fulfilling them all convincingly. In the following, I am going to illustrate how the author achieved this.

First, as with all research, we would expect that health systems research is technically excellent and meets high ethical standards of all countries involved. The study passed the ethic committees of both the Heidelberg Medical Faculty and the Comité d'Ethique of the Centre de Recherche en Santé in Nouna. As to the scientific quality, the author's publication record is the best guide: her doctoral dissertation yielded no fewer than 6 international peer-reviewed publications and achieved the highest distinction for doctoral dissertations Heidelberg University awards: summa cum laude.

Second, research should be relevant, for both the target community and for the district and national decision-makers. Access to health care for the poor is certainly one of the key challenges in health sector reform in most middle and low income countries, Oliver Razum pointed out in his foreword. But the fact that a piece of research works on a relevant topic is only a necessary, but not sufficient condition.

Third, health systems research should have a real impact on policies and eventually on the lives of the local population. Bertold Brecht expressed this both simply and powerfully: "Wissenschaft dient dazu, das Los der Menschen zu verbessern (Brecht, Das Leben des Galilei). Manuela showed the barriers that prevent households to enrol in a locally adapted and designed health insurance. Some factors were expected (low education, extreme poverty) others came to a surprise, such as the lack of ownership of the health care providers in the study area. The author's research and how it was fed back into the decision-making process were crucial for this to happen. I have witnessed how often the stakeholders referred to and used Manuela's results. This happened at all system levels: community: the "Comité de Pilotage" of the Insurance Association, (ii) the district health team, and (iii) the steering committee of Ministry of Health overseeing the research and its translation into national policy. This discussion has led to several changes in the implementation strategy. Manuela's findings of the lack of ownership the nurses felt vis-à-vis the insurance scheme have generated an intensified effort on the part of the district health team to win over the hearts of the nurses for the CBI-scheme. While nurses had been at best sceptical and at worst resisting the insurance scheme, they have now become

(2006/2007) the key agents to advertise for the insurance scheme in a village-to-village sensitization campaign, which is on its way as this book goes to print.

Fourth, we would like to see the choice of methods be consonant with the research question. The complex factors influencing health systems and their stakeholders from household to professional actors can often only be captured by combining quantitative and qualitative methods. Much research is like the proverbial hammer (method) that looks for a nail (study question). Manuela has used both approaches in a creative and very rigorous professional way. She trained in multilevel regression analysis to tease out the effects of individual, household and community variables which influence in a complex web the decision of the household head to enrol his family in community insurance. She applied the same methodological rigor to the qualitative study: an explicit sampling strategy ("factorial design"), an open almost artful interviewing technique and a rigorous qualitative analysis based on coded text which emanates from Strauss`s concept of "Grounded theory" belie the prejudice that qualitative analysis is "only" intuitive and can't be reproduced. Unfortunately much research using both qualitative and quantitative methods treats them strangely disconnected, both in analysis and in the discussion. Manuela managed to not only use, but combine the two approaches and showed that indeed the whole insight gained is more than the sum of both individual study approaches could have generated. As an example, the passive resistance of the nurses as a key factor confusing and discouraging the population to enrol would not have been easily picked up through household surveys. On the other hand, the consistently negative relationship between income quintile and enrolment probability could not have been shown as clearly and convincingly by using only in-depth qualitative interview techniques.

I trust the reader will enjoy both the work on the specific topic and how it is achieved in such a masterful way.

Prof. Rainer Sauerborn

Chair of the Department of Tropical Hygiene and Public Health
Faculty of Medicine
University of Heidelberg
Germany

Acknowledgements

This book is based on the dissertation which I completed as a requirement for obtaining my doctoral degree. Many people have contributed to making this research possible and although I ultimately wrote the manuscript on my own, I would have never been able to do so without their constant support, advice, and contribution to the overall research project.

First and foremost, I would like to express my sincere gratitude to the two people who guided me through the process of completing my dissertation: my academic supervisor, Prof. Rainer Sauerborn, and Dr. Bocar Kouyaté from the Centre de Recherche en Santé de Nouna. With them, I wish to thank the German Research Foundation (DFG) for supporting, within the framework of the SFB 544 on "The control of tropical infectious diseases", the study presented in this manuscript. Without the DFG financial support, my work would have never been possible.

During these three years, Prof. Sauerborn took care of building my academic character, always expecting the best and constantly encouraging me to conduct applied research abiding to the highest scientific standards. Dr. Kouyaté took care of building my Burkinabè character, making sure that I could successfully carry out my work in Burkina Faso and progressively helping me to become an "adopted" member of his team at the CRSN.

My special thanks go to Prof. Heiko Becher for building on my quantitative skills. I am grateful to him for allowing me to attend the post-graduate training program in Epidemiology and Public Health, but especially for always finding some time for individual tutoring whenever I was stuck on some piece of analysis. With him, I wish to thank his team, in particular Dr. Gael Hammer, Gisela Kynast-Wolf and Gabriele Stieglbauer, for all the times I just rushed into their offices with a question to be answered.

Special thanks also to Dr. Olaf Müller for taking me to be part of his team even before I had formally completed my doctorate. I am grateful to him for his support, for the time he allowed me to devote to my pending commitments, and for his confidence in my ability to engage in a new project while still completing my dissertation.

A very special thank you also goes to Prof. Steffen Flessa and to Dr. Hengjin Dong. Both of them saw the birth of my dissertation and supported me in a thousand different ways as I struggled to complete my work.

Thanks to Dr. John Bridges, who joined the Department once my doctoral work was already on its way towards an end. I am grateful to him for his challenging comments, which always encouraged me to question my own work to improve its quality.

A substantial contribution to my dissertation came from the comments of my peers, fellow doctoral students. I value our conversations as one of the most precious elements of the years spent in Heidelberg. As we completed our work and moved away in different directions, I will miss greatly all of them: Tin Tin Su, Anayo Akunne, Yazoumé Yé, Catherine Kyobutungi, Subhash Pokhrel, Malabika Sarker, Karolin Pfeiffer, and Budi Hidayat. I also wish to thank Dr. Mamadou Mariko for his support and friendship, and Dr. Valerie Louis for reading through my long manuscript to ensure that even those not familiar with the topic could follow my argument.

I also wish to thank everyone else both within the Department of Tropical Hygiene and Public Health and the SFB 544 broader research team. In one way or another in fact, through a word said at the right time or through a brief encounter in Nouna, many single persons in these teams made their contributions towards my work, even by simply making my experience as a foreigner in Germany easier and more pleasurable. In particular, I wish to thank all the people who helped me make sense of a complex foreign bureaucracy providing constant administrative support: Martina Weiss, Renate Deckner, Katharina Sommer, Angela Wende-Minch, Elke Braun, Anke Nitschke-Edert, and Deborah Douglas. A special thank you also to the two librarians, Ingo Glucker and Dietmar Fleischer, for always getting the one book or the one article I could not find myself. Special thanks also to Sandra Dannenberg, who has patiently assisted me in formatting this manuscript for wider publication.

I wish to thank the entire staff of the CRSN for their warm welcome and for always making me feel part of their team and truly at home. Our research has required the collaboration of so many interviewers, data entry clerks, transcribers, and translators that thanking each one individually is impossible. In my heart, however, I am grateful to each one of them personally.

Among the staff at the CRSN, my special thanks go to Mamadou Sanon, so to say, my partner in crime, the one person with whom I have worked most closely during my doctoral years. I am grateful to him for sharing with me his knowledge of the local culture and for always making our time together pleasurable, telling me old Burkinabè customs and stories. Thinking back on the time of my doctorate, I will recall lots of heated discussions between us, but also great laughs over a Burkinabè dinner or a German soccer match.

Special thanks also to Adjima Gbangou, Cheik Bagagnan, and Alphonse Zagané for their tiresome work on the household survey. I am grateful to each one of them for the promptness in answering my queries every time I incurred in a problem with the data. My very special thanks also go to late Dr. Florent Somé, who assumed the leadership of the insurance project towards the end of my dissertation. Although we did not work together extensively, I had enough time to learn to appreciate his effectiveness and his admirable negotiating skills. His unexpected premature death left an empty space for all of us working in Nouna.

Very special thanks to Yemalé Ghislain Tiawara, Mèma Sanogo, and Rahinata Bagagnan of the Assurance Maladie à Base Communautaire de Nouna (AMBC) and to Dr. Maurice Yé of the Nouna Health District. Our research has been possible only because of their hard work implementing the insurance scheme. I am grateful to them for their commitment to overcome any obstacle on the way to seeing our common dream, that of facilitating access to health care through insurance, realised.

Outside the CRSN, but still in the town of Nouna, many thanks to the sociologist who acted as my translator, Aline Bagayoyo, and to my Dioula teachers, Helen and Moussa Traoré. I am grateful to the three of them for their support in helping me make sense of the local language and culture, but also for their story-telling skills, which enhanced my understanding of the local context. With them, I also wish to thank the entire staff of the Association Tontine Nouna for their support while conducting our qualitative research.

Beyond the boundary of both Germany and Burkina Faso, I wish to express my very special thanks to Dr. Rosanna Tarricone from Università Luigi Bocconi in Milan. I am grateful to her not only for commenting extensively on some portions of my thesis, but also and most importantly for having encouraged me to pursue an academic career and engage in a PhD program. I also wish to thank Prof. Elio Borgonovi and Prof. Giovanni Fattore, also from Università Luigi Bocconi, for the distant support they have shown at different time during these three years.

As I wrote this manuscript, I came to see how much I still owe to my undergraduate instructors. Time after time, I looked back at some old notes or referred to some old lectures when trying to make sense of the events observed in Nouna and described in this dissertation. Although they may not even know that I have gone as far as completing my PhD, my heart is truly full of gratitude for the four people who initiated me to research and who constantly told me, starting my very first year in college, that I should consider no other career if not one in academics: Prof. Judith Porter, Prof. Robert Washington, Prof. David Karen, and Prof. Mary Osirim, all from Bryn Mawr College in the United States.

Last but surely not least, I wish to thank my friends … scattered between Germany, Italy, Burkina Faso, the United States, and everywhere else in the world. Without their constant emotional support, this manuscript would have never been completed. Out of fear of forgetting some, I will not mention any name, but my friends ought to know that they are all in my heart and that I am grateful to each one of them. I hope to be forgiven for all the times when they saw me stressed, in a bad mood, or did not dedicate to them the attention they deserved.

Finally, my biggest thanks go to my family, both old and new. My old family is made up of my parents, their spouses, my grandparents, and my very special younger brother Stefano who has often saved me from computer trouble during these years. I am grateful to all of them for always having encouraged me to pursue my dreams and to believe that I could attain anything I aimed at. I am grateful to my family for bearing the distance between us and having accepted rare visits at home during these years. My new family is made up of my husband, Dr. Uli Ronellenfitsch, and his entire family entourage, all living in and around Heidelberg. I am grateful to Uli and to all his family for their endless support during these difficult years. Having met Uli at the Department, I cannot help being grateful to this institution not only for having accompanied me in the beginning of my academic career, but also for having helped me to found my own family.

Table of contents

List of abbreviations

AMBC	Assurance Maladie à Base Communautaire de la Province de la Kossi
ATN	Association Tontines de Nouna
CAD	Centre Africain pour une Pratique Culturelle du Développement
CAMEG	Essential Generic Drugs and Medical Consumables Purchasing Pool
CHI	Community health insurance
COGES	Comité de Gestion
CRSN	Centre de Recherche en Santé de Nouna
CSPS	Centre de Santé et Promotion Social
DSS	Demographic surveillance system
FGD	Focus group discussion
GDP	Gross domestic product
GTZ	Deutsche Gesellschaft für Technische Zusammenarbeit
HMOs	Health maintenance organisations
ILO	International Labour Organisation
IMF	International Monetary Fund
NHDHS	Nouna Health District Household Survey
NGO	Non-governmental organisation
OR	Odds ratio
PROMUSAF	Programme d'Appui aux Mutuelles de Santé en Afrique
RAMS	Réseau d'Appui aux Mutuelles de Santé
SE	Standard error
WHO	World Health Organisation
WTP	Willingness to pay

List of figures

List of tables

1. Introduction

1.1 Background and problem statement

1.1.1 The problem of access to health care services

Every year across sub-Saharan Africa millions of people, many of which children, die because they lack access to basic health care. These people suffer from conditions, such as malaria, diarrhoea, or respiratory-tract infections, for which treatment has long been available. Still, they have no access to such treatment. The World Health Organisation (WHO), for example, has estimated that 92% of all deaths from communicable diseases in low income countries are in "excess" and are largely due to failures on the part of health systems to guarantee adequate access to the available treatment (World Health Organisation 2000a). Across sub-Saharan nations in fact, health service utilisation rates do not match the need for medical care and rarely even attain 0.5 per capita per year (Raberg and Jeene 2002; Stierle et al. 1999). This figure is well below the minimum of 2.0 visits per capita per year recommended by the WHO (World Health Organisation 2001). Low utilisation of health services remains therefore a serious concern in sub-Saharan Africa, as elsewhere in low income settings, where it is found to be responsible for the greatest loss of potentially effective treatment (Krause and Sauerborn 2000).

Both the World Health Report 2000 (World Health Organisation 2000a) and the report on Macroeconomics and Health (Sachs 2001) recently reinforced how reductions in mortality and improvements in health status are not possible unless and until health systems develop in such a way as to remove what substantial barriers to access continue to exist in most low income settings. The World Health Report 2000 put forward a framework for reform, explicitly encouraging the application of multi-facet interventions targeting all aspects of the health care system. The report recognised that improvements in health status can only be generated if countries commit themselves to a synergy of reforms. One aspect calling for reform across several low income countries is the financing of services. The Report called for a greater commitment towards ensuring greater fairness in the financial contribution of citizens, promoting the enhancement of risk- pooling and risk-management. The report envisioned reforms in the financing of the health care system as an essential step towards securing better health through expanded access to quality services and increased financial protection of households.

Community health insurance (CHI) has been recognised as a valuable alternative to prior systems of health financing in low and middle income settings, most notably user fees. Through the pooling of risks and resources in fact, CHI appears to allow low-income populations to gain better access to health services and to enjoy a higher degree of financial protection against the cost of illness. As such, CHI is expected to induce substantial improvements in health status.

In order to understand the emergence of CHI in sub-Saharan Africa and the problems relevant to its implementation, i.e. elements which constitute the focus of this dissertation, we first need to take a step back and consider the shortcoming of the prior prevailing health financing arrangement, i.e. cost-recovery through user fees.

Figure 1.1: Functions and objectives of the health system (Source: World Health Organisation, 2000a)

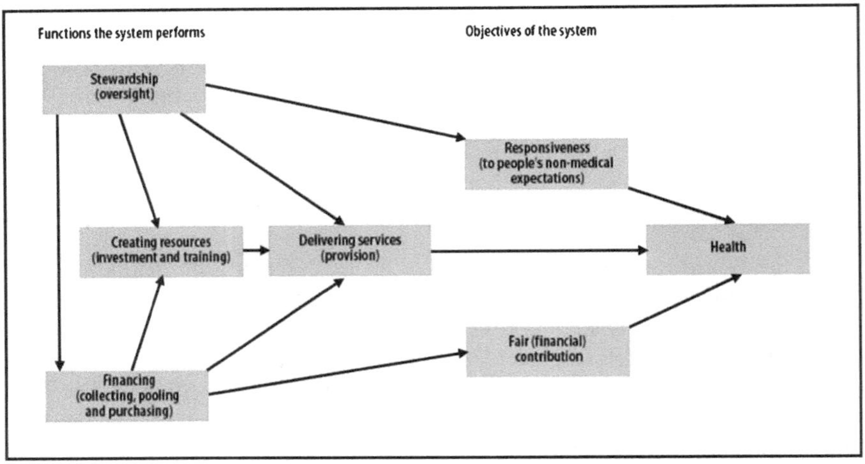

1.1.2 User fees in sub-Saharan Africa

1.1.2.1 Health care financing in sub-Saharan Africa: from free care to user fees

Following their independence, most countries in sub-Saharan Africa retained hope to be able to provide health care free of charge to their populations. For years, governments attempted to finance curative and preventive care both in urban and rural areas, offering services almost free of charge to their populations. Since its inception, however, such strategy proved to be problematic. Budgets allocated to the health care sector were insufficient to meet the cost of services. In addition, resources were often unevenly and inefficiently allocated, with more than 80% of the total health budget allocated to staff salaries and almost all the operating budget allocated to central hospitals (Soucat et al. 1997). The effect of such financing policies was reflected in the reality of everyday service provision. Many sub-Saharan countries experienced a striking urban bias in terms of health staff supply. Carrin noted, for example, that in Senegal as many as 70% of all physicians were employed in urban facilities (Carrin and Vereecke 1992). In addition, he noted that between 1.3 and 2.5 billion people lacked regular access to essential drugs because of the shortages induced in the rural facilities by the insufficient and uneven allocation of resources within the health care sector (Carrin and Vereecke 1992).

In the 1980s, the situation further deteriorated as health sector budgets declined in response to the severe macro-economic problems experienced by most sub-Saharan countries. At the same time, population growth, increasing successful social mobilisation, and the emergence of the AIDS epidemic were inducing an increase in the demand for health service, which the system was unable to meet (Korte et al. 1992; McPake et al. 1993). Per capita health expenditure in sub-Saharan Africa decreased from 5.17 US dollars in 1980 to 4.70 US dollars in 1985 (adjusted for declining purchasing power parity) (Korte et al. 1992). In many countries, this situation produced a severe crisis in the health sector with health staff not receiving salaries, critical shortages in drug supplies, and equipment and vehicles awaiting repair for long periods (McPake et al. 1993). Drug budgets were in some instances cut by 50% (Korte et al. 1992).

In response to national budget cuts, some experiments in self-financing of health services at the community level began to surface across West and Central Africa. Examples of such financing arrangements are the Kasongo project in the Democratic Republic of Congo, the Pikine Project in Senegal, and the Shomulu clinic in Lagos. These projects were financed by a combination of bilateral and non-governmental donor support and the implementation of cost-recovery schemes, imposing charges for the purchase of drugs and progressively leading to the establishment of revolving drug funds (Soucat et al. 1997).

The emergence of cost-recovery schemes in response to the health sector crisis was soon institutionalized through two separate, although parallel, events. On one side, a meeting of African Ministries of Health sponsored by WHO and UNICEF in 1987 launched the Bamako Initiative (McPake et al. 1993). On the other side, given the overall deteriorating economic situation, the World Bank and the International Monetary Fund (IMF) imposed structural adjustment policies on many sub-Saharan countries (Korte et al. 1992; Sekwat 2003). Structural adjustment policies were recommended by the World Bank and the IMF to address unsustainable macroeconomic imbalances. They entailed structural changes which imposed a shift from the public to the private sector (Korte et al. 1992). Although rooted in different philosophical approaches, in practice, the Bamako Initiative and the structural adjustment policies led to very similar health sector reforms and marked the large-scale introduction of user fees across the continent.

The Bamako Initiative promoted the introduction of user fees within the framework of the African experience of poor primary care. Not having been able to achieve the goals set by the Alma Ata Conference of 1978 because of insufficient resources, African Ministries of Health saw in the Bamako Initiative an opportunity to accelerate and strengthen the large-scale implementation of primary health care, aiming to achieve universal accessibility to these services (Gilson 1997; Gilson et al. 2001; Korte et al. 1992). The Bamako Initiative sought to achieve its goal through three main strategies: (1) the decentralisation of decision making including the empowerment of community members in managing primary health care activities; (2) the implementation of user-financing of health services under community control; and (3) the provision of essential drugs within the framework of a national drug policy and through the establishment of revolving drug funds (Gilson 1997; Gilson et al. 2001; McPake et al. 1993). In principle, the focus on community participation proposed by the Bamako Initiative should have allowed single communities to decide independently the level of the fees to be charged as well as the exemption mechanisms to be applied for the very poor. Community participation was expected to result with time in social and political emancipation as well as in greater equity (Korte et al. 1992).

The introduction of user fees promoted by structural adjustment policies did not focus on the promotion of primary health care nor on the implementation of revolving drug funds. The model proposed by the World Bank was rooted in a neo-liberal economic approach and rested upon the assumption that the introduction of fees would not only increase the amount of resources available to the health sector, but would also induce efficiency and equity benefits (Criel et al. 1996). Efficiency benefits would result from the introduction of price signals which would offer an incentive for the appropriate use of the referral system and which would limit demand for "frivolous" care (Shepard and Benjamin 1988). Equity benefits would result from the introduction of exemptions and differential payment scales, favouring health service utilisation by all strata in society (Gilson 1997; Gilson and Mills 1995). The underlying assumption of the model was that, with the exception of the very poor, people were able and willing to pay for health care and that such purchasing power had never been fully exploited (Carrin 1987; Shepard and Benjamin 1988). The World Bank model proposed the introduction of a uniform user fee model to be defined at the central level and then implemented by all facilities in a country (Gilson and Mills 1995).

In spite of their different philosophical approach, in practice, the two models of cost-recovery have often been blurred and applied concurrently. Francophone countries have been more likely to adopt cost-recovery schemes which, at least in principle, were in line with the ambitions of the Bamako Initiative. Anglophone and Lusophone countries, instead, have truly adopted the two models at once (Gilson 1997; Gilson and Mills 1995).

1.1.2.2 Exemptions mechanisms

In principle, both the Bamako Initiative and the World Bank cost-recovery model disposed for the introduction of exemption mechanisms, meant to lower the additional barrier to access potentially faced by the very poor after the introduction of user fees. Both the Bamako Initiative and the World Bank cost-recovery model based their judgement on the experience of mission hospitals, which had already been charging fees and operating effective exemption schemes with the result of providing good quality care (Korte et al. 1992). In practice, however, the implementation of exemption mechanisms on a large scale has proven more difficult than expected and has rarely been successful in securing access to care for the poor (Gilson 1997; Gilson et al. 2001; Raberg and Jeene 2002; Stierle et al. 1999).

The application of exemption mechanisms rests in fact, on the prior establishment of well-defined criteria for eligibility for benefits and on the ability to identify individuals that meet such criteria (Leighton and Diop 1995). Administrative mechanisms used to identify an individual's income for purposes of determining his/her eligibility for benefits are usually referred to as "means testing" (Willis and Leighton 1995). In practice, "means testing" has proved to be an extremely challenging task. The conditions for the effective implementation of "means testing", i.e. formal wage records, steady income, and strong administrative and information systems, are largely lacking in most sub-Saharan countries (Leighton and Diop 1995). Thus, field experience has shown that "means testing" and the subsequent implementation of exemption mechanisms have often been improvised rather than implemented according to a carefully designed policy (Bitran and Giedion 2003).

Part of the problem also rests with attributing responsibility over defining the exemption criteria to national governments, local management committees, or providers, all entities who are often not responsive to the real needs of the local community and are rather concerned with the protection of their own interests (Hutton 2004; Kivumbi and Kintu 2002; McPake 1993; Russell 1996). In some instances, exemption mechanisms have not been implemented at all. This is the case of health facilities or local health systems whose financial sustainability relies completely on the revenues raised through user fees (Gilson 1997). In other instances, exemption mechanisms have been implemented, but have ended up favouring the wealthy rather than the poor (Gilson 1997; Hutton 2004; McPake 1993). In many African countries, for example, civil servants are exempted from paying user charges although they often enjoy a much higher socio-economic status than the vast majority of the population. Across sub-Saharan Africa, the implementation of effective exemption mechanisms has been further hampered by corrupt practices and by the inability of the poor, due to their weak knowledge of the system and their often complete lack of empowerment, to claim the benefits they are entitled to (Bitran and Giedion 2003; Hutton 2004).

1.1.2.3 The impact of user fees on resource mobilisation and community empowerment

Although rarely stated explicitly, once implemented, cost-recovery policies across sub-Saharan Africa focused on the dominant objective of raising revenues for the health care sector, largely neglecting the original aims of empowering communities and promoting efficiency in service provision.

In principle, unless demand for health services drops to zero, the introduction of user fees in a country which has previously provided care free of charge, should inevitably lead to increased resource mobilisation (McPake 1993). In practice, however, user fees have been found to be a weak mechanism of raising substantial revenues, since, as discussed in greater detail in the following section, they do deter health service utilisation (Sekwat 2003). What revenues they generate are therefore minimal and often not sufficient to recover recurrent costs in rural health facilities.

Experience indicates that, other than a few successful cases, user fees generate on average only around 5% of total recurrent health sector expenditure, gross of administrative costs (Creese 1991; Gilson 1997; Vogel 1993). The extent to which cost-recovery is possible largely depends on the capacity of the local market. A pricing structure which is not affordable to the vast majority of a community inevitably limits the ability of the local health system to operate cost-recovery effectively (McPake et al. 1993). The administrative cost of implementing a fee system combined with weak accounting and managerial capacity further undermines revenue generation (Gilson 1997). The potential of user fees to generate substantial resources for the health sector is even weaker when fees are applied exclusively to the sale of drugs. For instance, Soucat et al. (1997) noted that in Benin and in Guinea, revolving drug funds were able to generate enough revenues to cover the cost of drugs, but, given that fees deterred utilisation, not enough drugs were sold to generate the resources needed to cover, as expected, other health sector costs.

In addition to not being able to generate sufficient resources for the health system, the implementation of user fees centred around revolving drug funds has been sharply criticised from its inception for privileging curative rather than preventive care, implicitly introducing an incentive for providers to prescribe drugs in order to raise the health facility revenues (McPake et al. 1993; Korte et al. 1992). Field evidence appears to be in line with this criticism. Unlike what originally expected, price structures have not promoted the use of cost-effective interventions, such as preventive care and treatment of communicable diseases, but have rather promoted the use of high-cost treatments (Gilson and Mills 1995; Sepehri et al. 2005). For instance, in areas where user fees have been applied, preventive care coverage has been observed to be lower than average (Soucat et al. 1997). Similarly, the efficiency gains envisioned by policy makers in relation to a more adequate use of the referral system have not always translated into practice. In spite of the application of a differential fee system across levels of care, evidence shows that people continue to bypass first-level facilities, seeking care directly at the secondary or tertiary level (Gilson and Mills 1995). The underutilisation of first-line facilities may be partly explained by the poor quality of care (McPake et al. 1993). Field experience in fact, has also shown that the introduction of user fees does not directly translate into quality improvements, unless specific efforts in this direction are made, therefore providing an additional disincentive to use facilities at the lowest level in the health system (Gilson and Mills 1995).

The focus on community participation embedded in the Bamako Initiative has also yielded results well below expectations. Community participation presupposes in fact, the existence of an extensive managerial capacity at the community level, an expectation which may not always be realistic. If communities ought to take charge of their own health care systems, they ought to have the adequate means to do so (Korte et al. 1992). Very little explicit effort has been made, however, to ensure that communities would be up to the challenge set by the new health sector reform. Field experience has shown that the expectations imposed on the community by the implementation of cost-recovery in each country have often not been clear and therefore, communities not ready to manage the local health system (Criel et al.1996; McPake et al. 1993). In addition, in several instances, the decision-making bodies at the community level have been found to reflect an elite within society rather all groups served by the relevant health facilities (Gilson et al. 2000). In principle, the Bamako Initiative prescribed that the funds generated though user fees ought to be retained at the community level, but in practice this has not always been the case as communities have been asked to turn to national governments a portion of their revenues (McPake et al. 1993). Given their relative poor training and empowerment, communities have rarely been able to influence decision-making substantially and to a great extent, they have accepted and adapted to what imposed by national guidelines or preferred by local health providers. Community financing has therefore often been reduced to a mere instrument for generating additional resources, failing to exploit the potential originally envisioned by the Bamako Initiative to empower communities with the aim of achieving wider socio-political objectives (Criel et al.1996).

1.1.2.4 The impact of user fees on health service utilisation

The price of health services has been identified as one of the major barriers to access to care in sub-Saharan Africa. User fees have been found to dissuade health service utilisation, to delay the process of seeking care, and to increase the use of self-medication and informal care (Asenso-Okyere et al. 1998; Gilson 1997; Hutton 2004). A study in Zaire showed that a rapid increase in the price of health care led to a sharp drop in the demand for curative, prenatal, and under-five clinical services, with utilisation falling from 37% to 31% for curative services and from 95% to 84% for prenatal services (De Béthune 1989). Similarly, following the large scale implementation of user fees in Ghana in 1985, service utilisation dropped steadily over time in all rural government facilities (Waddington and Enyimayew 1989). In Kenya, the 1989 outpatient registration fee led to an average reduction in utilisation of 27% in provincial hospitals, 45% in district hospitals, and 33% in health centres (Collins et al. 1996).

Changes in utilisation following the introduction of fees have been found to be associated not only with severity of disease, but also with the characteristics of the patient, causing children and the elderly suffering the most from the introduction of user fees (Creese 1991; Hutton 2004). Experience both from Ghana and from Burkina Faso confirmed that the economic active group continued to use health services even after the implementation of fees, but that utilisation dropped dramatically among children and elderly people (Sauerborn et al. 1994; Waddington and Enyimayew 1990). Across sub-Saharan Africa, as expected, poor people have been found to suffer the most from the introduction of user fees (Creese 1991; Gilson 1997; Hutton 2004). Against the argument that low cost drugs are affordable for all (Carrin 1987), field experience has shown that in communities where per capita annual income may very well be below 100 US dollars, even the cost of a simple generic drug used to treat a common condition, such as a malaria episode, may exceed the capacity to pay of many people (Bennett et al. 1998; Creese 1991; Raberg and Jeene 2002). A study conducted in Zambia confirmed that, even years after their introduction, user fees continued to discourage health service utilisation disproportionately more among economically disadvantaged groups (Hjortsberg 2003). Similarly, a study in Mozambique found that those in the lowest income quartile were twice less likely as those in the highest income quartile to seek care in case of a fever episode (Hutton 2004). A review investigating patterns of health care utilisation in eight low and middle income countries found that richer groups were consistently more likely, as compared to poorer groups, to obtain care when sick, to be seen by a doctor, and to receive medicines (Makinen et al. 2000).

The impact of user fees in restricting access to care is exacerbated by seasonal and annual fluctuations in income, a factor that can be explained in terms of the almost exclusive dependence of rural communities on the sale of crops. Seasonal fluctuations refer to the fact that rural communities enjoy a certain wealth only following the harvest season, but have close to no access to any other source of income during other months of the year. Seasonal fluctuations are linked to variations both in climatic conditions and in the market price of crops, two elements which may change considerably from one year to the next and that inevitably affect the amount of revenues that can be generated through the sale of crops (Sauerborn et al. 1996c). Consumption smoothing is adopted as a coping mechanism. The term consumption smoothing is used to indicate the practice of spending the income accrued at one point in time over the whole year, by controlling and limiting immediate consumption, in such a way as to ensure that households can always meet their basic needs (Gertler and Gruber 2002; Morduch 1995; Townsend 1995). Consumption smoothing, however, is insufficient to secure that households have enough money to cope with unexpected events, such as illness, especially if such events occur at a time of the year when most resources have already been consumed. In some settings, the time of the year when households face the greatest health care needs corresponds to the time of the year when they also enjoy the least cash availability (Sauerborn et al. 1995; Sauerborn et al. 1996c). This unfortunate combination of events undoubtedly imposes yet another insurmountable obstacle to access to care, especially among the economically disadvantaged groups who have the least access to any form of saving or credit (Baltussen et al. 2002; Ensor and Cooper 2004).

Communities in sub-Saharan Africa are well aware of the additional barrier to access imposed by the introduction of user charges. People often report lack of money as the main reason for resorting to self-treatment rather than seeking professional care. In Benin, two consecutive studies were conducted to investigate the impact of user fees among the poor. In 1989, one half of all people not seeking care on the occasion of an illness episode identified lack of financial means as the main reason for forgoing treatment. By 1991, the proportion of respondents attributing their choice not to seek professional care to the same reason had risen to one third (Gilson et al. 2000). A similar pattern was observed in Mali where 33% of people interviewed attributed to lack of money the reason for not seeking professional care for a fever episode (Hutton 2004). In a study in Mozambique, 52% of all respondents defined as difficult the need to meet the payment for the care received. Significant differences were observed across income groups, with 65% of those in the lowest and 45% of those in the highest socio-economic quartile respectively defining paying for care as difficult (Hutton 2004).

The bulk of the evidence available suggests that user fees deter health service utilisation and enhance existing inequalities in access to health care. An average health service utilisation rate of 0.5 visits per capita per year across sub-Saharan Africa (Raberg and Jeene 2002; Stierle et al. 1999) suggests that it is not only frivolous care that is being diverted, but rather that sick people forgo treatment because of their inability to pay (Creese 1991; Korte et al. 1992; Raberg and Jeene 2002; World Health Organisation 2000a). The price of medical services in relation to people's income and ability to pay is not the only barrier to access, but it is definitely one of the most important (Ensor and Cooper 2004), recognised as such by people themselves (Hutton 2004). Several other factors contribute to limit access to health services in low income settings: (1) poor quality of health services (Carrin 1987; Haddad and Fournier 1995; Reerink and Sauerborn 1996; Baltussen et al. 2002; DiPrete Brown et al. 2004); (2) lack of access to adequate information on what services are available and on how to use them (Ensor and Cooper 2004; Hutton 2004); (3) distance to the health facilities (Baltussen et al. 2002; Diop et al. 1995; Hjortsberg 2003; Nabyonga et al. 2005); (4) cultural beliefs and practices (Pokhrel et al. 2005; Rashid et al. 2001; Sauerborn et al. 1996b; Sauerborn et al. 1994). Critics of cost-recovery policies argue that other barriers to access, such as the distance to the health facility and the opportunity cost of seeking care, already act as deterrents and limit utilisation, making it unnecessary, if not unethical, to impose yet another barrier to access through the application of user charges.

In spite of the abundant evidence against user fees, a few authors and policy makers have consistently argued in favour of their implementation, supporting their argument with a few studies reporting an increase rather than a decrease in utilisation, following the implementation of cost-recovery (Griffin 1988; Litvack and Bodart 1993; Shepard and Benjamin 1988). Proponents of user fees fail to acknowledge, however, that this health financing option has induced increases in service utilisation only in instances where it has been accompanied by additional health care reforms, such as substantial quality improvements (Chawla and Ellis 2000; Leighton 1995; McPake 1993; Shepard and Benjamin 1988). When quality and price are positively correlated, the failure to find a negative association between increased fees and utilisation becomes questionable as a result of unaccounted quality (McPake 1993). Studies which documented no decrease in utilisation following the introduction of fees were conducted under pilot conditions (Chawla and Ellis 2000; Hutton 2004; Leighton 1995), where either government or external agents invested in substantial quality improvements, focusing in particular on upgrading infrastructures and increasing the availability of drugs. These studies, however, did not explicitly acknowledge the fact that the meagre revenues generated through user charges could alone not sustain such quality improvements in the long term. They also ignored the fact that increased revenues alone do not provide an answer to the problem of low quality as more systematic and multi-level approaches are needed to induce quality improvements in service provision (Haddad and Fournier 1995). At most in fact, increased revenues can act to improve the structural component of the quality of care, increasing availability of equipment and drugs, but can do little to improve the process of service delivery (Donabedian 1980).

Besides a few pilot projects, however, sub-Saharan Africa has experienced the implementation of cost-recovery as a stand-alone health sector reform, rarely accompanied by methodical efforts towards substantial quality improvements, therefore inevitably inducing decreases in health service utilisation rates, especially among the most vulnerable groups in society, i.e. the poor, the children, and the elderly. Also to be noted as a weakness of the studies describing an increase in utilisation is the inability to identify which proportion of the reported increase may have been due to providers' induced demand. The implementation of a fee system inevitably entails perverse incentives for providers (Sepehri et al. 2005), especially if revenues from the fees are retained at the level of the single facility (Gilson 1997). Providers in fact, may have an incentive to encourage utilisation of certain services, usually the most profitable ones, accounting at least for a portion of the increase in demand reported in some studies. To the present day, however, the role of provider-induced demand following the implementation of user charges has not been addressed in the literature. The reason may be found in the fact that, given the difficulty in collecting the necessary information, it is hard to estimate if and to what extent formal user fees have substituted informal payments to providers. The empirical evidence to this regard is almost non-existent, leaving unexplained some of the potentially relevant impact of user fees on health service utilisation.

1.1.2.5 The impact of user fees on poverty

The literature criticizing cost-recovery has focused mostly on the negative impact of user fees on health service utilisation, largely neglecting, at first, the link between the price of medical services and poverty. The literature on poverty has in fact traditionally identified a link between low income and ill health, but it has until recently paid limited attention to the causal relationship running in the opposite direction, linking ill health to low income. In recent years, however, there has been growing recognition of the fact that poverty and ill health are intimately related, and that the causal relationship runs in both directions. Poor countries, and poor people within countries, suffer from a multiplicity of deprivations that translate into high levels of ill health. At the same time, ill health sustains, and in some instance induces, poverty (Raberg and Jeene 2002; The World Bank 2001; Wagstaff 2002). Although both elements are of extreme importance, hereafter we will focus primarily on the latter as most relevant to our discussion on the shortcomings of user fees and the emergence of CHI.

The literature recognises three major pathways through which illness can act to keep or to lead households into poverty (Meessen et al. 2003; Russell 2004; Sachs and Malaney 2002; Wagstaff 2002). The first is through the income forgone because of illness. A simple episode of malaria may not jeopardize household income excessively, but repeated malaria episodes, long term chronic diseases, and/or illness clustering within households may very well limit the capacity of a household income earner to contribute to the welfare of his/her family. The second is through the death or permanent disability of a household income earner. Death or disability may in fact lead to changes in the structure of the household which hold profound effects on schooling, demography, and migration. The third is through the cost of treatment itself which, following the implementation of user charges, has been found to impose a substantial burden on households facing illness.

The effect of illness on poverty is exacerbated by the complete lack of access to social security systems for the vast majority of people living in low income countries (Preker et al. 2002a; Preker et al. 2002b; Preker et al. 2004; van Ginneken 1996). In high income countries, the impact of illness on households is buffered by well-functioning social security systems. In low income countries, such systems are either inexistent or pertain exclusively to certain strata of the population, usually civil servants and government employees. The rural population, those employed in the informal sector, and the urban poor, in spite of being the must vulnerable groups in society, are all left alone to cope with illness, relying exclusively on their own resources.

Prior to the introduction of user charges, households already faced severe costs in case of illness: the opportunity cost of seeking care, the opportunity cost of taking care of the sick, and the cost of transportation. Following the introduction of user fees, households found themselves facing yet an additional burden, having to pay for treatment. As described in the section above, households may choose to forgo care, facing potentially dramatic effects on their health status, or may choose to seek care, in this case facing potentially catastrophic effects on their overall financial stability. Households choosing to seek care in fact, may sacrifice other basic needs, such as food and education, to mobilise enough resources to pay for treatment (Russell 1996).

For the most part, households are able to cope with a confined illness episode. They manage to meet the price of treatment and all additional costs by temporarily reducing consumption of other goods or by seeking assistance from informal support networks (Besley 1995; Dercon 2002; Gertler and Gruber 2002; Meessen et al. 2003; Morduch 1995; Russell 1996; Russell 2004; Sauerborn et al. 1996a). Repeated illness episodes, illness clustering within households, chronic conditions, and severe diseases requiring costly interventions, such as surgery, are all instances which may be well beyond the coping capacity of households (Fabricant et al. 1999; Meessen et al. 2003). Single households already living at the edge of poverty may not be able to mobilise enough resources to cope with them given that their own incomes are too meagre and that, because of contract constraints, informal credit institutions may also be unwilling to lend money beyond a certain threshold (Foster and Rosenzweig 2001; Goldstein et al. 2001; Russell 2004). In this case, households may be forced to sell or mortgage productive assets. Some households may recover, but others may not and, because of illness, may fall deeper into poverty. Households not owning extensive assets may either forgo care or, if well connected in social networks, indebt themselves to the point of never recovering from the health shock (McPake et al. 1993; Meessen et al.2003; Russell 2004). Investing disproportionate amounts of resources towards the consumption of health care means that households are not able to invest in productive activities to generate economic wellbeing in the long run. The impact of the price of care on forgone investment and therefore on the long term wealth both of single households and of entire communities is still to be investigated (McPake et al. 1993; Sachs and Malaney 2002).

Ability to cope with the cost of illness is influenced by the type, the severity, and the duration of the disease, but also by a household financial and non-financial assets (Russell 2004; Sauerborn 1994). Non-financial assets include education as well as access to social networks. A household's ability to mobilise sufficient resources in times of illness is in fact, largely dependent upon their ability to know where to seek support and how to obtain it (Russell 1996; Russell 2004; Sauerborn 1994). Financial assets include all the economic resources of a household. Given the failure to establish effective exemption mechanisms, user fees have been found to be regressive, imposing the greatest burden on households who are already very poor (Russell 2004). Gertler et al. (1987) argued that the regressive impact of user fees ought to be measured not only in terms of price elasticity, but also in terms of welfare loss. Their argument was based on a model that demonstrated how even if all individuals were equally price sensitive, the welfare loss induced by user fees would be greater for the poor relative to their income than for the rich. Thus, they concluded that user fees are regressive both in terms of access and in terms of welfare loss, on one side discouraging health service utilisation and on the other side producing a substantial reduction in consumer welfare with the burden falling disproportionately on the poor.

A review of the empirical literature appears to strengthen their argument. Although the poor in general spend less on treatment than other income groups, because in most instances they forgo care, their spending represents a higher proportion of their overall income (Russell 2004). A multi-country analysis consistently found that across settings, lower income groups spend a greater proportion of their income on health care than higher income groups (Makinen et al. 2000). In Sierra Leone, a study found that average expenditure on curative services was 6.9% of average household income. The proportion of income spent on health care however, was more than six times as large among the poorest income quartile than among the wealthiest one (Fabricant et al. 1999). In the Gambia, household spending on health care was found to be 6% of annual income, but significant differences existed across income groups with low income and high income households spending respectively 10% and 3.4% of their earnings on health services (Williams 1994).

A recent development in the literature exploring the relationship between the price of care and illness attempts to estimate what proportion of illness episodes may cause households previously not defined as poor, to fall into poverty. Studies exploring the direct relationship between health expenditure and poverty define as catastrophic expenditure any health expenditure that may cause households to exceed their coping capacity and/or to fall below the poverty line. No agreement has been reached as to where to set the threshold defining the poverty line realistically nor deciding the size of expenditure to be defined as catastrophic. Given the relative novelty of the approach, empirical evidence is still scarce. The studies published so far suggest that catastrophic health expenditure is closely related to the proportion of the total cost of care recovered through user fees (Wagstaff and van Doorslaer 2003; Xu et al. 2003).

A recent multi-country study defining as catastrophic any health expenditure exceeding 40% of a household capacity to pay[1], found that a 1% increase in the proportion of total health expenditure covered through out-of-pocket payments is associated with an average increase of 2.2% in the proportion of households facing catastrophic expenditure (Xu et al. 2003). It is important to consider these estimates in relation to the consideration that while in high income countries, on average less the 20% of all health care costs are recovered through out-of-pocket payments, in sub-Saharan Africa this proportion is in most cases close to 50% (Raberg and Jeene 2002). In the light of such findings, the potential impact of

---

[1] The study defined as "capacity to pay" the income left after paying for the household basic food and clothing needs.

user fees on sustaining and inducing poverty in sub-Saharan countries is, to say the least, alarming.

1.1.3 The emergence of community health insurance in sub-Saharan Africa

1.1.3.1 Health insurance coverage in sub-Saharan Africa

The failure of user fees to provide an adequate solution to the problem of health financing in sub-Saharan Africa is today widely acknowledged. Recognising that user fees restrict access to care and jeopardise the financial stability of households, international organisations have repeatedly argued against the financing of health systems based on out-of-pocket payments (Sachs 2001; The World Bank 2001; World Health Organisation 2000a). As mentioned at the very beginning of this chapter, particularly the World Health Report 2000 explicitly valued fairness in financing and protection against the financial risk associated with illness as intrinsic aims of any health system. It encouraged low income countries to create conditions for adequate risk-sharing and pooling of resources relying on collection mechanisms that allow the time of payment to be disassociated from the time of service use (World Health Organisation 2000a).

Awareness of the limits imposed by a system based on the application of user fees has in recent years stirred up debate in sub-Saharan Africa regarding what health financing reform may meet WHO expectations, securing better access to health services and greater financial protection against the cost of illness. In the light of the successful experience of Western Europe (Barnighausen and Sauerborn 2002), the most natural solution would seem to switch from a financing system based on out-of-pocket payments to one based on national-level risk-sharing and pooling, either through increased tax collection and/or through the development of social health insurance. A few sub-Saharan countries are currently investing in the development of social health insurance (Task Force on Establishment of Mandatory National Social Health Insurance 2005), but for the vast majority of countries, this option remains a distant objective as several constraints impede its development in the short term.

Contextual limitations shape what policy options for health financing are concretely available to decision-makers in sub-Saharan countries (Preker et al. 2004). First of all, taxation capacity is severely hampered as the vast majority of the population is employed in the informal sector (Shepard and Benjamin 1988). Enhancing taxation capacity would entail developing a sophisticated infrastructure, one that also allows for the collection of consumption taxes (Carrin 1987), which may simply be too costly and too complex for several low income nations (Carrin and Vereecke 1992; Jütting 1999). When a country taxation capacity is as low as 10% of GDP or less, it would take 30% of government revenues to meet a target of 3% of GDP health expenditure through formal collective health financing channels (Preker et al. 2004). This appears to be an unrealistic objective given that on average, all countries pooled together, public health spending across sub-Saharan Africa rests at 1.6% of GDP (Peters et al. 2000). In some countries the situation is even more severe with less than 10% of public expenditure, i.e. less than 1% of GDP resources, devoted to health care (Preker et al. 2004). The option of shifting existing government resources towards higher health care budgets has also long been recognised as highly unlikely (Carrin 1987). Similarly, scepticism surrounds the question of whether additional resources generated through increased taxation would then really be earmarked for the health care sector (Carrin 1987).

An additional set of problems relevant to the implementation of large scale coverage in sub-Saharan Africa stems from the pooling of financial resources. Pooling entails that resources are transferred from the rich to the poor, from the healthy to the sick, and from active to inactive groups in society. In sub-Saharan Africa, however, tax evasion is widespread among the rich and the middle class, allowing higher socio-economic groups, those who could potentially contribute the most, to limit their participation in a national scheme (Preker et al. 2004). The government's ability to effectively mobilise resources for health care is also largely hampered by a general dissatisfaction with the quality of the service provided, so that those wealthy enough to potentially contribute to a national insurance scheme, are discouraged from doing so as they prefer to seek care at private facilities (Preker et al. 2002b). Governments often also lack the accountability for setting up an effective large scale administrative system, which constitutes a *sine qua non* for the management of a national scheme (Carrin 1987; Carrin 1988; Vogel 1993).

Furthermore, certain unwillingness to pool resources across income levels has been observed in sub-Saharan Africa. This entails that what little pooling does occur is fragmented along socio-economic status, preventing the effective cross-subsidy necessary for the implementation of national schemes (Preker et al. 2002b). A few African countries have successfully established social health insurance, but these schemes are highly fragmented and offer coverage exclusively to civil servants and in some instances to a few formal sector employees (Huber et al.2002). Overall coverage rates are still very low and vary from less than 1% in Ethiopia to 11% in Kenya (Huber et al.2002; Vogel 1993).

In sub-Saharan Africa, private health insurance, defined as voluntary for-profit insurance coverage, also offers only a partial solution to the problems of access to health care and financial protection against the cost of illness. In some countries, such as Namibia, Zimbabwe, South Africa, Botswana, Kenya, Mali, Ivory Coast, and Madagascar, private health insurance coverage is growing, reimbursing as much as 20% of all health care costs (Sekhri and Savedoff 2005; Vogel 1993). Private health insurance remains available exclusively to the minority working in the formal sector, covering only a very limited percentage of a country's total population. Its price remains prohibitive for the vast majority of the African people employed in rural areas and in the informal sector.

1.1.3.2 Definition and rationale of community health insurance in sub Saharan Africa

CHI in sub-Saharan Africa has evolved as a response to the problems of access to care and financial protection faced by those excluded from formal insurance systems. Both social health insurance for government and formal sector employees and private health insurance have in fact enhanced existing inequalities by facilitating access to health services for those who would need the least support. Given that health facilities remain heavily subsidised across sub-Saharan Africa, easing access for the rich and the middle class has implied that, paradoxically, those with the most means also capture the greatest share of public subsidies (Huber et al. 2002; Makinen et al. 2000; Shepard and Benjamin 1988; Wagstaff 2002).

CHI has emerged in an attempt to bridge the gap in access and social protection between people covered by formal schemes and those left to pay for care out of their own pocket. CHI is a general expression used to indicate community insurance arrangements described in the literature with a variety of terms: community-based health insurance, micro-insurance, medical aid schemes, mutual health organisations, community health funds, and rural health insurance (Atim 1998; Bennett et al. 1998; Criel et al. 2004; Dror 2002; Preker et al. 2004; Waelkens and Criel 2004). The different terms developed are representative of the variety of contexts where CHI has emerged, but all stand to indicate a "voluntary, non-profit insurance scheme, formed on the basis of an ethic of mutual aid, solidarity and the collective pooling of health risks, in which the members participate effectively in its management and functioning" (Atim 1998). The concept of insurance is applied at the micro-level to favour risk-sharing and the pooling of resources across a community, in such a way as to facilitate access to care and offer financial protection against the cost of illness, by favouring a transfer from the healthy to the sick and by disassociating payment from the time of care.

Dror identified simplicity, affordability, and proximity as the three core characteristics of any CHI scheme (Dror 2002). Simplicity refers to limiting procedural complexities to a minimum in order to secure greatest acceptance and participation on the part of communities, where many people may be illiterate and generally unaccustomed to deal with bureaucratic formalities. Affordability refers both to the price of the premium and to the perceived return on the money paid. Participation in the scheme is only possible if the premium is judged to be fair, is known to be the same for all members of a community, and meets the capacity to pay of the population the scheme caters to. Proximity refers to the operational base of CHI schemes, located within and often managed directly by the very same community they serve.

An important distinction ought to be made between CHI and pre-payment programs. Pre-payment schemes have in fact also been proposed as a health financing option alternative to out-of-pocket payments, but ought to be clearly distinguished, in the framework of our discussion, from CHI. Pre-payment schemes, at times also referred to as medical savings accounts, are plans that encourage or coerce people to save to meet future health care costs. They refer exclusively to an inter-temporal transfer of current consumption to future consumption, but do not constitute a form of inter-personal transfer as they entail neither risk-sharing nor pooling. CHI schemes instead apply the traditional concept of insurance which refers to a trade across states of nature, from good to bad, and across different individuals (Besley 1991). CHI is therefore different from mere pre-payment as it entails a mechanism for pooling resources and spreading risk across income, age, gender, or health status differences of an entire group (Dror 2002).

Although the fundamental aim of CHI remains that of facilitating access to care and increasing financial protection against the cost of illness through the abolishment of payment at point of delivery, proponents of this financing option are confident that schemes can also act to reduce others barriers to access. CHI in fact, is expected to induce changes in the quality of services through two separate, although related, processes. On the one hand, schemes can help stabilise providers' revenues, allowing for a more efficient and effective planning both of daily activities and of long term investments (Atim 1998; Criel 1998a; Musau 1999). On the other hand, the emphasis on group mobilisation can be instrumental in empowering communities to voice their needs, forcing health systems to become more responsive to their requests (Bennett et al. 1998; Huber et al.2002; Musau 1999; Preker et al. 2004; World Health Organisation 2000a). Likewise, schemes are also likely to facilitate the flow of information among members of a community, potentially levelling off the barrier to access currently imposed by lack of knowledge and education (Fonteneau 2000; Waelkens and Criel 2004). Informed individuals can more easily identify their health needs and the relevant services available in the community to respond to such needs promptly.

1.1.3.3 Brief history of community health insurance in sub-Saharan Africa

The very first CHI schemes appeared in sub-Saharan Africa in the second half of the 1980s. Examples of these pioneer experiences are the *Mutuelles des travailleurs de l'education et de la culture (MUTEC)* founded in Mali in 1987 (Atim 1998) and the Bwamanda Hospital Insurance Scheme founded in the Democratic Republic of Congo in 1986 (Criel 1998b). The beginning of the 1990s saw a rapid increase in the development of similar schemes throughout the continent. An exact count of how many schemes currently exist in sub-Saharan Africa is not available. Many experiences in fact, are not documented. The most recent review indicated the existence of approximately nine hundred schemes, but this figure was based exclusively on the schemes described in the literature and can therefore by no means be considered exhaustive of the field experience (Waelkens and Criel 2004).

Most CHI schemes have emerged as entities of their own, but others have grown out of pre-existing mutual aid organisations initially set up to provide their members with a range of social security benefits, such as funeral grants, marriage and birth allowances, and retirement benefits (Atim 1998). The Bwamanda scheme in the Democratic Republic of Congo constitutes an example of CHI set up exclusively to address the problem of access to health care. MUTEC in Mali instead, was originally formed to address the teachers' need for retirement benefits, but progressively grew to include health care coverage as well. Unlike the experience of South-East Asia (Balkenhol and Churchill 2002; Bennett et al. 1998; Desmet et al. 1999; Ranson 2004), very few schemes in sub-Saharan Africa have until recently stemmed out of micro-credit institutions. This can most probably be attributed to the fact that large scale organised micro-credit institutions are only a recent development in the African context. Thus, in the late 1980s and early 1990s, the premises for the development of CHI in conjunction with micro-finance simply did not exist in the continent.

CHI schemes also differ insofar as their initiator is concerned. Some schemes have been initiated by health care providers, others by cooperation agencies and NGOs, and yet others by communities themselves.

In the late 1980s, reliance on user fees constituted a problem also for providers who faced daily the problem of access to care by the poor and found themselves unable to raise enough revenues to operate their facilities effectively. In an attempt to pool risks, create a wider revenue base, and increase community access to health care, some providers initiated their own CHI scheme (Atim 1999; Bennett et al. 1998; Criel 1998a). The most notable example of a scheme initiated by providers is again the Bwamanda Hospital Insurance Scheme in the Democratic Republic of Congo. In the 1980s, due to inflation, the Bwamanda hospital had been forced to increase fees several times, inducing an inevitable drop in health care utilisation on the part of the rural community it served. In order to increase utilisation and at the same time stabilise the hospital funding, the health district management initiated an insurance scheme, setting premium at the equivalent of the cost of two kilograms of soy beans, a common local crop, and imposing a co-payment of 20%. Having applied only small modifications to its original design, the scheme is still active nowadays. Although initiated by providers, the scheme counts on the active contribution of community members for its management (Criel 1998b; Criel and Kegels 1997).

The PRIMA project in Guinea-Conakry provides the example of a scheme born out of a partnership between NGOs, cooperation agencies, and local health authorities. The scheme was initiated by the NGO Medicus Mundi Belgium and the German Agency for Technical Cooperation (GTZ) in collaboration with the Guinean Ministry of Health. The objective was to design and test a model for the sharing of risks in health in order to optimise access to care and increase financial protection against the cost of illness by strengthening existing solidarity mechanisms in the community. In spite of the substantial efforts invested in the project, the insurance scheme was discontinued after only two years of operation. Enrolment in the scheme dropped below sustainable levels, a rebel incursion provoked severe damage to much of the local health infrastructure, and a generally unstable political situation endangered the operations of the project (Criel et al. 2002).

One of the most successful examples of schemes initiated directly by the community comes from the Thiès region in Senegal. The first health insurance scheme was autonomously founded by community members in 1990 in a town called Fandène. Witnessing the success of this first experience, several surrounding communities mobilised to establish similar schemes. The presence of several schemes within a region enhanced their contractual capacity with the local private non-profit health provider, the Catholic Hospital St.Jean de Dieu, which came to offer a reduction on fees up to 50% for the treatment of insured members. In 1994, schemes joined to set up their own technical support structure, *Groupe de Recherche et d'Appui aux Initiatives Mutualistes*, which was complemented in 1997 by a regional coordination structure, the *Coordination Régionale des Mutuelles de Santé de Thiès*. The former developed into an NGO specialised as a management support structure, offering technical and teaching expertise to emerging schemes and to foreign donors interested in investing in the development of CHI. The latter developed into a federal structure, representing the interests of the health care users of the Thiès region at the national level (Huber et al.2002; Jütting 2004).

Earlier schemes developed primarily with the aim of offering their members coverage against high-cost low-frequency events, such as inpatient care and surgery. The rationale was that of protecting households against truly catastrophic health care costs, the assumption being that households could cope with the lower costs associated with the treatment of more common conditions, such as malaria and uncomplicated respiratory tract infections (Bennett et al. 1998; Carrin 2003). The Bwamanda scheme in the Democratic Republic of Congo and the schemes in the Thiès region in Senegal both constitute examples of CHIs set up to cover exclusively hospital-based services (Criel 1998b; Huber et al.2002; Jütting 2004).

With time, however, it became clear that the price of treatment also constitutes a problem due to clustering of illness within households and/or to repeated episodes of a common condition (Hutton 2004; Sauerborn 1994). In poor communities, where cash flows are unreliable and subject to seasonal fluctuations, even paying for first-line services may be impossible for some households, especially at specific times during the year (Bennett et al. 1998; Carrin 2003). In addition, exclusive coverage of hospital-based services induces a shift from first-line to second-line facilities, with many people waiting to be severely sick before seeking medical care (Abel-Smith 1992; Ahuja and Jütting 2003b). Due to community pressures, schemes progressively evolved to include basic services provided by first-line facilities. This also facilitates adequate referral across levels of care, ensuring that patients report more promptly to their closest facility. The PRIMA project in Guinea-Conakry constitutes an example of how the community negotiated the inclusion of first-line services in the benefit package from the very onset of the scheme (Criel et al. 2002). The experience of the Thiès region constitutes an example of how the benefit package can be reviewed *in itinere* to include also first-line services (Huber et al.2002; Jütting 2004).

At first, CHI schemes developed in an environment where government involvement and commitment towards finding an alternative to user fees was minimal (Atim 1998; Bennett et al. 1998). Nowadays, most sub-Saharan governments have recognised the important contribution that CHI can play as a mechanism of facilitating access to services and offering financial protection against the cost of illness, while at the same time raising revenues for the health care sector. Governmental responses to the emergence of schemes, however, have been very different across countries.

Some countries, such as Mali, have been pioneers in developing legislation regulating the emergence of CHI schemes. The general Law on Mutuality was passed in February 1996 and was followed by a number of decrees specifying implementation details such as the model rules and regulations, the procedures for registration, and the management of funds (Atim 1998). Still, the initiative for the creation of the single schemes was always left to the community. In other countries, such as Ghana, Ministries of Health are currently seeking to achieve national coverage by enforcing and subsidising the large scale implementation of single CHI schemes (Ministry of Health of Ghana 2003). Other countries, such as Senegal, recognised the need to construct a legislation that could guide the development of CHI schemes, but opted to discuss the legislation only after witnessing the first field experiences. They did so in recognition of the fact that legislation ought not to precede the development of schemes, but rather to follow it in order to be informed and enriched by the field experience (Atim 1998). In other countries, such as Burkina Faso, Benin, and Guinea Conakry, a clear legislation regulating CHI is still missing, but the government actively encourages and supports schemes by favouring foreign aid investments in the insurance sector and by supporting the development of private organisations offering technical assistance (Atim 1998; Waelkens and Criel 2004). In countries where government support is minimal and a clear legislation is still missing, CHI schemes tend to register under the laws governing the registration of associations, cooperatives, or social welfare organisations (Atim 1998).

The trend towards the development of a clear national policy accompanied by a precise legislation regulating the emergence of CHI is bound to expand also in response to international pressure (Bennett et al. 1998; Carrin 2003; Carrin et al. 2001; World Health Organisation 2000a). International organisations are pushing for CHI to be considered more and more not as an end in itself, but rather as a step towards achieving universal coverage in countries which are unable to strive for social health insurance at once (Carrin 2002; Carrin et al. 2001). In the long run in fact, a nation-wide financing scheme is advisable since small scale scattered community schemes, although providing a solution to the problem of access in the short term, still imply fragmented risk-sharing and pooling and may induce or sustain inequalities across different regions within a country (Carrin and Vereecke 1992).

In a recent document, Carrin suggested that, in an attempt to favour the development of CHI schemes as a step towards the establishment of national health insurance coverage, governments should assume four basic functions: (1) to promote not-for-profit schemes which include in their design measures to ensure coverage of the poorest; (2) to monitor the activities of these schemes as to be able to adjust their performance; (3) to train interested not-for-profit groups wishing to set up not-for-profit schemes; (4) to co-finance, if necessary by relying also on foreign aid, health insurance operations (Carrin et al. 2001). Needless to say, government commitment to CHI is plausible only in nations that enjoy a certain political, economic, and social stability, a condition unfortunately not met by all African countries. A sad example comes from the experience of the Ivory Coast, where the recent socio-political unrest has jeopardised the government long standing plans to achieve universal coverage through the development of small scale schemes (Huber et al. 2002).

1.1.3.4 Assessment of community health insurance schemes in sub-Saharan Africa

Early investigations into the role of CHI in sub-Saharan Africa focused primarily on the managerial and financial analysis of the existing experiences. The aim was clearly that of identifying guidelines to inform the design of schemes. Several pioneer projects in fact, had failed to survive because of weaknesses in their design. Whether initiated by NGOs, providers, or communities themselves, those early experiences were often born out of the good will of a restricted group of individuals who, lacking expertise in the practice of insurance, failed to address issues, such as adverse selection, fraud, cost-escalation, and community preferences, essential for the survival of any scheme (Atim 1998; Bennett et al. 1998). Those early investigations converged towards establishing the criteria for the development of viable insurance schemes and were thus dominated by discussions on design flaws, managerial and administrative malfunctioning, adverse selection, moral hazard, irrational prescribing, and contractual capacity *vis à vis* the providers (Atim 1998; Atim and Madjiguene 2000; Bennett et al. 1998; Brown and Churchill 2000; Fonteneau 2000; Huber et al. 2002; Musau 1999; Wiesmann and Jütting 2000; Wiesmann and Jütting 2001).

Today, emerging schemes have access to a wide network of international and local agencies, offering expertise assistance and having developed clear guidelines as to how to address potential insurance pitfalls in the scheme design (Ahuja and Jütting 2003b; International Labour Organisation 2001; International Labour Organisation 2002; Waelkens and Criel 2004). Provided that interested groups seek the support of such agencies, design flaws linked to the theory and practice of insurance can for the most part be avoided (Arhin-Tenkorang 2004; Criel et al. 2004). More recent investigations into the performance of CHI have therefore shifted towards the analysis of its impact in terms of access to care and protection against the financial cost of illness. The promotion of CHI relies in fact on the ability to prove that such financing option lives up to the expectations of its proponents and offers a concrete solution to the problems of access and financial protection. Although there is still paucity of systematic evidence on the impact of CHI (Ekman 2004; Palmer et al. 2004), a few studies have recently been published exploring the relationship between enrolment status, health service utilisation, and out-of-pocket health expenditure (Criel et al. 1999; Jakab et al. 2004; Jütting 2004; Schneider and Diop 2004).

1.1.3.5 Low coverage rates: the unresolved problem of CHI in sub-Saharan Africa

A feature of CHI which has not yet received much attention in the literature is the problem of low enrolment. Apart from a few successful experiences, the most notable of which is the Bwamanda Hospital Scheme in the Democratic Republic of Congo (Criel 1998b), CHI schemes in sub-Saharan Africa rarely even attain 10% coverage rate among their target population. For the vast majority of schemes, the literature has consistently reported coverage rates that range between 1% and 10% (Atim 1998; Bennett et al. 1998; Carrin 2003; Criel et al. 2002; Criel and Waelkens 2003; Musau 1999; Tabor 2005; Waelkens and Criel 2004). The most recent review of CHI pooled together all documented experiences in the continent to assess that the overall coverage rate of the target population rests at 8.2% (Waelkens and Criel 2004). The same review also highlighted how the lowest coverage rates are among schemes which are community-based, meaning those schemes that are initiated and managed by the communities themselves, as opposed to schemes initiated and managed by either NGOs or providers. Among community-based schemes, the average enrolment rate was found to be as low as 3.2% (Waelkens and Criel 2004).

Given its focus on community mobilisation and empowerment beyond the mere objective of facilitating access to care and offering financial protection against the cost of illness, the community-based model has been identified as the most promising and therefore the one most often promoted by international and local agencies committed to the development of CHI (Huber et al.2002; Waelkens and Criel 2004). The extremely low enrolment rates among community-based schemes are therefore disconcerting.

Low enrolment rates constitute one of the major weaknesses of CHI on several fronts. First of all, low enrolment rates inevitably entail feeble levels of resource mobilization. Although there is evidence that CHI schemes can have a positive effect on resource mobilisation, the actual amounts raised are often limited and therefore not sufficient to ensure the long term viability of the schemes nor a stabilisation of the financial resources made available to providers (Ekman 2004).

The theory and the practice of insurance rest on the principle that in order to function effectively, schemes ought to pool together the risks of large number of individuals. Insurance premiums are in fact calculated as a function of two factors: the cost of care and the expected health service utilisation of a given population, determined also by the disease pattern of a given region. When membership is low, schemes more easily face random fluctuations in the number of claims. A greater exposure to high-severity claims translates into a higher risk of insolvency, which is instead avoided in larger groups where there is a higher convergence around the average value of claims. Insolvency translates into a higher risk of bankruptcy, thus threatening severely the survival of schemes (Dror 2002; Folland et al. 2001; The Health Insurance Association of America 2001).

Figure 1.2: Claim fluctuation (Source: Dror, D. M., 2002)

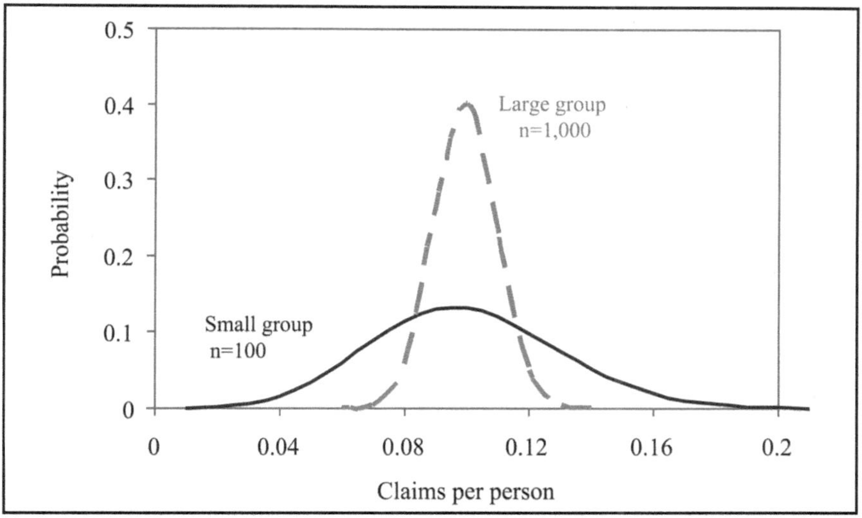

Low membership rates may also be a warning that adverse selection is taking place, meaning that only high-risk individuals are enrolling in a scheme (Carrin 2003; Jakab and Krishnan 2004). Adverse selection can constitute a severe problem for schemes, again jeopardising their financial viability, because health service utilisation by high-risk individuals may differ substantially from the average on the basis of which the actuarial calculations have been made. Furthermore, low enrolment rates may also signify that only the most affluent members of a community are joining the scheme. Facilitating access to care and offering financial protection against the cost of illness only to a limited number of individuals within a community may yield potentially catastrophic effects, reinforcing existing inequalities in health service utilisation (Carrin 2003; Preker et al. 2004).

Low membership may also introduce conflicts in the health care system as schemes may come to represent exclusively the objectives of a restricted groups of individuals. It is not to be excluded that low membership may cause the scheme objectives to develop in overt conflict with the overall social objective of enhancing health service utilisation, and thus health status, for the population as a whole (Bennett 2004). CHI is conceived as an effective health financing option if it can serve to overcome the experience of exclusion, measured in terms of lack to access to care and financial exposure to health risks, currently so common to many sub-Saharan nations (Preker et al. 2004). Exclusion, however, can be overcome if and only if CHI schemes manage to secure broad participation among their target populations.

In spite of the fact that low enrolment has long been reported in the literature as a key limitation of schemes in sub-Saharan Africa (Atim 1998; Bennett et al. 1998; Carrin 2003; Tabor 2005; Waelkens and Criel 2004), limited systematic effort has been challenged towards understanding what motivates the decision of people to enrol or not to enrol in schemes. Earlier investigations into CHI attributed low enrolment rates either to flaws in the design and promotion of schemes or to the lack of a market for health insurance in sub-Saharan Africa (Atim 1998; Bennett et al. 1998; Carrin 1988). In the light of the progress that has been made in terms of the design of schemes and the increase in the insurance offer throughout the continent, these motives are no longer sufficient to explain low enrolment rates (Criel et al. 2004). Understanding what motivates low enrolment remains therefore a relevant research question. The puzzle is to disclose why a health financing model offering in principle such a suitable solution to the well-recognised problem of access and financial protection, generates in practice such little interest. Low enrolment rates appear almost paradoxical given that CHI rests its foundation in the same ethic of solidarity and mutual aid which represents the core of a long-standing tradition of risk-sharing arrangements in the continent (Atim 1998; Waelkens and Criel 2004).

1.2 Study objective

This study presents a systematic investigation into decision to enrol in community health insurance in sub-Saharan Africa. Specifically, the study explores decision to enrol in a community-based health insurance scheme launched in the Nouna Health District, Burkina Faso, in 2004.

The specific objectives of the study can be summarised as follows:

a) to ascertain which individual, household, and community factors influence household decision to enrol in CHI;

b) to assess the extent to which community understanding and perceptions both of the scheme and of the insurance principle in general affect household decision to enrol in CHI;

c) to investigate the extent to which preferences for the single elements of the scheme influence household decision to enrol in CHI.

The conceptual framework guiding the conduct of this study was informed by the review of the theoretical literature discussing insurance purchase, by the empirical studies having explored demand for health insurance, with special focus on sub-Saharan Africa, and by an in-depth exploration of the research setting, with specific reference to the reality of the health care system and the recent emergence of the community-based health insurance scheme in the area. The presentation of our methodology is therefore preceded by a review of each of these elements.

1.3 Understanding decision to purchase health insurance: theory and practice

Both the theoretical and the empirical literature discussing decision to purchase health insurance are undoubtedly dominated by the field of economics. It is only in recent years, and exclusively with reference to the experience of low income countries, that alternative explanatory models, focused on social dynamics and capacity for collective mobilisation, have been applied to the understanding of decision to purchase health insurance. Thus, the following sections, dedicated to the review of the theoretical and the empirical literature, inevitably draws more heavily from the field of health economics.

1.3.1 Theoretical explanatory models in health economics

Orthodox economic consumer theory assumes that perfectly informed individuals enter the marketplace with a definite set of preferences. In the light of the relative price of goods, individuals allocate their income across goods to best serve these preferences[2]. Changes in prices and income are therefore expected to influence the quantities purchased of each good (Frank 2002). Standard economic analysis assumes that the products and the benefits which can be derived from them are well known and understood by the consumer

---

[2] We are aware that by excluding the discussion of how consumers distribute their income between savings/investments and direct consumption, we are simplifying consumer theory. However, we trust that the level of detail provided is sufficient to illustrate the most important conceptual differences between theories of decision-making under certainty (orthodox consumer theory) and theories of decision-making under uncertainty (all the other theoretical approaches described in this section).

(Folland et al. 2001). Thus, demand for most commodities, such as food or clothing, appears to be steady in origin, regular, and predictable by the consumer (Arrow 1963).

This assumption, however, does not hold true in the health care market (Arrow 1963). The consumer in fact, can in most instances not predict future consumption of health care because of his/her inability to predict future illness episodes and/or the benefit he/she may derive from the consumption of health services. The case of demand for health insurance represents a further departure from standard economic analysis as insurance is also not desired *per se*, but as a means towards satisfying other needs. In the case of health care, it is future access to medical services that the individual is securing through the purchase of insurance. In turn, the consumption of medical services produces a benefit, by protecting or restoring health, only in the case of illness (Arrow 1963). Thus, treating demand for health insurance in the same way as demand for any other good appears to be unfeasible. Since the decision to purchase insurance is not reached under conditions of certainty, i.e. at time of purchase the individual does not know whether he/she will fall sick and whether the available services will always suffice to restore his/her health, much of the economic literature attempting to explain demand for health insurance has therefore relied on theories of decision-making under uncertainty.

Figure 1.3: Relationship between health insurance, health care, and health

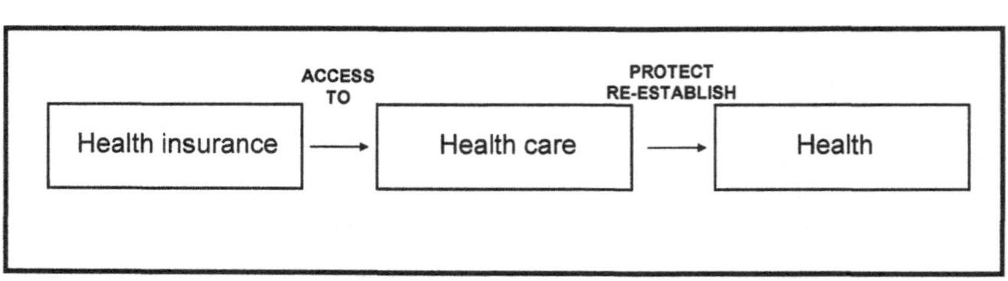

The most prominent theories of decision-making under uncertainty are: expected utility, state-dependent utility, endowment effect, status quo bias, regret and disappointment paradigms, and prospect theory.

Expected utility theory assumes that individuals act to maximise their utility[3]. When faced with an uncertain prospect, they will choose between two alternatives depending upon which one of the two offers the highest total expected utility. Expected utility theory postulates that individuals derive utility from their income and that the cost of medical care can act as a random deduction from this income. The theory further assumes that individuals are risk-averse, meaning that they are reluctant to choose an alternative that involves risk (Schoemaker 1982). Risk aversion is usually quantified by the mathematical expected value that one is willing to forego in order to get greater certainty (Folland et al. 2001). Individuals demand health insurance as a means of maximising their utility over a long period of time, protecting their income from the potentially catastrophic impact of medical costs. They prefer to undergo a certain loss today, i.e. paying the health insurance premium, rather than facing the uncertainty of a loss of potentially greater entity, which may occur in the future should they fall sick, need medical care, and still be uninsured (Arrow 1963). The implication of this model is that the more risk-averse an individual is the more insurance coverage he/she will purchase.

Figure 1.4: Simplified illustration of the concept of risk aversion

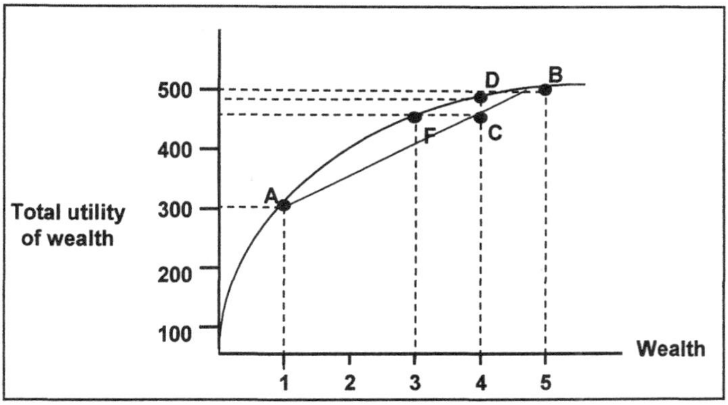

At a wealth level of 5, the individual enjoys a utility of 500 (B). However, knowing that he/she faces the probability of falling sick and that his wealth may decline to wealth level 1 due to medical expenses (A), he/she can only enjoy a lower total expected utility than the one his/her wealth could actually afford him/her (C). By forgoing a certain loss every month, i.e. paying the insurance premium, so that his/her income is stable at level 4 even in the event of illness, the individual can enjoy a total higher expected utility (D) than the one he/she enjoys when facing the uncertain prospect of falling sick and experiencing a substantial decline in wealth (C). In fact, the individual is willing to purchase insurance up to the point where the wealth remaining after paying the premium still grants him/her a total expected utility (F) that equals the expected utility he/she derives when facing the uncertain prospect of falling sick (C).

Expected utility theory as such is silent about the impact of the individual's income on decision to purchase insurance. It does not discuss how one's income may affect risk-aversion and thus, the decision to purchase insurance (Schneider 2004). The literature on poverty, however, has described how household socio-economic status may shape risk-aversion and therefore influence the decision to purchase insurance. The model proposed suggests that the closer the households are to the poverty line, the more risk-averse they will be. Any further drop in income may in fact easily cause them to exceed their coping capacity and drop below the poverty line (Morduch 1995; The World Bank 2001). It follows that poorer households may be more willing to insurance to protect their meagre assets from future shocks (Schneider 2004). Yet another explanatory model comes from the work of Ahuja and Jütting, who claimed that in spite of their potentially greater willingness to purchase insurance, the poor may not be able to do so because of institutional constraints. Ahuja and Jütting argued that low demand for health insurance in poor settings and especially among poor people is not the consequence of poverty *per se*, but rather of institutional constraints liming opportunities to ease insurance purchase[4] (Ahuja and Jütting 2003a).

Expected utility theory has been criticised as the principles and axioms on which it is based do not seem to hold true in laboratory studies nor in real life (Schoemaker 1982). People's perceptions of the probability and magnitude of a potential loss, as well as their perception as to the cost of insurance, may differ from what valued to be realistic and included in actuarial calculations. It follows that people's perception of the probability with which an event is likely to occur, i.e. their subjective view of risk, will in practice affect the decision to purchase insurance to a different extent than what postulated by the expected utility model. In addition, in some instances, for example in the case of low-probability high-loss events, people may find it particularly difficult to assess the probability of a certain risk occurring. The fact that at times people ignore low probability events whereas at other times they focus on the magnitude of the potential loss raises substantial doubts against the assumption that preferences are as consistent and coherent as claimed by expected utility theory. A potential

---

[4] It is true that due to the positive association that exists between low-income and poor health (Wagstaff et al. 2001; Wagstaff 2002), less wealthy individuals may indirectly be excluded from insurance plans through underwriting practices. In high-income countries in fact, insurance companies may limit access for sicker individuals, i.e. who are also likely to be the least wealthy, by imposing on them a higher premium (Cutler and Zeckhauser 1999). Given our exclusive focus on theories of demand for health insurance, however, we do not discuss in this section supply-side, i.e. the insurer, incentives. In addition, the focus of our study is on low-income settings, where insurance premiums tend to be community rather than individually rated. Thus, underwriting practices limiting access to insurance plans play only a very marginal role within the context of a discussion on CHI in Africa.

explanation for the discrepancy observed between what would be predicted by the model and what is observed in real life may be due to the fact that people's preferences do not hold in a vacuum, but are context-dependent, influenced by marketing, labelling, and by the specific circumstances surrounding the decision-making process. Unlike what assumed by the model, decisions are often made is a decomposed manner which relies on relative comparisons across options available rather than on the existence of absolute preferences (Schoemaker 1982). Cultural norms and values are powerful in shaping individual risk-perceptions as well as response mechanisms (Sommerfeld et al. 2002b).

State-dependent utility theory refers precisely to the contextual situation which frames the decision-making process. Like expected utility theory, this model recognises the existence of risk-aversion. In addition, however, this model acknowledges that insurance purchase does not occur exclusively as a function of risk-aversion, but it is also influenced by the state of the individual, specifically by his/her socio-economic status and his/her health, which in turn influences the anticipated need for medical care. The decision is thus made in terms of the expected pay-off that the insurance contract will yield. It follows that individuals who anticipate a higher pay-off, most likely those in a worse-off health status, will purchase more insurance. In contrast, those in good health not expecting a great need for medical care, may choose to remain uninsured (Farley and Monheit 1985).

Endowment effect, status quo bias, and regret theory also all recognise the contextual nature of the decision-making process under uncertainty. Rather than focusing on the pay-off of insurance calculated as a function of one's expected demand for medical services, all three paradigms relate to the concept of loss aversion, i.e. an indication that the disutility of giving up an object is greater than the utility that would be associated with acquiring it (Kahneman et al. 1991). All three theoretical models recognise that when making a decision between alternatives, individuals hold one option, usually the current one or the known one, as a reference point, against which they judge the potential advantages and disadvantages of the other alternatives (Kahneman et al. 1991).

Specifically, endowment effect theory postulates that individuals may be unwilling to give up something they currently hold, i.e. a portion of their income to pay a premium, when they are not sure of the entity of the gains of the alternative they know the least, i.e. the insurance and its potential benefits (Kahneman et al. 1991). It follows that individuals may demand more to purchase insurance than the mere coverage of health services. They may require, for example, additional facilitations to access or improvements in the quality of the care provided (Schneider 2004). Status quo bias and regret theory both frame the concept of loss aversion with reference to how individuals often perceive the disadvantages of leaving a known status as being larger than its potential advantages (Kahneman et al. 1991; Salkeld et al. 2000; Samuelson and Zeckhauser 1998). In this case, innovations in the provision and delivery of health services are simply not valued sufficiently by the individual, who is reluctant to abandon the known for the unknown. If applied to insurance purchase, this theoretical approach may explain why some people will continue to refuse to purchase insurance coverage, always preferring direct out-of-pocket payments at point of delivery even though they may also perceive the latter as inconvenient. The new alternative, in this case insurance purchase, may also not be chosen out of fear of regret or disappointment, in case the choice to join a scheme should prove to have been wrong or the benefits should not correspond to one's expectations (Salkeld et al. 2000; Smith 1996).

Yet another criticism directed against expected utility theory comes from proponents of prospect theory (Kahneman and Tversky 1979) . Prospect theory postulates that the way individuals frame an outcome or a transaction in their mind affects the utility they expect to derive from a given prospect. Unlike expected utility theory, the model recognises that the preference order is not invariant across contexts and that the same prospect can be edited and valued in different ways depending of the context in which it appears. An important feature of this model is its focus on the process, measured in terms of gains and losses as perceived by the individual, rather than exclusively on the utility associated with the final states. Applied to the concept of insurance purchase, this model suggests that individuals demand insurance not because they wish to minimise uncertainty, but rather because they expect a certain gain from their status of being insured. Given a premium level, individuals assess their own health status and health care needs and decide to insure if they feel that future deviations from the current status will with certainty cause them to incur a loss. In this case, they choose to purchase insurance because they expect their decision to result in a certain gain (Kahneman and Tversky 1979). Cumulative prospect theory represents a further development of prospect theory, incorporating in addition elements of state-dependent theory (Tversky and Kahneman 1992). This more recent model postulates that decisions between prospects are made by weighting the probability of potential gains and losses. This model assumes that demand for health insurance will therefore also depend upon an individual's perception of his/her probability to fall sick.

The access motive paradigm is in clear disagreement with the notion that insurance purchase is determined exclusively by a valuation of gains and losses. This model postulates that the benefits derived from health insurance are not limited to the gain from the avoidance of financial risk by risk-averse individuals, but that additional benefits are derived from the ability of the insurance to grant access to medical services that would otherwise not be affordable at all. Nyman argued that there is no financial risk for unaffordable health care purchase simply because such purchase cannot *a priori* occur privately. Therefore, individuals purchase health insurance as the only mechanism available to gain access to medical care that they would otherwise have to forgo (Nyman 1999). Households, especially in poor settings, may have access to alternative methods of securing enough money to access medical services, such as credit or self-insurance though consumption smoothing, but such strategies may still be insufficient in case of severe diseases, requiring expensive treatment (Besley 1995; Dercon 2002; Morduch 1995; Townsend 1995).

The economic literature recognises that insurance purchase may also be influenced by an individual's time preferences. The concept of time preferences refers to a preference for either present or future consumption of available resources. Decision to purchase insurance implies in fact a trade-off between current and future consumption, giving up a portion of income today in order to safeguard income in the future. Individuals who attribute a higher value to future protection than current consumption are more likely to purchase insurance than individuals who attribute a higher value to present consumption than future protection (Schneider 2004; The World Bank 2001). Time preferences, however, have in turn been found to be influenced by socio-economic status, with poorer individuals and/or poorer societies consistently displaying a preference for present rather than future consumption (Gbangou et al. 2005; Lawrance 1991; Wladarsch 2003). This is likely to be the effect of an inability to consider future needs when preoccupied with meeting the most immediate ones rather than the expression of a real preference to privilege present above future consumption. It is probable that even if interested to purchase insurance, poorer people may simply be unable to afford such purchase without jeopardising their immediate survival (Schneider 2004). Although not often mentioned in the economic literature, cultural norms and beliefs as well as past experience have been found to be powerful in shaping time preferences (Wladarsch 2003).

1.3.2 Alternative explanatory models

Alternative explanatory models discussing insurance purchase rarely adopt the same terminology employed by economists. Rather than referring to demand for health insurance, non-economists most often refer to insurance purchase in terms of decision to enrol or to participate in a scheme. The different terminology adopted reveals the origin of these alternative approaches, which have emerged out the literature on development and have until now been applied almost exclusively to studies in low income settings. Talking of decision to enrol or to participate in a scheme rather than of demand for health insurance appears to address the issue more holistically, taking into account the specificities of settings where insurance is offered by non-profit organisations often managed by community members themselves. In addition, this alternative terminology denotes an attention to the importance of factors beyond those traditionally recognised as relevant by economists. Alternative explanatory models aim in fact at combining different disciplines, such as sociology, anthropology, and social history, without excluding health economics, in an attempt to answer the question as to why people may choose to enrol in a given scheme or not (Waelkens and Criel 2004). Alternative approaches to the study of insurance purchase have not been described in the literature as stand-alone theoretical arguments, as it has been the case in the field of health economics. Alternative explanatory models have emerged primarily out of empirical studies (Atim 1999; Criel et al. 1998; Criel et al. 2002; Criel and Waelkens 2003; Fonteneau 2000; Ron 1999), which have later been grouped together and defined to be representative of a distinct theoretical approach (Waelkens and Criel 2004).

The focus of the studies looking at insurance purchase beyond the standard economic approach, is no longer on the net benefit that the individual may gain by insuring, but rather on the social dynamics which shape collective interests and processes and thus decision to enrol in a scheme (Fonteneau 2000; Waelkens and Criel 2004). What is recognised is that not all social behaviour is influenced by factors to which one can explicitly attribute a monetary value. Some social behaviour can better be explained in relation to the specificity of a given context and to a need to fulfil social norms, to respect traditional beliefs, and to meet collective expectations. An example prior to the emergence of health insurance in low income settings, comes from analysing participation in civic organisations, where decision to join is shaped on one side by considerations of self-interest, those traditionally acknowledged by economists as well, and on the other side by social norms regulating principles of solidarity, reciprocal engagement, and volunteerism (Weinberger 2000). With specific reference to the field of insurance, the decision to enrol in a scheme is assumed to be influenced by social capital, defined as a web of cooperating and trusting relationships between people that facilitates collaborative action to meet common needs (Veenstra 2005), by social class dynamics, by the perceived quality of the medical services to which the insurance promises to grant access, and by the trust the community has both in providers and in the insurance promoters (Schneider 2004; Waelkens and Criel 2004).

1.3.3 Review of empirical research

1.3.3.1 Review of empirical research in high income countries

Although the focus of this dissertation is on sub-Saharan Africa, it is nevertheless useful for the purpose of our discussion to take a brief look at studies having explored the decision to purchase health insurance in other countries. While the literature specific to sub-Saharan Africa, and in general to low income countries, is still very limited, much attention has been devoted to understand insurance purchase in high income settings. Looking at the design of the major studies conducted in high income settings, as well as at the conclusions they have reached, has proved to be informative in establishing the conceptual framework and the methodology guiding our own work.

The theoretical discussion on insurance purchase which has been taking place within the field of health economics, and which we have described in the section above, is not necessarily reflected in the empirical literature. Most empirical studies modelled demand for health insurance without explicitly referring to one single theoretical approach (Browne 1992; Ettner 1997; Harmon and Nolan 2001; McCall et al. 1997; McCall et al. 1998; Paulin and Dietz 1995; Shea and Stewart 1995; Shmueli 1998; Wilcox-Gok and Rubin 1994). In spite of the considerable criticism directed towards it, the few studies that explicitly incorporated theoretical considerations in the construction of their models, all did so starting from a discussion of expected utility theory (Cameron et al. 1988; Hopkins and Kidd 1996; Liu and Chen 2002; Marquis and Long 1995; Propper 1989; Rhine and Ng 1998). Marquis and Holmer attempted to model demand for health insurance using alternative theoretical approaches, but since their estimation data consisted of responses to hypothetical insurance offers, one may question how well the estimated models would really predict actual behaviour (Marquis and Holmer 1996).

Most studies treated demand for health insurance as a discrete choice problem and applied a one stage empirical model. One stage models rely on the application of one single equation and assume that the individual decides at once whether or not to purchase insurance and how much insurance coverage to purchase. Some studies applying a one stage model used maximum likelihood logistic regression (Cameron et al. 1988; Hopkins and Kidd 1996; McCall et al. 1998; Propper 1989), while others applied probit regression (Harmon and Nolan 2001; Marquis and Long 1995; Shea and Stewart 1995; Shmueli 1998; Wilcox-Gok and Rubin 1994). Three studies focused on differential coverage, measured in terms of insurance typology, i.e. public vs. private, or insurance level, i.e. complete vs. partial coverage, thus they applied multinomial logistic regression (Ettner 1997; Paulin and Dietz 1995; Rhine and Ng 1998). Only one study treated decision to purchase insurance as sequential. The model estimation was based on the assumption that an individual is first faced with the decision of whether to purchase insurance or not and then, in case he/she should have decided to purchase insurance, he/she has to decide what amount of insurance to purchase. The paper applying this model relied on logistic regression to estimate the first step in the decision-making process, i.e. whether to purchase insurance at all, and, for those having chosen to purchase insurance, on ordinary least square regression to estimate the second step, i.e. what amount of insurance to purchase (Liu and Chen 2002). With the exception of one study which used pseudo-panel data derived from repeated cross-sectional surveys (Propper et al. 1999), all other papers used cross-sectional data, most often derived from large scale national surveys. Only two studies incorporated a price variable in their regression model (Ettner 1997; Marquis and Long 1995).

Two strands of studies emerge from the review of the empirical literature on insurance purchase. On one side, a number of studies have looked at the amount of coverage purchased by individuals in settings where voluntary private health insurance represents the only option available to consumers. On the other side, in settings where health financing relies primarily on tax-based or social insurance systems, studies have looked at the purchase of supplemental health insurance. Although the focus of this dissertation is more in line with the first set of studies, since we look at insurance purchase in a context where CHI represents the only alternative to user fees for the vast majority of the population, we shall in this section take a brief look at both set of studies. Some themes in fact, for example knowledge of benefits, have been investigated exclusively in the second set of studies.

The first attempt to explore demand for health insurance dates back to 1973. Based on household survey data from 1963, Phelps explored demand for health insurance among families in the United States. He found a positive correlation between choice of insurance plan and income, education, urban residency, and race. Using aggregate (annual) time-series data, holding average population coverage as the outcome variable, he identified a positive correlation between insurance purchase and both user fees and the mean level of illness recorded in a region. His study also detected a negative association between insurance purchase and premium level (Phelps 1973).

Following Phelps' first analysis of demand for health insurance, a number of authors explored the issue within the context of a country, the United Stated, that, unlike European nations, has chosen to fund health care provision primarily through private insurance, but where one out of six citizens below 65 years of age still has no coverage (Rhine and Ng 1998). All studies consistently reported a positive association between insurance status and high income, with low income individuals being more likely to be uninsured, only partially insured, or covered exclusively through some sort of government social security program

(Marquis and Long 1995; Paulin and Dietz 1995; Rhine and Ng 1998). Similarly, studies reported a positive association between insurance coverage and occupational status, indicating that the number of earners in a family as well as the nature of the job contract, full-time vs. part-time, significantly increased the probability of being insured (Paulin and Dietz 1995; Rhine and Ng 1998).

In line with Phelps' first analysis, other authors also consistently found a positive association between ethnicity and insurance coverage, with minorities enjoying the least probability of being insured (Paulin and Dietz 1995; Rhine and Ng 1998). Across studies, findings were not consistent when looking at the impact of the age of the household head, one study suggesting that younger heads tend to purchase more insurance (Marquis and Long 1995) and one study suggesting exactly the opposite (Paulin and Dietz 1995). Only one study looked exclusively at the role of health status in determining insurance purchase. By comparing insurance purchase in the individual and in the group, i.e. employer-based, markets, Browne concluded that, given government subsidies, low-risk individuals end up purchasing more insurance in the group market than they would have otherwise purchased in the individual market, favouring this way cross-subsidisation from low to high-risk people (Browne 1992). Marquis et al. (1995) found that families having indicated at least one member as being in poor health were less likely to have insurance, probably not out of their own will, but rather because of effective underwriting practices limiting purchase in the individual insurance market (Marquis and Long 1995). Across studies, region and/or location of residency were found to be significantly associated with insurance coverage (Marquis and Long 1995; Paulin and Dietz 1995; Rhine and Ng 1998).

In the late 1970s, Australia provided the ideal setting for the study of demand for health insurance as it allowed its citizens to opt out of a government-sponsored plan and purchase, as an alternative, private coverage in a highly regulated market. Based on data from the 1977-1978 National Health Survey, Cameron et al. (1988) developed a model to estimate demand for health insurance and demand for health services jointly. Their findings indicated a positive association between insurance purchase and socio-economic characteristics, in particular education and income. Variables measuring health status, although important predictors of health service utilisation, appeared to have only a minor role in predicting insurance purchase. In line with studies from the United States, Cameron et al. also identified significant differences associated with region of residency (Cameron et al. 1988).

As mentioned earlier in this section, an important market for supplemental health insurance exists in several countries where national coverage of basic services is secured either through a tax-based or a social insurance system. Although plans may vary considerably across countries, supplemental health insurance is usually, but not always, supplied by private for-profit insurance companies. These companies enter the market offering coverage for what services are not reimbursed by the national system, such as dental or long-term residential care, or providing additional benefits to patients, such as the possibility of bypassing waiting lists or being hospitalised in a private room.

Propper has investigated demand for private supplemental health insurance in England over a 20 year period, her first study being published already in 1989 (Propper 1989). Although the methodology differed from one study to the next, Propper consistently found a significant association between the decision to purchase supplemental health insurance and socio-economic characteristics, in particular income, education, and occupational status (Propper 1989; Propper 1993). While findings from her first study were not conclusive as to the role of health status, findings from the second study suggested that poor health status was associated with a reduced probability of purchasing supplemental insurance. In line with finding by Marquis (1995), Propper attributed the association between poor health status and reduced insurance purchase to underwriting practices restricting entry into the schemes. Using pseudo-panel data derived from repeated cross-sectional surveys, her latest study broadened the perspective on demand for health insurance, incorporating contextual factors, such as institutional and quality changes over time, into the analysis. The findings continued to indicate the importance of socio-demographic characteristics, but also highlighted how the relative quality of services in the public and private health sectors affected the decision to purchase private supplemental health insurance (Propper et al. 1999). In all three studies, Propper identified important differences in insurance coverage across regions.

Based on an adaptation of the model developed by Propper in 1989, Harmon and Nolan investigated determinants of demand for supplemental private health insurance in Ireland. Their results were consistent with those by Propper. They identified a positive association between insurance purchase and socio-demographic characteristics, such as income and education, and a negative association between insurance purchase and health status. They also found that gender and age were important determinants of purchase, with women and younger people having a higher probability of being insured when compared respectively to men and older people (Harmon and Nolan 2001). The effect of age and gender observed in this study, but not in others (Cameron et al. 1988; Propper 1989), may be due to the fact that Harmon and Nolan analysed data at the individual level, while other studies aggregated data at the family level, choosing as outcome variable household rather than individual insurance status.

Based on data from the 1998 Survey of Family Income and Expenditure, Liu and Chen (2002) looked at demand for private supplemental health insurance in Taiwan (Liu and Chen 2002). Their findings were consistent with those of studies conducted in Western Europe and North America, as they also identified higher income, higher education, and being employed as important predictors of insurance purchase. Their study included no measure of health status, but it did include a measure of previous health care utilisation, which was found to be insignificant in predicting insurance purchase. Their study also highlighted an important association between insurance coverage and location of residency, measured in terms of region and urban vs. rural.

In 1984, Australia established a universal, tax-financed public health insurance scheme which provides basic standard care in public hospitals and subsidises the cost of medical care in private outpatient practices outside hospitals. Following the introduction of national coverage, private health insurance ownership dropped dramatically. Based on data from the 1989-1990 National Health Survey, Hopkins and Kidd (1996) took a second look at determinants of demand for health insurance in Australia, now under different policy conditions from the ones described by Cameron et al. (1988). Their findings confirmed the positive association between insurance purchase and socio-economic status, measured in terms of education and income, and recent health care utilisation. They also confirmed the existence of important regional differences, which the authors explained in terms of the interstate differences in the relative supply of public vs. private facilities and in the price of health insurance, two variables not included in their model (Hopkins and Kidd 1996).

A final set of five studies, of which four were conducted in the United States and one in Israel, looked at supplemental insurance purchase exclusively among the elderly. All studies consistently identified a significant association between insurance purchase and higher income, higher education, better health status, and being female (Ettner 1997; McCall et al. 1998; Shea and Stewart 1995; Shmueli 1998; Wilcox-Gok and Rubin 1994). Three studies found a negative association between insurance purchase and minority status, with whites being the ones who enjoyed the highest probability of purchasing additional coverage (Ettner 1997; Shea and Stewart 1995; Wilcox-Gok and Rubin 1994). Two studies identified a positive association between insurance purchase and health service utilisation (Ettner 1997; Wilcox-Gok and Rubin 1994). One study also incorporated a set of variables to measure the respondents' knowledge of long-term care in relation to the benefits covered by the standard insurance scheme and those covered only by supplemental coverage. This study found that the better the knowledge, the higher the probability of purchasing additional coverage (McCall et al. 1998). Only two out of five studies explicitly modelled regional differences, finding, yet again, significant variations in insurance coverage across regions (Shea and Stewart 1995; Wilcox-Gok and Rubin 1994).

In summary, the review of the literature identifies that major determinants of insurance purchase in high-income settings are socio-demographic characteristics, such as education, income, employment status, sex, and ethnicity (when relevant). Previous health service utilisation also appears to be associated with the decision to purchase insurance. The empirical evidence on the existence of adverse selection, when measured exclusively in terms of health status, is rather weak, with the vast majority of studies having identified that individuals in better health also tend to purchase more insurance. This is probably due to underwriting procedures which effectively limit access for sicker people in the private insurance market. There is some evidence that knowledge of health benefits in the public vs. the private system may also influence the decision to purchase insurance. Location of residency, whether measured at the town, district, or regional level, consistently appears to be an important predictor of insurance purchase.

1.3.3.2 Review of empirical research in sub-Saharan Africa

The research on insurance purchase in sub-Saharan Africa does by no means match the wealth of research conducted on the same topic in high income countries. Given that low participation has long been identified as a fundamental obstacle to the successful implementation of CHI across sub-Saharan nations (Atim 1998; Bennett et al. 1998; Waelkens and Criel 2004), the almost complete lack of scientific attention dedicated to the matter appears surprising. Most early analyses and reviews of CHI, mainly consultancy reports commissioned by donor agencies and/or international organisations, have considered possible reasons motivating the low enrolment, but they have rarely presented a scientific investigation into its causes, thus providing only limited sound evidence for policy discussion (Atim 1998; Bennett et al. 1998; Fonteneau 2000). One isolated attempt was made in the late 1980s to understand what differentiated insured from non-insured households living in the catchment area of the Bwamanda Hospital Insurance Scheme. Based on data from a survey conducted on 518 households, Moens concluded that on average insured households tended to be wealthier, have fewer cattle, and be headed by individuals between 30 and 50 years of age (Moens 1990). His analysis, however, was based on a basic comparison of the socio-demographic characteristics between insured and non-insured households, rather than on the construction of a multivariate model, as the ones described in the section above, to allow for the exploration of the effect on demand for CHI of several factors at once. Therefore, his findings have to be interpreted with caution and, as such, they are rarely referred to in the literature on decision to enrol in CHI.

A detailed review of the published and unpublished literature led us to the identification of only three studies having conducted a systematic analysis of demand for CHI along the lines of the research on insurance purchase carried out in high income countries. One unpublished study focused exclusively on understanding demand for voluntary health insurance in rural Ghana (Osei-Akoto 2004). The other two studies looked at demand for voluntary health insurance within the framework of a broader study whose primary objective was to assess the impact of insurance status on access to care and health expenditure (Jütting 2004; Schneider and Diop 2004). All three studies relied on cross-sectional data. None of the studies included the price of the premium nor any other information on the insurance product in the model. In all three cases, however, the authors pooled together information on different schemes, where the insurance product, including the quality of the services contracted, and the price of the premium differed. By not controlling for such elements in their models, all three studies are likely to have introduced a source of bias in their analyses as they did not take into explicit account the fact that people respond to differences in prices and in the attributes of the products to be purchased.

Osei-Akoto presented an analysis of demand for CHI pooling together information on two districts in Ghana, Nkoranza and West Gonia (Osei-Akoto 2004). At the time of the analysis, a hospital-based scheme had been operative for 10 years in Nkoranza and for 7 years in West Gonia. Enrolment rates varied considerably between districts, with 33% of the population enrolled in Nkoranza and 13% enrolled in West Gonia. Based on survey data from 485 households, Osei-Akoto applied a zero-inflated Poisson regression with logit specification to understand which individual, household, and community characteristics affected the decision to participate in CHI. He chose to use zero-inflated Poisson regression model over simple logistic regression because, already prior to his study, he had observed that several households had bypassed CHI regulations enforcing household enrolment and had insured only a restricted number of family members. Therefore, his interest was in estimating simultaneously the probability of enrolment and the probability of the number of household members being enrolled. His findings indicated that the probability of enrolment in CHI was associated with socio-economic, employment, and migration statuses as well as with the location of the household relative to the location of the referral health facility. Households where adults held several jobs were more likely to enrol in the scheme, while poor households, migrant households, rural households, and households living far from the facility were much less likely to enrol. Household size and composition did not significantly influence the probability of a household to be enrolled, but they did influence the number of family members being insured within a household. The number of women living within a household and the number of illness episodes reported in the last six-months were both associated with a decrease in the number of household members being insured, while the opposite was true when considering the effect of the number of household members above age 60. Socio-economic, employment, and migrant statuses were not significant predictors of the number of family members being insured. Greater distance to the facility and rural residency were also significantly associated with the probability of enrolling fewer members of the household in the scheme.

Jütting investigated determinants of membership in CHI pooling together information on four villages in the Thiès region in Senegal, each village operating its own scheme, but all contracting services with the same provider, the St. Jean de Dieu Hospital (Jütting 2004). Enrolment across villages varied from 37.4% to 90.3%. Based on a weighed sample of 346 households, Jütting estimated the impact on household enrolment of individual and household characteristics using a probit regression model. He treated decision to enrol in CHI as a discrete choice problem although he also found that in some cases households had not enrolled all of their members. His findings identified a positive association between enrolment and socio-economic status, indicating that the poorer were excluded from the schemes. Among all household head socio-demographic characteristics (age, sex, literacy, religion, ethnicity), only religion and ethnicity were found to be significant in predicting enrolment. Christian and Wolof people were found to be more likely to enrol their households than people from all other religious and ethnic groups. Membership in another organisation was also found to be associated with a greater probability of enrolment in CHI. Jütting's findings also reported no evidence of adverse selection into the scheme as illness ratio, measured in terms of the number of illness cases per household over the number of household members, was found not to be associated with enrolment. Village of residency constituted a significant predictor of enrolment.

Similarly to Jütting, Schneider and Diop also treated household decision to enrol in CHI in Rwanda as a discrete choice problem. However, they applied a logistic rather than a probit regression model to examine the effect of individual and household characteristics on decision to enrol (Schneider and Diop 2004). They based their analysis on data from 2,518 households resident in three districts where CHI was being piloted, each district operating its own distinct community-based scheme. Their findings identified as important determinants of enrolment in CHI, household head's level of education, family size, distance to the health facility, and radio ownership. Households whose heads had attended school, larger households, households living closer to the health facility, and households owning a radio were all found to enjoy a much greater probability of enrolling in CHI. In line with the two previous studies, their findings also detected no adverse selection. However, they used rather broad indicators of health status: (1) having experienced a pregnancy; and (2) having spent more than four days in bed in the previous year. The most striking result, however, pertains to the fact that, unlike all others studies on insurance purchase; the study in Rwanda found no association between socio-economic status and enrolment. Explaining the discrepancy with all prior research appears rather difficult given that the authors used a standard measure of socio-economic status, i.e. per capita monthly expenditure. The authors justified this surprising result in relation to the fact that the community under study was homogenously poor so that real differences in wealth across income groups (quartiles) were minimal. Schneider and Diop also observed significant differences in the probability of being insured across districts.

An alternative approach to the understanding of decision to enrol in CHI was pursued in three studies, which relied on qualitative rather than quantitative methods of analysis. In these studies, the investigators engaged the community in an active discussion regarding the reasons for having enrolled or not enrolled in a scheme, exploring social dynamics and touching upon a series of themes, such as payment modalities, unit of enrolment, and quality of care, which cannot easily be included in standard econometric modelling.

The most noteworthy of these three studies looked at the decision to enrol in the Maliando Mutual Health Organisation, a CHI scheme set up around the catchment area of the Yende health centre in the Kissidougou district in Guinea-Conakry (Criel et al. 2002; Criel and Waelkens 2003). The scheme was only operative over a period of two years, from 1998 to 2000. At the time when the study was conducted, enrolment rates had dropped from 8% to 6%. This drop motivated the scheme initiators to conduct a series of focus group discussions in order to understand the reasons behind the low enrolment. In total, 16 focus group discussions (FGD) were conducted with four different groups of people: (1) those having subscribed in two subsequent years; (2) those having subscribed only during the first year; (3) those having subscribed only during the second year; and (4) those never having subscribed to the scheme. The transcribed text of all 16 FGD was coded along three different lines, allowing for the same portion of text to be classified by different investigators and more than once. This allowed crosschecking the validity of the findings by comparing classifications across groups to verify the interpretation of the material collected.

Respondents in Guinea-Conakry showed a clear understanding of the insurance principle and an appreciation for the effort to establish a system that would facilitate access to care in their community. Affordability of the premium was cited as the main reason for not enrolling in the scheme, especially for the very poor, the physically disabled, and the chronically ill. In addition, respondents identified household enrolment as an important obstacle to participation in the scheme, especially for large households having to cover the premium for too large a number of people. The community in Yende also showed no appreciation for the quality of care provided and therefore no incentive to enrol. Criticisms were directed both towards the availability of services and drugs and the providers' attitudes towards patients. In particular, respondents found that the services on offer for the insured at the contracted health facility were of inferior quality to the services on offer for the non-insured at other facilities in the area. Respondents recognised possible similarities between the insurance scheme and traditional forms of risk-sharing. Nevertheless, they expressed a certain scepticism towards engaging in institutionalised arrangements. Given their previous negative experiences with institutionalised forms of risk-sharing, such as micro-credit schemes, several respondents admitted to be sceptical and wished to wait to see how the scheme would develop before enrolling. Two years after the launch of the scheme, respondents expressed no lack of confidence in the integrity and management skills of the Maliando directorate, but rather criticised the organisation for not having achieved its promised objective of making high quality care available to all.

The other two studies were not conducted as *ad hoc* scientific investigations into the problem of low enrolment, but were the by-product of broader consultancy efforts set to evaluate the achievements of two schemes, the Nkoranza Community Health Insurance Scheme in Ghana and the Community Health Fund in the Hanang District in Tanzania. In both instances, the discussion of what factors might have influenced the decision to enrol was only one among the many issues addressed, receiving secondary attention when compared to the most prominent focus on managerial and financial matters.

The first of these two consultancy reports examined the decision to enrol in the Nkoranza hospital-based scheme in Ghana (Atim and Madjiguene 2000). Atim and Sock (2000) discussed the results of 43 FGD conducted with community members at a time when 30% of the eligible population was enrolled in the scheme. In the study report, the authors described how groups were formed taking into account the respondents' gender, age, and occupation. Unlike Criel et al. (2003), however, Atim and Sock provided no information regarding the systematic inclusion or exclusion of different community constituencies, such as enrolled and non-enrolled individuals and/or health service users and non-users. Thus, the presentation of the findings turns out at times to be unclear since the reader cannot easily identify to whom to attribute a certain opinion or concern. In addition, it appears that the groups were not conducted in a standardised manner across health zones within the District. Furthermore, the authors did not describe in detail how they conducted data analysis. The presentation of the results appears as if all FGD consistently generated unanimous responses and participants never contested each other's statements.

In spite of the fact that the description of the methods appears unclear, the authors offered an interesting discussion of the decision to enrol in CHI. They identified three major factors constraining enrolment: (1) the erroneous timing of the registration; (2) the community poor perception of the scheme objectives; and (3) adverse selection. Unlike the study by Criel and Waelkens (2003), the community did not mention lack of means as the main reason for not enrolling in the scheme. The community did recognise, however, that affordability was severely hampered by the timing of the campaign, which did not match the harvest season. Atim and Sock found that the perceived quality of care did not *per se* constitute a problem in the Nkoranza district. During the discussions, the community expressed appreciation for the quality of the services available and confidence in the medical capacity of the providers. However, respondents indicated that they did not trust the motives behind the initiation of the insurance scheme nor the management of the hospital. Although their belief did not match the reality of service provision, as records consistently showed that enrolees received better care than non-enrolees, respondents, especially non-members, often attributed their decision not to enrol to the feeling that, in order to maximise profits, hospital managers would intentionally trim down the length of hospitalisation and the quality of services for CHI enrolees. The authors attributed this misrepresentation of the scheme objectives to the fact that the local population had no active role in the scheme management, in spite of their widespread and persistent claim to assume one. The measure of adverse selection used in the study is questionable given that the authors had no access to accurate information on the health status of respondents. Nevertheless, they examined enrolment trends over time and saw that in spite of compulsory household enrolment, households enrolled only a selected number of individuals and that membership patterns changed remarkably one year to the next. This led the authors to believe that each year, households chose to register only the sickest members and by doing so, they inevitably constrained the overall enrolment rate in the region.

In the case of the study conducted in the Hanang District in Tanzania, the analysis of the decision to enrol was based on information collected through 4 FGD with scheme members and 5 FGD with non-members as well as a number of exit interviews conducted with patients at district facilities (Chee et al. 2002). The study was conducted in 2001, at a time when average enrolment rate was 5% although remarkable differences were observed across regions within the District, with rates ranging from 0.3% to 13%. Similarly to the study by Atim and Sock (2000), the report by Chee et al. describing the experience in Tanzania also offers no details on the methodological approach to data analysis. The presentation of responses, however, is clearly differentiated between scheme members and non-members. Chee et al. found that although most respondents had heard of the scheme and expressed appreciation for its objective, their knowledge of its specific features was rather poor and the sense of community ownership was basically non-existent. The most common reason indicated for not enrolling was lack of means, as respondents felt that it was easier to pay a smaller amount at time of illness than to pay a larger amount once a year. Non-members also felt that they may simply not utilise health services frequently enough to make up for the money paid as yearly premium. The study reported no systematic investigation of the community perception of the quality of care. It remains unclear, however, whether specific questions linking quality of care to enrolment were not asked or whether communities were satisfied with the care on offer. The authors provided no extensive explanation to justify the different enrolment rates observed across regions within the District.

Drawing any conclusion on the reasons motivating or discouraging enrolment in CHI on the basis of only six studies, two of which are consultancy reports and not scientific evaluation, is extremely difficult. Although most studies agree on the role of certain factors in influencing enrolment, for example income, they do disagree on several others, for example education, health status, and quality of care. This discrepancy may suggest that the decision to enrol is contextual and not influenced by exactly the same set of factors in all settings. The consistency with which location of residency appears to influence insurance purchase, both in high income countries and in sub-Saharan Africa, also seems to suggest that context is an important determinant of enrolment. However, in the case of the quantitative studies presented above, where information on different schemes was pooled together, the observed difference in enrolment rates across villages, districts, and/or regions could also indicate that different insurance packages may appear more or less attractive to the population, encouraging or discouraging enrolment. None of the studies conducted so far, however, has systematically looked into community preferences for the different elements of an insurance package, leaving much still to be explained in terms of enrolment decision. Likewise, none of the studies presented has systematically looked at how social norms and cultural beliefs may influence the decision to enrol. Only the study conducted in Guinea-Conakry has done so partially (Criel and Waelkens 2003). Its analysis, however, focused mainly on the community understanding of the insurance principle and the perceptions of the scheme, rather than on the broader socio-cultural discourse on health, health care, and access to health services.

The conclusion of this literature review is that more research is urgently needed to understand enrolment in CHI. Given the paucity of the evidence available, no conclusive statement can at present be made with regard to what policies may favour or disfavour enrolment in CHI. Research is therefore needed to build an evidence-base for policy-making. The focus ought to be on clarifying the role of certain factors, for example education and health status, in influencing enrolment and on exploring areas, such as social norms and cultural beliefs, which have so far not been addressed sufficiently by the relevant research. Given the central role that context can play in determining enrolment, the description of our methodology is preceded by a description of the setting where our study took place, with specific reference to the emergence of the CHI scheme at the core of our investigation.

1.4 The research setting

The research described in this dissertation was conducted in the Nouna Health District, one of the 53 health districts in Burkina Faso, West Africa. In order to set the research within its wider socio-political context, the description of the Nouna Health District is preceded by a general description of the country Burkina Faso. Our description of Burkina Faso focuses in particular on the performance of the health sector, the pitfalls in current health financing policies, and the recent emergence of CHI in the country.

Figure 1.5: Map of Burkina Faso

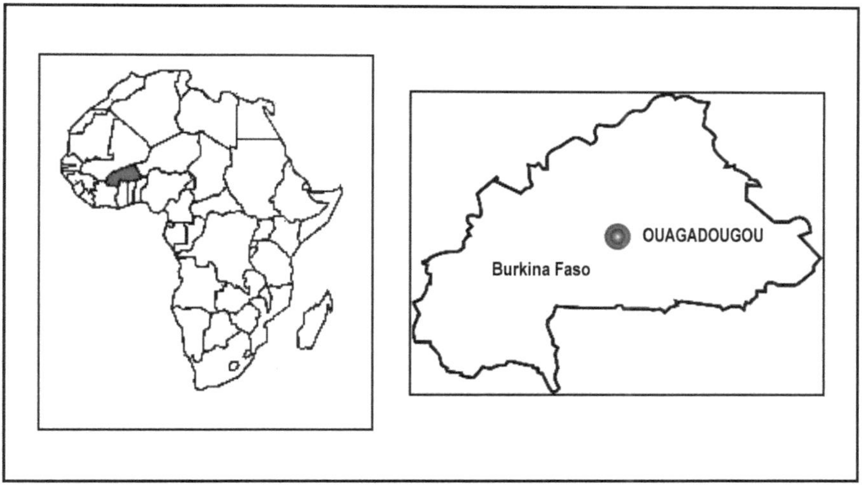

1.4.1 Burkina Faso

1.4.1.1 The Country

Burkina Faso is a landlocked country located in the Sahel region of West Africa. From 1897 to 1958, the country was a French colony, known as Upper Volta, a name that was retained even after gaining independence in 1960. It was only in 1984, after the revolution promoted among others by Thomas Sankara, that the country was renamed Burkina Faso. If translated literally, the name means "land of the incorruptible" or "land of the upright people". The composition of the name is derived from the two main local languages: Burkina is a Mooré word which indicates "pure" or "incorruptible", Faso is a Dioula word which indicates "homeland". People from Burkina Faso are known as Burkinabè, with the *bè* suffix being borrowed from the third main local language Fufulde. The inclusion of all three main local languages in the name of the country and its people is representative of an explicit choice to symbolise the end of colonisation as well equality among ethnic groups, a sign against the traditional dominance of the Mooré-speaking Mossi, the largest ethnic group in the country (Wladarsch 2003).

Burkina Faso is a presidential republic with President Blaise Compaoré as the head of state and an elected national assembly. The capital Ouagadougou is the largest town, followed by Bobo-Diolasso, the formal capital and still somewhat the cultural centre of the country. Burkina Faso counts a population of nearly 14 million inhabitants distributed over an area of 274, 200 (Central Intelligence Agency 2005). Of Burkina Faso's total population, nearly 20% currently live in urban areas. The population growth rate is still high and stands at 2.53% per year (Central Intelligence Agency 2005). The country is divided in 45 provinces. Each province is made up of several administrative departments, which in turn are made up of several villages and/or urban centres. The whole country counts 33 urban centres and approximately 8000 villages (World Health Organization 2000b).

Using the human development index, a measure of a country's achievements in terms of life expectancy, educational attainment, and adjusted real income, the United Nations ranks Burkina Faso at the 175th position, indicating it as one of the least developed countries in the world (United Nations Development Program 2005). In spite of a clear growth in per capita gross domestic product (GDP) since the launching of structural adjustment policies in 1991, Burkina Faso remains one of the poorest countries in the world with a per capita GDP of 1,100 US dollars (adjusted for purchasing power parity) (United Nations Development Program 2005). The economy remains fragile, with almost 80% of the total population employed in the agricultural sector, mostly in subsistence farming with millet as the main staple crop and cotton, sesame, and peanuts as the main cash crops. A recent survey estimates that 45.3% of the country population lives below the poverty line. As much as 27.5% of the total population lives in conditions of extreme poverty. Nearly 95% of the poor live in rural areas (Edmond et al. 2002) and only 13% of the population is literate (United Nations Development Program 2005).

The society is characterised by great ethnic variety, with more than 60 different ethnic groups peacefully cohabiting within the country. Nearly 50% of the population is Muslim, 40% is Animist, and 10% Christian. Each ethnic group has its own language and customs, but groups interact freely and inter-marriage is no longer uncommon, especially in the larger urban centres. Few are the villages made up of one ethnic group only. Usually, several groups cohabit within the same village, each one of them occupying a given neighbourhood, but meeting the other groups in all daily activities. The society is hierarchically structured according to seniority, with the age pyramid matching the authority pyramid. Each village has its own official administrative representative, the *délégué*, as well as one or several, depending on the ethnic composition of the village, traditional chiefs, known in Dioula as *dugutigi*. It is not uncommon for a *dugutigi* also to be elected by his population as the village *délégué*.

The official language French is not widely spoken in the rural areas, where a wealth of local languages prevails. The three main local languages, Mooré, Dioula, and Fufulde allow for communication across ethnic groups. Dioula, in particular, is a *lingua franca* commonly spoken across West Africa. Within Burkina Faso, Dioula is not the mother tongue of any ethnic group, but exclusively a language of commerce and trade which facilitates communication between people of different ethnic groups.

1.4.1.2 The health system

Most of the health system in Burkina Faso is operated by the State. The Ministry of Health performs a dual function, both normative, i.e. setting legislation and policy, and executive, planning and managing the supply of services. The private supply of health services exists, whether for-profit or not-for-profit, but it is negligible in comparison to public services. It mainly consists of private for-profit practices located in the main cities and religious or not-for-profit organisations scattered throughout the country, which work in close collaboration with the Ministry of Health (World Health Organization 2000b). As in most countries in sub-Saharan Africa, Burkina Faso also enjoys a long standing tradition of healers. However, little is known about the organisation of their work and the extent to which they really act as a substitute to modern medical services (World Health Organization 2000b).

The health system is subdivided into 11 Regional Health Directorates, whose geographical coverage corresponds to the catchment area of the 11 functional hospitals located in the country. Each Regional Health Directorate is in turn subdivided into Health Districts. Each Health District comprises a district hospital, in most cases a medical centre with a surgical unit (CMA), and several first line facilities, known as *Centres de Santé et Promotion Sociale* (CSPS), literally translated as Centres for Health and Social Promotion. Each CSPS covers between 10,000 and 20,000 people (Fonteneau 2000). The Health District is the most decentralised health unit, in charge of planning and managing health service provision at the local level. Each Health District covers a population of approximately 200,000 to 300,000 people. The autonomy with which each Health District can make decisions regarding health care provision in a given area is largely limited by administrative and legal constraints as well as by the fact that the government, through its Civil Service Ministry, remains the exclusive employer of medical staff for all public facilities in the country (World Health Organization 2000b).

The Bamako Initiative was launched in Burkina Faso in 1992-1993. Its primary objective was to revive primary health care, by increasing the resources available to the health system, through the application of user charges, and improving availability and access to primary services, through the development of community participation. Responsibility was assigned to the local communities through the establishment of *Comités de Gestion* (COGES), committees comprising of a mixture of community members and local health care providers in charge of managing the local CSPS (World Health Organization 2000b). Although highly effective in principle, in practice the COGES have not proved to be an adequate means of empowering communities to manage their own health care system. The Health District still retains authority over most decisions made at the local level and the single providers participating to the COGES tend to dominate decision-making at the level of the community.

The adoption in 1996 of a National Drugs Policy Framework Document and the establishment in 1998 of an Essential Generic Drugs and Medical Consumables Purchasing Pool (CAMEG) have substantially improved the pharmaceutical supply across the country, making drug shortages a memory of the past. Still, the resources available to the health sector are insufficient to meet the need of a growing population. Total health expenditure rests at 2.0% of GDP (United Nations Development Program 2005). The World Health Organisation estimates that in Burkina Faso, the State and external aid cover respectively 18% and 28% of all health expenditure, meaning that the remaining 54% is financed directly by the public, mostly through the payment of user fees (World Health Organization 2000b). User charges are applied in the form of fee-for-service, with rates defined by national guidelines for the various clinical, laboratory, and hospitalisation services. In addition, people are asked to pay for drugs even if dispensed directly by government facilities. Referral hospitals ought to comply with the national fee scale. First-line facilities, i.e. CSPS, are allowed to vary by 5% the price set for drugs by national guidelines and are also allowed to decide freely, within certain limits, the price for clinical and laboratory examinations (World Health Organization 2000b).

1.4.1.3 Access to care

In Burkina Faso, as elsewhere in sub-Saharan Africa, problems of access to care linked to geographical and cultural accessibility as well as to the poor quality of the services available, are exacerbated by the application of user fees (Edmond et al. 2002; World Health Organization 2000b). The vast majority of the population in fact, has no access to any social security and is left to pay for care out of pocket at point of delivery. Only civil servants enjoy insurance coverage through a plan that reimburses 80% of the cost of hospital fees. In addition, the government, though its National Social Security Fund, offers coverage for industrial accidents and occupational illnesses, but only to those workers who are employed in the formal sector and have paid their contribution (World Health Organization 2000b). A number of private companies such as SONAR, FONCIAS, and UAB offer private insurance contracts, but the prices remain prohibitive for the vast majority of the population. Officially, the Ministry of Health takes charge of the cost of the care for the very poor. In practice, however, there is no system to translate this policy into a programme that concretely secures pro-poor exemptions (World Health Organization 2000b).

Studies in Burkina Faso have repeatedly reported low utilisation rates following the introduction of user fees. In the Kongoussi District, between 1997 and 2000, the number of curative consultations fell on average by 15% in all CSPS charging fees, while, within the same district, it increased by 30% in all CSPS not charging fees. The trend was never reversed and people who decided to abandon their preferred facility following the introduction of fees, never went back (Ridde 2003). According to the Demographic and Health Survey (DHS) of 1998/1999, out of all pregnant women as many as 40% did not attend any prenatal visit and nearly 70% delivered without the assistance of trained personnel. Great differences were observed across socio-economic groups, with only 36.3% of women in the poorest quintile attending at least two prenatal visits as compared to 85.4% of those in the wealthiest quintile (Edmond et al. 2002).

According to the same survey, only 28% of children aged 12 to 23 months received all recommended immunisations (Edmond et al. 2002). Pooling together information on several provinces, Makinen et al. (2000) estimated that in Burkina Faso only 13% of those reporting ill seek modern medical care. They found that the rich are consistently more likely than the poor to seek care, to be seen by a doctor, and to report to a hospital in case of illness. Although the wealthy spend more on health services in absolute terms, health care spending clearly appears to be regressive as people in the poorest and in the richest quintile spend respectively more than 10% and less than 3% of their annual expenditure on health care (Makinen et al. 2000).

1.4.1.4 Community health insurance in Burkina Faso

In order to facilitate access to services and offer financial protection against the cost of illness, a number of CHI initiatives have emerged, starting in the late 1980s, across the country. Traditional forms of risk-sharing are abundant in the country, but have proven to be insufficient in assisting people in case of illness (Fonteneau 2000). Traditional risk-sharing networks in fact, are bound by socio-cultural norms which limit their field of action. Thus, they rarely include coverage of health care in their benefits (Sommerfeld et al. 2002a). In addition, they are usually small, based on shared ethnicity and kin, making it impossible to pool risks and resources to an extent that is sufficient to meet the cost of health care. Traditional forms of risk-sharing are based on the concept of balanced reciprocity, meaning that one contributes to a network, but expects a direct return from that very same network (Fonteneau 2000; Sommerfeld et al. 2002a). For example, in the case of a *tontine*, i.e. the traditional semi-formal micro-credit institution, money is paid into a group where all members know each other, trust each other, and are bound by familiar and/or ethnic ties. What money is collected is then assigned on a rotation basis to each one of the group members, so that each person contributing to the *tontine* can be sure that within months, he/she will be the beneficiary and receive a consistent sum of money which will allow him/her to satisfy a certain need.

The concept of insurance represents a clear departure from the tradition of customary forms of risk-sharing. First of all, in order to be functional, insurance needs large pools, thus it forces people to pool into a form of risk-sharing that reaches beyond shared ethnicity and kin. This entails making a great leap and trust that unknown individuals, people of a different ethnic group, will not abuse the system. In addition, insurance does not entail balanced reciprocity. A person pays his/her contribution, in the form of the premium, into the pool, but his/her probability of receiving support in exchange for this payment is strictly linked to the odds of falling sick and needing medical assistance. There is therefore no guarantee that what one has paid into the insurance scheme will hold a direct return as people may at times spend years without falling sick.

In Burkina Faso, CHI schemes are clearly differentiated from traditional risk-sharing networks and are usually known either as *mutuelle de santé*, equivalent to mutual health organisation, or as *assurance maladie*, equivalent to health insurance. The oldest CHI scheme in the country is the *Mutuelle pharmaceutique de Tounama*, which was founded in 1985 by workers of the Tounama parish in the town of Bobo-Dioulasso and that is still active today (Fonteneau 2000). In 2003, the West African CHI consultancy network, *La Concertation*, estimated that in Burkina Faso there were 36 active schemes and 51 in process of development. The fact that in 1997, the same network had counted only 6 operative schemes in the entire country shows the rapidity with which the new health financing option is expanding in the nation (La Concertation 2004). Like elsewhere in sub-Saharan Africa, schemes are at times initiated by providers, at times by NGOs, and at times by communities themselves (Fonteneau 2000). More than 80% of all operative schemes are embedded within a larger pre-existing organisation, most frequently either a NGO or a health facility (La Concertation 2004).

Apart from a few exceptions, the most notable of which is the *Mutuelle de Bobo-Dioulasso*, initiated by the Regional Health Director himself in collaboration with the French cooperation, most CHI schemes in Burkina Faso are born out of the good will of a restricted number of individuals. Although bridging ethnic and kin boundaries, most scheme are geographically confined so their pooling capacity, before even considering the problem of low enrolment, is severely hampered (Fonteneau 2000; La Concertation 2004). Of all 36 operative schemes, only 6 are directed at populations above 10,000 individuals while more than half of all scheme are directed at populations below 5,000 individuals (La Concertation 2004).

The constraints imposed by a small target population are exacerbated by low enrolment. Out of 36 operative schemes, 30 count less than 2,000 enrolees having paid their current membership (La Concertation 2004). In the light of such numbers, it is not difficult to imagine why a lot of schemes do not survive much after their launching. As discussed earlier in this chapter, small pools and low membership rates leave schemes exposed to extreme financial fluctuations bearing a high risk of bankruptcy. Additional difficulties restricting the effective implementation of CHI schemes in Burkina Faso are linked to weaknesses in managerial and administrative capacity, to the poor quality of the health care services, and to the lack of community empowerment *vis à vis* the providers (Fonteneau 2000; La Concertation 2004).

Although a clear legislation regulating the establishment of schemes in still missing, the government of Burkina Faso, probably in response to internal as well as external pressure, has recognised the potential role that CHI can play in facilitating access to care and in protecting its citizens against the financial cost of illness. The most recent policy documents by the Ministry of Health refer explicitly to CHI as a valuable health financing alternative, one that ought to be promoted as a step towards achieving better health care coverage at the national level (Secretariat General du Ministère de la Santé du Burkina Faso 2000a; Secretariat General du Ministère de la Santé du Burkina Faso 2000b).

Although not directly involved in the development of schemes, the government is supporting CHI by encouraging foreign intervention in the field. Burkina Faso has in recent years largely benefited from the support of the French, the Belgian, and the Dutch cooperation, all investing in the creation of local organisations specialised in providing assistance and training to emerging schemes. The largest of these organisations are the *Réseau d'Appui aux Mutuelles de Santé* (RAMS), the *Programme d'Appui aux Mutuelles de Santé en Afrique* (PROMUSAF), and the *Centre Africain pour une Pratique Culturelle du Développement* (CAD) (Waelkens and Criel 2004). Also very active in Burkina Faso in providing training and assistance to emerging schemes is the International Labour Organisation (Waelkens and Criel 2004), which, through its Poverty Reduction Strategy, proposes a worldwide standard model for the implementation of CHI (International Labour Organisation 2001).

1.4.2 The Nouna Health District

Before proceeding with the description of the CHI scheme which constitutes the focus of this dissertation, we take a brief look at the social, economic, and cultural context of the Nouna Health District. In particular, we focus on a sub-portion of the District currently under demographic surveillance. We discuss health service provision and access to care to show how, in spite of small inevitable differences due to regional variation, the situation of this region is not dissimilar from the one described above for the country as a whole.

1.4.2.1 The demographic surveillance system

The Nouna Health District, which administratively is equivalent to the Kossi Province, is located in the North-West of the country, about 300 km from the capital Ouagadougou. It counts a population of approximately 230,000 inhabitants of which 22,000 live in the district capital, the town of Nouna. The Nouna Health District comprises: (1) 22 first-line facilities, i.e. CSPS; (2) a medical centre in Djibasso, a semi-urban settlement at the border with Mali; and (3) a medical centre with surgical facilities, also known as the district hospital, located in the town of Nouna.

A sub-portion of the whole District, comprising the catchment area of the district hospital and of six first-line facilities is under demographic surveillance by the *Centre de Recherche en Santé de Nouna* (CRSN), a renowned research institution which responds directly to the Burkinabè Ministry of Health and which has enjoyed a long-standing collaboration with the University of Heidelberg since 1989.

Figure 1.6: The Kossi Province

This area counts a population of 70,000 individuals distributed in 41 villages and in the town of Nouna. The CRSN, in collaboration both with the University of Heidelberg and with other universities and international organisations, is committed to clinical and health system research in the area. The aim is to provide adequate evidence-base for policy-making in public health. The demographic surveillance system (DSS) represents the core of all CRSN activities. Demographic surveillance entails that births, deaths, and migrations both in and out of the area are constantly monitored (Kynast-Wolf et al. 2001). Verbal autopsy is used to ascertain the cause of all deaths recorded in the area (Hammer et al. 2005). The DSS provides the sampling frame for all studies conducted in the area.

1.4.2.2 The social, economic, and cultural context

The DSS area is a dry orchard Savannah, where subsistence agriculture and pastoralism remain the main economic activities. The economy of the area is closely linked to the cycles of a typical Soudano-Sahelian climate, characterized by two main seasons: the rainy season from May to October and the dry season from October to May. In the town of Nouna, there are an important market, visited by residents of the entire region, as well as several public and private offices, a police station, a post office, and several banks, making this town the administrative centre of the province and a place of extensive monetary transactions. All secondary schools and professional training schools are located in the town of Nouna, so children who have the opportunity to continue their studies leave their villages, where there are at most primary schools, to reside in town. In 2001, average household monthly expenditure, used as the most reliable indication of socio-economic status in low income countries (Morduch 1995), was 17,723 CFA[5], equivalent, after adjustment for purchasing power parity, to 110 US dollars (Su et al. 2005). An average household is composed of eight people, usually four adults and four children (Dong et al. 2003).

Five major ethnic groups inhabit the area: the Dafing, the Samo, the Mossi, the Bwaba, and the Peulh. Each group has its peculiar socio-economic organisation and its own language. The Bwaba, traditionally Christian, are known to have less restrictive social structures, with women enjoying a higher degree of emancipation than women in other ethnic groups (Kevane and Wydick 2001). The Peulh, known in English as Fulani, are nomadic cattle-raisers who easily migrate in and out of the District. Christianity peacefully coexists with Islam and traditional beliefs. Inter-marriage, across ethnic and religious groups, is not uncommon, especially in the town of Nouna. Dioula constitutes the *lingua franca* used in the region to facilitate communication between different ethnic groups.

Families are bound together by a closely knitted web of traditional risk-sharing networks. A recent systematic investigation conducted in the region distinguished between informal risk-sharing arrangements, such as *tchibla* (rotating labour arrangements) and *faso-bara* (village-wide collective work parties), and semi-formal and formal networks, such as *groupements* (cooperatives), *tontines* (rotating saving and credit associations), and associations (Sommerfeld et al. 2002a). With the exception of the associations, which often serve cultural or charity purposes, all other informal and semi-formal risk-sharing arrangements cited above mainly serve functions related to the economic activities of the community. People come together to plant, harvest, and/or sell their crops. In the case of the *tontines*, people come together to sustain each other in the effort of establishing small revenue-generating activities or to assist families in the event of common festivities (e.g. births, marriages) or common sorrows (e.g. funerals).

Prior to the launch of the CHI scheme in 2004, no mutual health insurance existed in the Nouna Health District. Likewise, other than one single exception, no formal risk-sharing arrangement explicitly offered its members support in case of illness (Sommerfeld et al. 2002a). Sickness is traditionally considered an

---

[5] The exchange rate between euro and CFA, the local currency, is fixed at 1 Euro = 655 CFA.

individual problem, thus people are generally expected to cope with it on their own, seeking support at most from family members and friends (Sommerfeld et al. 2002a).

1.4.2.3 The health care system

In the Nouna Health District, the government is the only provider of health services. There are no NGOs active in the region and the Catholic Church has traditionally only intervened in the health care sector by supporting the provision of ophthalmologic services within government facilities.

Following the introduction of the Bamako Initiative at the national level, the Nouna Health District also introduced a policy of user fees. The district hospital applies fees which abide to national guidelines, but differences in fee levels exist across CSPS. Within the DSS area, the price of a consultation varies between 200 and 500 CFA, a normal delivery ranges between 1,500 CFA and 3,000 CFA, while a Caesarean section, only practiced in the district hospital, costs as much as 30,000 CFA. In recent years, national drug policies have substantially reduced drug shortages. Facilities in the area are generally well-equipped and drug shortages are an extremely rare instance.

Each CSPS is staffed by one head nurses and either one or two additional aids. The district hospital is currently staffed by five physicians, one in each of five main hospital units (maternity, paediatrics, general medicine, ophthalmology, and surgery), and by several trained nurses and aids. In addition, the Chief Medical Officer and several physicians working at the CRSN occasionally also render service at the hospital. Ambulance transport is available from the rural facilities to the district hospital. Given its prohibitive price, however, most people, unless severely injured or sick, travel by foot, by bike, or on trolleys carried by donkeys both to the local first-line facility and to the urban medical centre. There are no official estimates regarding under-the-table payments, therefore it is difficult to assess the extent to which it plays a role in health service provision, imposing yet an additional burden on poor people seeking care.

Health services in the area suffer from extreme under-utilisation. The most recent official statistics available revealed an utilisation rate among the lowest in the country, with 0.16 contacts per capita per year (Secretariat General du Ministère de la Santé du Burkina Faso 2002). A recent study indicated that out of all the people reporting ill, less than 20% sought care at a facility, more then 50% resorted to self-medication, 10% visited a traditional healers, and 17% did nothing (Dong et al. 2004a). The decision regarding treatment choice has repeatedly been found to be influenced by the individual characteristics of the patient, by the household socio-economic status as well as by the perceived severity of the disease (Dong et al. 2004a; Sauerborn 1994; Sauerborn et al. 1996a). Distance to the health facility and a poor judgement on the quality of the services available have been identified as additional barriers to access (Baltussen et al. 2002). A study focused on malaria suggested that in case of a self-diagnosed malaria episode, an even greater percentage of people, 81% of all those reporting ill, resorted to self-medication, potentially treating as malaria a different disease (Mugisha et al. 2002b). It needs to be noted that across studies, "self-medication" did not distinguish between people purchasing drugs at a pharmacy or at the local market and people treating themselves with traditional herbal infusions. This makes it very difficult to estimate with accuracy the potential impact of inappropriate treatment on elements such as disease aggravation and/or increasing drug resistance.

Residents in the area have repeatedly reported lack of financial means as the main reason for not seeking care at a facility and rather resorting to self-medication (Dong et al. 2004a; Mugisha et al. 2002b; Sauerborn 1994). The regressive impact of user fees is illustrated by the fact that, although people in the highest income quintile spend more on health care in absolute terms, they still only spends 2.1% of their annual income on health services compared to 14.3% of annual income spent by those in the lowest quintile (Su and Flessa 2005). Depending on the threshold used, between 5% and 15% of all households seeking care in the Nouna Health District face catastrophic spending due to illness, with poor households being the most likely to incur into catastrophic expenditure (Su et al. 2005).

1.4.3 The emergence of community health insurance in the Nouna Health District

1.4.3.1 The scheme rationale and its initiators

Plans to initiate a CHI scheme in the Nouna Health District followed the request of the Burkinabè Ministry of Health. Having recognised the failure and the difficulties faced by small scale schemes everywhere in the nation, the Ministry showed interest in promoting the development of schemes that pool risks at the district level, since those constitute an essential step towards the establishment of national coverage (Carrin 2003; Carrin et al.2001; Criel 1998a). The presence of the CRSN, its long standing collaboration with the University of Heidelberg, and the dynamism of the local District management team made of the Nouna Health District a unique setting where to "experiment", under controlled conditions, the development of a district-wide scheme. The aim of this joint initiative is that of developing, in a context of close monitoring and continuous support, a model scheme that, once functional, can be adapted and replicated elsewhere in the country.

1.4.3.2 Research preceding the implementation of the scheme

Extensive research and continuous discussion among the scheme initiators and the community preceded the implementation of the scheme, informing its institutional set up and guiding the definition of its main objectives. Between 1999 and 2002, research was conducted in all of the following areas: community perceptions of the quality of care; risk perceptions and traditional networks of risk-sharing; community preferences and willingness to pay for a benefit package; cost estimation analysis; health demand and health need assessment.

An investigation into perceived quality of care revealed that communities across the region are dissatisfied with the services, not because equipment or drugs are unavailable, but mainly because providers do not address patients respectfully and are not motivated to treat them well (Baltussen et al. 2002). As described in greater detail earlier in this section, an investigation into existing risk-sharing networks revealed that health is usually excluded from the range of benefits offered by these networks. The study indicated that the implementation of CHI is urgently needed, but may encounter a certain socio-cultural resistance as communities may be unaccustomed to it (Sommerfeld et al. 2002a). Counteracting this resistance may be the fact that people are well aware of the risk of falling sick and perceive themselves vulnerable to such risk. When asked to rate risks according to perceived vulnerability, communities consistently identified getting malaria and lacking funds to buy medications when sick respectively as the most likely and the second most likely risks faced in their daily life (Sommerfeld et al. 2002b).

A mixture of qualitative and quantitative methods was used to assess which health care services the community would prefer to see included in a potential benefit package. Responses consistently indicated a preference for inclusion of both first-line and second-line services, clearly recognising the inability of households to meet moderate health care costs due to simple, but repeated, illness episodes, as in the case of malaria (Kouyaté et al. 2001). A willingness-to-pay (WTP) study was conducted on the basis of the results of the study on community preferences for the benefit package. The WTP study identified a median WTP for the preferred benefit package of 7,500 CFA per household per year. The median value was calculated in relation to the average size of households in the area, i.e. eight people (generally four adults and four children). The WTP study also highlighted important differences across household members, showing that household heads were willing to pay much more to insure themselves than to insure any other member of the household, especially children (Dong et al. 2003; Dong et al. 2004c; Dong et al. 2005).

Based on current demand and on the unit cost of health services, the per capita cost of the benefit package identified as the preferred one by the community, was estimated to be 1,673 CFA. The study further estimated that of this amount, nearly 60% was covered by government and foreign aid subsidies while 40% was recovered through user fees (Mugisha et al. 2002a). Based on data from the household survey, three physicians independently rated and later agreed upon an estimate of health care needs in the region. If based on health care need rather than on current demand, i.e. treating all illness episodes worthy of medical attention at a District facility, the cost of the benefit package was estimated to raise nearly six-fold up to 9,630 CFA per capita per year, of which of course 60% still covered by government and foreign aid subsidies (Dong et al. 2004d).

In 2001, in addition to the research conducted by the CRSN and the University of Heidelberg in collaboration with the staff of the Nouna Health District, a lawyer was contracted to explore the legal feasibility of setting up an insurance scheme within the framework of a country which has still not passed a clear legislation concerning the legal status of CHI. His recommendation, which was later adopted, was to register the emerging scheme as a not-for-profit association devoted to the provision of mutual aid in the field of health care (Zio 2001).

1.4.3.3 How research informed policy

In 2002 and 2003, the staff of the CRSN and of the Health District initiated several meetings to discuss with the community the design of the scheme in the light of the research results. The CRSN and the Health District selected and appointed an *ad interim* committee of three people, who worked full time on the development of the scheme details by reconciling the results of the research with the interests and opinions of the various stakeholders. The initiators aimed at meeting community preferences without jeopardising the managerial and financial viability of the scheme. This was done by ensuring that adequate mechanisms to control potential insurance pitfalls, such as adverse selection and moral hazard, were explained to the community and incorporated in the implementation plan.

Several workshops were held with health care providers to negotiate contracting between the insurance scheme and the single facilities. In spite of the fact that the Health District management team and the Regional Health Director had been among the programme initiators, the single health providers, meaning the head nurses controlling the single CSPS or the single units of the hospital, had until that point not been actively involved in the development of the scheme.

Table 1.1: How research informed policy

Research component	Relevance to policy
Quality of care	Design interventions to improve quality of services
Risk perception	Understand community discourse on risk
	Identify importance that community attributes to risk of illness
	Identify possible socio-cultural resistance to CHI
Risk-sharing arrangements	Identify existing community support in case of illness
	Assess need for CHI
	Identify possible socio-cultural resistance to CHI
	Identify managerial aspects to be incorporated in CHI structure
Benefit package	Inform design of benefit package to include both first and second-line services
	Serve as basis for WTP study
WTP	Assess value that community attributes to CHI
	Inform premium setting (in the light of community preferences)
	Inform need for differential premium levels
Cost estimation analysis	Inform premium setting (in the light of cost of services)
Health need assessment	Inform premium setting (to secure access to care beyond current demand)

In 2002 and 2003, much was done to offer training to providers on the principle and practice of insurance and to discuss with them the most adequate contracting arrangement. At first, the single health providers resisted the implementation of the scheme, claiming that they would have not complied with the Health District request to sign the contract and engage in collaboration with the insurance scheme. As a justification for their stance, they argued that they had not been sufficiently involved in the preparatory phases of the project and that the suggested payment modality, i.e. capitation, would have turned out in a loss for their facilities. Following months of intense negotiations and training, however, all providers accepted to sign the contract with the insurance scheme and, under the pressure of higher health authorities, also accepted to be paid on a capitation basis.

In October 2003, a workshop was held just outside the town of Nouna to discuss a final draft of the scheme implementation plan. The workshop was attended not only by representatives of all initiating agencies, i.e. the CRSN, the Nouna Health District, the Regional Health Directorate, and the University of Heidelberg, but also by all head nurses affected by the scheme, by a number of community leaders, by representatives of the Burkinabè Ministry of Health and Ministry of Finance, by the acting director of RAMS and by the ILO employee in charge of the social security section in Burkina Faso. The workshop offered the opportunity for all stakeholders to come together, discussing with a wider audience concerns which had only been raised in smaller groups. Following the end of the workshop, the implementation plan was finalised, the contract with providers signed, and a communication and sensitisation campaign prepared with the support of a health promotion specialist who had already worked on the marketing of CHI in Ghana.

The end of the workshop also marked the official naming of the CHI initiative in the District. Between the two terms adopted in French-speaking West Africa, *mutuelle* and *assurance*, the scheme initiators privileged the latter and named the emerging scheme *Assurance Maladie à Base Communautaire de la Province de la Kossi*. A few hours later, an acronym had already been created so that the long form was reduced to *AMBC Nouna*. A few days later, the scheme began to be known among the community either as *AMBC* or *assurance-ci*, the ci suffix borrowed from the local language Dioula, showing how quickly people incorporated a French word, most probably also foreign in principle, into their everyday life. Hereafter, for simplicity, we refer to the CHI scheme of the Nouna Health District simply as the AMBC.

1.4.4 Main features of the Assurance Maladie à Base Communautaire

Understanding the research that follows with regard to the reasons people indicated for having chosen to join or not to join the scheme is impossible, unless the reader is familiar with the basic elements of the institutional design of the AMBC. In this section, we briefly describe the main features of the scheme set up and, when relevant, we explain how choices were made in the light of research results, community preferences, and/or principles of insurance theory and practice.

1.4.4.1 The step-wedge implementation of the AMBC

Although, as mentioned earlier in this chapter, the ultimate aim is to set up a district-wide health insurance scheme, the AMBC is currently operative only in the area under demographic surveillance by the CRSN. In order to facilitate implementation and at the same time ensure the scientific assessment of the impact of insurance on utilisation and protection against the cost of illness, offer to insure is set to follow a step-wedge design with villages being incorporated progressively into the scheme[6].

Figure 1.7: The step-wedge implementation of the AMBC

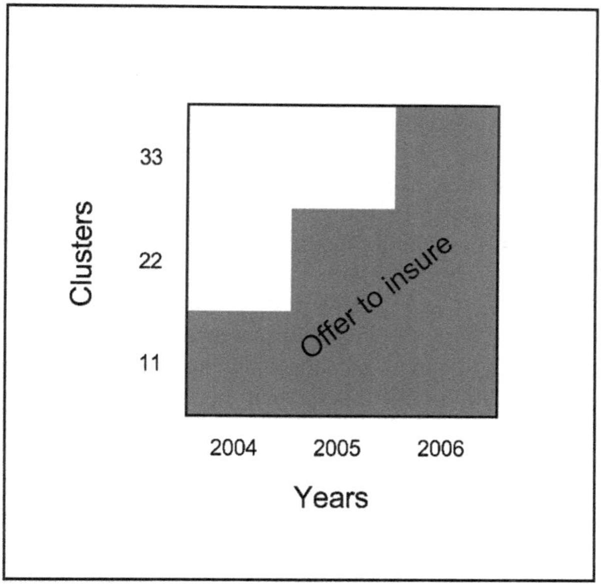

[6] The step-wedge randomised implementation of the AMBC has a precise rationale and direct implications for the research to assess the impact of insurance on health service utilisation and financial protection against the cost of illness. The discussion of these elements, however, is beyond the scope of this dissertation as it is only marginally relevant to our study on decision to enrol. The relevance of the step-wedge design with regard to our study on enrolment is limited to the fact that we observed enrolment decision only within the framework of the first set of 11 clusters (comprising 12 villages and 3 town sectors) having received the offer to insure in 2004.

The area under demographic surveillance has been subdivided into 24 rural (villages) and 9 urban (town of Nouna) clusters of approximately equal size. These 33 clusters have then been randomized to intervention and control so that, from 2004 to 2006, each year 11 clusters, corresponding to a variable number of villages and town sectors, are offered the opportunity to join the scheme.

Discussion is currently ongoing regarding the inclusion of villages outside the CRSN research area starting from 2007. Expansion is only possible if the scheme proves to be functional and effective in meeting its objectives. The greatest challenge comes from the need to continue with the progressive incorporation of villages in such a way as to minimise community conflict and respect, to the extent possibly, equity across villages.

1.4.4.2 The institutional set up of the AMBC

As its name indicates, the AMBC is community-based, meaning that the community itself is in charge of managing the scheme. All the project initiators in fact, agreed from the very beginning that although willing to support the program technically as long as needed, ownership should rest in the hands of the community, which ought to be trained to progressively take full charge of all managerial functions. Community leaders agreed on the proposition as they also felt that the only way for the scheme to reach its full potential was through community mobilisation and greater involvement in matters of health care. Communities felt that since COGES are in practice dominated by the opinion and the action of the CSPS head nurse, people could benefit from the creation of an independent institution with the authority to counteract the absolute power that providers often seem to hold in the region within the health sector.

- The AMBC enjoys the legal status of a not-for-profit association whose management is entrusted upon the following organs:

- General Assembly – a body including all the members enrolled in each village or town sector;

- Plenary – a body composed of the presidents of all General Assemblies;

- Steering Committee – a body composed of five elected representatives from the Plenary;

- Health Insurance Management Unit – hired personnel to manage the everyday insurance activities.

The General Assembly represents the venue for all AMBC members in each village or town sector to meet regularly, discuss matters of interest to the community, and put forward propositions and/or complaints to be brought to higher bodies in the managerial structure of the scheme. The Plenary is the legislative body of the AMBC and it has the authority to vote over modifications to be applied to any one component of the insurance scheme. The Plenary also has the authority to choose to discontinue the AMBC.

The Steering Committee is the executive body of the AMBC. In addition to the five representatives elected from the Plenary, one representative from the Health District and one from the CRSN also sit on the Steering Committee. These two representatives, however, do not vote on decisions and maintain exclusively the function of technical advisors. The Steering Committee is legally liable for the administration of the insurance funds. In addition, it has the responsibility to hire the insurance personnel for the Management Unit, to set up contracts with providers, and to actively work to ensure that the quality of the services delivered meets adequate standards.

Figure 1.8: The AMBC institutional set up

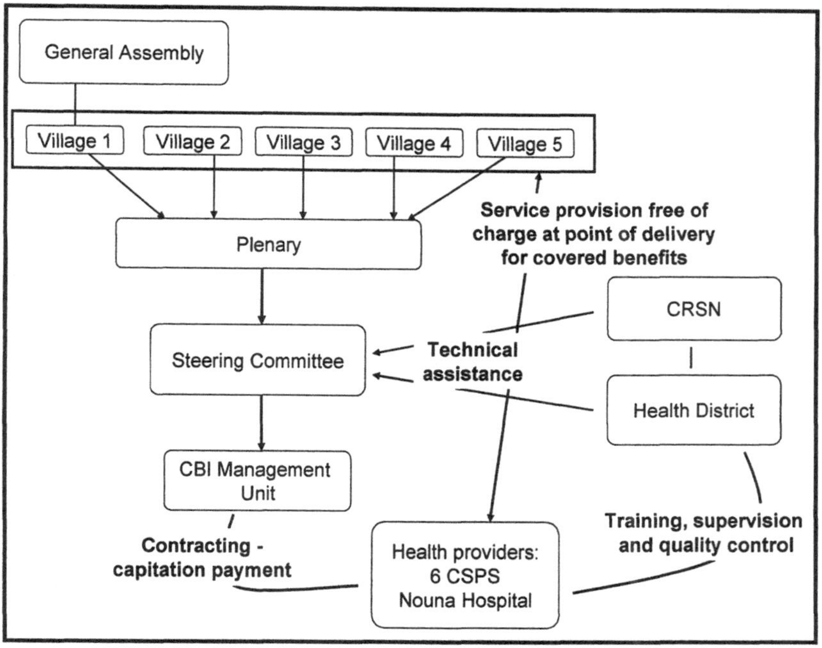

The Management Unit is the organ in charge of the everyday management of the AMBC. The Management Unit includes three people, all of whom are hired full-time on an annual basis: a coordinator, a marketing/social mobilization specialist, and a treasurer. In 2004, the three members of the *ad interim* committee previously selected by the Health District and the CRSN were re-appointed as the Health Insurance Management Unit by the newly elected Steering Committee. The coordinator of the Management Unit is currently a law graduate who has matured an extensive experience in community mobilisation having worked for the *Association Tontines de Nouna* (ATN) for several years. The figure below provides a simplified illustration of the institutional set up of the AMBC, schematically describing the links between the various organs and parties involved.

1.4.4.3 The enrolment unit and the payment modalities

Enrolment in the scheme is voluntary. In order to limit adverse selection, the unit of enrolment is the household. For uniformity purposes, the definition of household applied by the AMBC is the same as the one applied by the DSS. The term household is therefore used to refer to the basic socio-economic unit, within which individuals living together in a house or compound, share resources and jointly satisfy their needs under the authority of the household head (Würthwein et al. 2001). When registering households, the AMBC management team refers to the DSS records, checking the consistency of the information provided by the household head. This is done to ensure that no household attempts to register exclusively some of its members. If new births or recent deaths are recorded upon enrolment, they are immediately reported to the DSS personnel, who take care of updating the population registers.

Given that households vary considerably in size, the premium is set on an individual basis. The premium is set just above the median value elicited by the WTP study (Dong et al. 2003) so that the average household of eight people pays 8,000 CFA per year. Given that the WTP study had identified differential WTP values across members of a household (Dong et al. 2004c; Dong et al. 2005), it was decided that children should pay only one third of the adult premium. In practice, this means that households wishing to enrol pay 1,500 CFA for each adult and 500 CFA for each child. Upon joining the scheme, each household also contributes an additional flat quota of 200 CFA as membership fee. Membership is renewable on a yearly basis and people renewing their enrolment are not expected to contribute the membership fee in subsequent years. The premium for the entire household is to be paid in one single instalment directly to the AMBC Management Unit during the enrolment campaign. In principle, the campaign is set to follow the harvest season.

Actuarial projections have shown that in order to break-even, the premium for the average household of eight people would need to be 10,000 CFA (Flessa 2005). This sum would allow the insurance to cover administrative as well as medical costs and already accounts for the possibility that health service utilisation may double compared to current demand. The scheme initiators debated the choice of an adequate premium level for a long time and in the end, they decided to privilege community preferences and set the premium around the median level identified by the WTP study. They felt that a raise in premium, to meet actuarial projections, compared to the level identified as affordable by the community, would have discouraged many people from enrolling. At present, the Burkinabè Ministry of Health is subsidising the scheme, covering what costs the premium paid by the community cannot cover.

1.4.4.4 The benefit package and the modalities of health service provision

Membership gives right to a wide range of first-line and second-line medical services available within the Nouna Health District system. The AMBC does not cover costs for referrals outside the District, either to the regional or to the national hospital. Likewise, the AMBC contracts services exclusively with government facilities as those are the only authorised health care providers in the District. The AMBC applies no co-payment policy nor it ceils the number of contacts enrolled members are entitled to. When discussing this choice, community leaders were afraid that the application of either co-payments or ceiling would have been very difficult for people to conceptualise and therefore to accept. They insisted on maintaining the scheme regulations as simple as possible, relying for the control of over-utilisation on social pressure rather than on standard insurance tools.

Community preferences, elicited through the relevant study (Kouyaté et al. 2001), with regard to what services to include and what services to exclude from the benefit package were for the most part respected. One modification was applied as just before the implementation of the scheme, the Burkinabè Ministry of Health passed a decree prescribing that all Health Districts ought to offer antenatal services free of charge. This made the inclusion of antenatal care in the AMBC benefit package meaningless. While negotiating contracts, providers also insisted to exclude delivery from the benefit package. They argued that delivering a child is a predictable, and therefore not insurable, event.

In all other instances, the *ad interim* committee and its technical advisors made an explicit effort to protect the community's concern to include both first-line and second-line services in the benefit package. An obvious limit to the inclusion of services was linked to the capacity of the District facilities. In the case of surgery, for example, only emergency surgery was included in the benefit package because it was the only type of surgery for which capacity existed at the time when the benefit package was set. This is not to say that, in following years, the benefit package, like other elements of the AMBC set up, may not be revisited in the light of what development may take place in the District.

Table 1.2: The AMBC benefit package

Services included in benefit package	Services excluded from benefit package
General and specialised consultation	Ophthalmology services
Essential and generic drugs (if prescribed)	Dental care
Laboratory tests (also for antenatal care)	Circumcision
Inpatient hospital stays (up to 15 days per episode of care)	Family Planning
X-rays	Sanitation
Emergency surgery	AIDS treatment
Ambulance transport (when authorised by provider)	Injury resulting from individual responsibility (e.g. drunkenness)

In order to limit fraud, upon joining the scheme, a separate photo ID card is issued for each person in a household. Members are entitled to receive services free of charge only once they have shown this card to the health personnel. In addition, the nurses at the single facilities are asked to verify on their own records the enrolment status of the patients presenting at the facility with a card. In order to limit adverse selection, upon enrolment, members are asked to observe a three-month waiting period before being able to access services. In order to limit over-utilisation and to ensure adequate use of the referral system, the AMBC imposes strict observance of a gate-keeping mechanism. Members are expected to seek care first at the CSPS and then, only if referred by the facility personnel, at the district hospital. In the town of Nouna, the first-line facility, the equivalent of the rural CSPS, is within the compounds of the district hospital, but it is clearly differentiated, also administratively, from the hospital as such.

In order to ensure an even distribution of cases across facilities and simplify reimbursement procedures, people have been assigned to a CSPS according to the official catchment's areas set by the Health District. This is to say that, depending on the village where they reside, people are asked to seek care exclusively at a given CSPS. This restriction can be bypassed only in case of severe emergency, for example a person incurring in an accident while visiting family in a different village.

1.4.4.5 Providers' payment

In the months preceding the launch of the scheme, in an attempt to improve the quality of care available, treatment guidelines were revised and discussed with providers, who also received extensive additional training in rational prescribing. After negotiations that lasted several months, providers accepted to be paid on a capitation basis. The scheme initiators insisted on a capitation rather than a fee-for-service payment mechanism as they felt that this was the only tool to limit over-provision by transferring part of the risk to the providers themselves. Given that a possible consequence of capitation payments is the under-provision of services, the AMBC Management Unit invests in a continuous monitoring of the quality of the services delivered, systematically checking that enrolled members receive what care they are entitled to. The AMBC Management Unit promptly reports directly to the District staff any case of malpractice or refusal to treat, asking that either the Chief Medical Officer himself or one of his deputies intervene by reproaching the interested facility and/or the single provider.

What money is raised through the payment of the premium is transferred almost entirely to providers. The AMBC retains only 5% to cover administrative costs and 5% to devote to an emergency fund. Although as mentioned earlier in this section, the scheme is currently subsidised by the Burkinabè Ministry of Health, which covers most administrative costs, the scheme initiators insisted on setting standard management procedures from the very onset of the AMBC, so that in the years to come, the practice of devoting a given sum to non-medical costs will already be effectively in place. The capitation fee paid to providers was calculated by averaging the adult and the child premium, the rationale being that of giving no incentive to providers to treat children any less than adults. Taking into account what portion of overall service delivery is absorbed by each level of care as well as what differences exist in average expenditure per episode between the first-line facilities and the district hospital, it was decided that for each person enrolled, 75% of the capitation fee be transferred to the referral CSPS and 25% to the district hospital. Each CSPS receives an amount equal to 75% of the capitation fee multiplied by the number of AMBC enrolees in its catchment's area. The district hospital receives an amount equal to 25% of the capitation fee multiplied by the total number of AMBC enrolees.

To illustrate the principle described above, we assume that an equal number of adults and children enrol in the AMBC. Thus, the average AMBC premium results into 1000 CFA per person enrolled. Out of these 1000 CFA, 50 CFA are retained by the AMBC Management Unit for administrative costs and an additional 50 CFA are retained to set up an emergency fund. The remaining 900 CFA, i.e. the capitation fee, are transferred to the providers immediately after the end of the enrolment campaign. Of these 900 CFA, 75%, equivalent to 675 CFA, is transferred to the referral CSPS and the remaining 25%, equivalent to 225 CFA, to the district hospital.

Figure 1.9: Providers' payment within the framework of the AMBC
The illustration below assumes an average (adult and child combined) premium of 1000 CFA per person

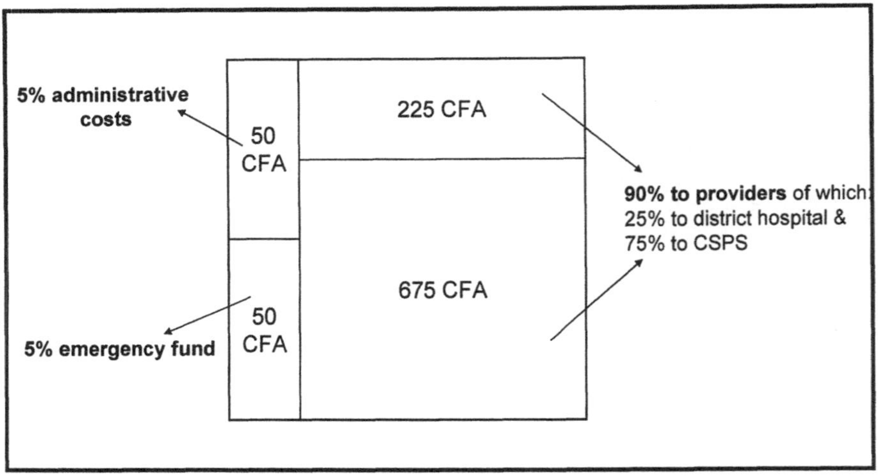

1.4.4.6 Additional remarks

Although not directly managed by the AMBC team, it is important to note here that substantial efforts are currently under way to improve the quality of services available at facilities in the District. Having recognised poor quality of care as a central problem in the region, the Health District, the CRSN, and the University of Heidelberg have joined in a formal program which addresses concrete concerns regarding health service provision. Since the inception of this program, for example, staffing at the hospital has increased and stabilised, weekly meetings to discuss cases have been made compulsory, on-the-job continuous training has been institutionalised, and an emergency room, where people can receive care even before paying for it, has been set up. The AMBC team participates as an associate partner to the programme. Its main function, being the community agent, is to report people's complains and suggestions, actively contributing to the discussion on what needs to be done to improve service delivery.

1.4.5 The first enrolment campaign

The AMBC was launched on February 3, 2004 with a great ceremony attended by provincial and regional authorities and celebrated by several hundreds of community members. The first enrolment campaign stretched from February to May 2004.

Figure 1.10: Villages and facilities in the first enrolment campaign

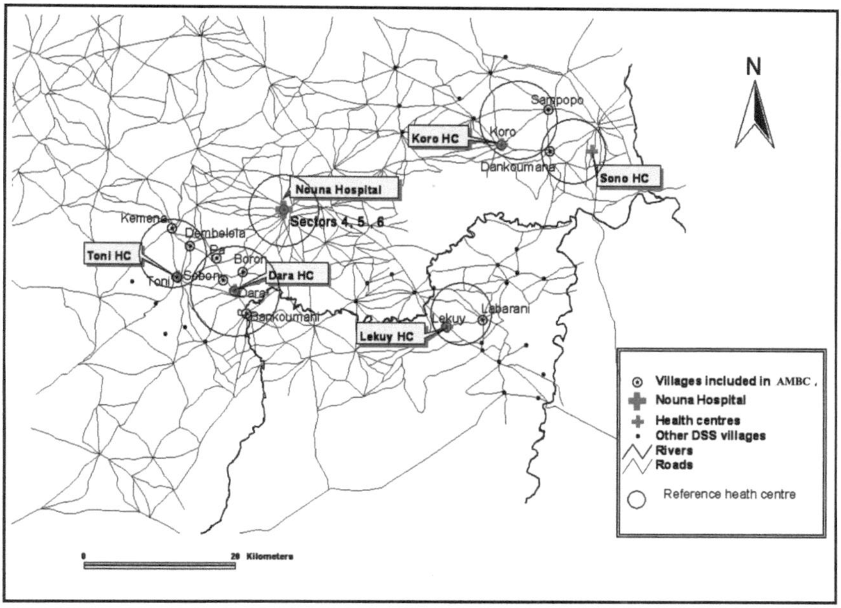

Health insurance was offered to residents of the first 11 clusters, corresponding to a total of 12 villages and 3 town sectors. Given the distribution of villages in the first round of enrolment, in addition to the district hospital, only five out of six CSPS in the DSS area were concerned: Dara, Toni, Koro, Sono, and Lékuy.

The communication and sensitization campaign was designed by the AMBC team in consultation with the Health District staff, the CRSN staff, and staff from the University of Heidelberg. A communication specialist with extensive experience in the promotion of CHI in Ghana assisted the AMBC Management Unit both in the preparation and throughout the implementation of the communication and sensitization campaign. Activities included the use of theatre and frequent radio broadcasting, repeated community gatherings in all the villages and town sectors, and targeted meetings with community leaders, such as local political figures and teachers, who could act as the scheme promoters.

It is not to be forgotten that the community had already been exposed to the concept and modalities of health insurance through the extensive research and discussion which preceded the implementation of the scheme. Therefore, the communication and sensitization campaign did not find the population completely unprepared and focused mainly on reinforcing knowledge and understanding of insurance concepts, openly discussing with the community the potential benefits as well as the limitations of health insurance with specific reference to the set up of the AMBC. The construction of messages was largely informed by the previous research conducted to explore risk perception and perceived vulnerability as well as participation in traditional risk-sharing arrangements. In this dissertation, we do not discuss the content of the communication and sensitisation campaign in much detail given that it is the object of a separate study.

In spite of the great effort to promote the initiative and in spite of the initial apparent enthusiasm of the population, by May 2004, only 4.9% of the eligible population enrolled. As illustrated in the table below, we observed great variations in enrolment rates across villages, with a minimum of 1% of households enrolled in Bankoumani and a maximum of over 22% of households enrolled in Lékuy. This variation appeared disconcerting both for the AMBC and for the research team.

Table 1.3: Enrolment rates at the end of first AMBC

Village/Town sector	Population (in households)	Households in AMBC	Percentage households in AMBC
Nouna 4	525	29	5.5
Nouna 5	457	20	4.4
Nouna 6	479	21	4.4
Bankoumani	197	2	1
Boron	64	10	15.6
Dara	287	8	2.8
Dankoumana	71	2	2.8
Dembéléla	28	6	21.4
Kéména	299	10	3.3
Koro	213	4	1.9
Labarani	73	6	8.2
Lékuy	99	22	22.2
Pâ	126	6	4.7
Sampopo	73	3	4.1
Sobon	134	5	3.7
TOTAL	3125	154	4.9

2. Study population and methods

We open this chapter by presenting a brief outline of the conceptual framework guiding our research. Understanding the theoretical assumptions regarding which factors influence decision to enrol in CHI is essential to understanding the methodological choices described later in the chapter. This dissertation aims in fact at capturing the complexity of factors influencing decision to enrol in CHI. Therefore we have relied on a combination of quantitative and qualitative methods of analysis. In addition, we have also adopted an innovative statistical technique, multilevel logistic regression, which had not been applied before to model demand for health insurance. Given the novelty of our methodological approach, we will not only describe the methods, but will also, when necessary, explain and justify their application. A comprehensive discussion of the strengths and weaknesses of the methods adopted, however, will only follow in the later discussion chapter.

2.1 The conceptual framework

The conceptual framework guiding the conduct of this study was informed by the theoretical and the empirical discussion on insurance purchase presented in the previous chapter. Our conceptual framework recognises that decision to enrol in CHI is the result of the interaction of several factors acting at different levels. Given that AMBC does not allow single individuals to enrol in the scheme, decision to enrol in CHI was treated as a household decision. Figure 2.1 provides an illustration of the factors considered in our conceptual framework: household head, household, community, health service, and product characteristics.

When faced with the decision of whether to enrol in CHI, household heads weigh the potential costs and benefits of membership. The underlying assumption is that, under a prospect of uncertainty, not knowing whether they will fall sick and need medical care, household heads seek to maximise utility, i.e. obtain the maximum benefit possible, for themselves and for other members of their household (Arrow 1963). We recognise, however, that decisions are context dependent and considerations regarding the potential utility of a given prospect may not always be the simple product of a rational decision making process (Jakab et al. 2004; Kahneman and Tversky 1979; Schoemaker 1982). We assume that the household head's perception of the potential costs and benefits of enrolment is influenced by product characteristics as well as by individual, household, and community factors.

Figure 2.1: Conceptual framework
The dashed line indicates the link between the various factors

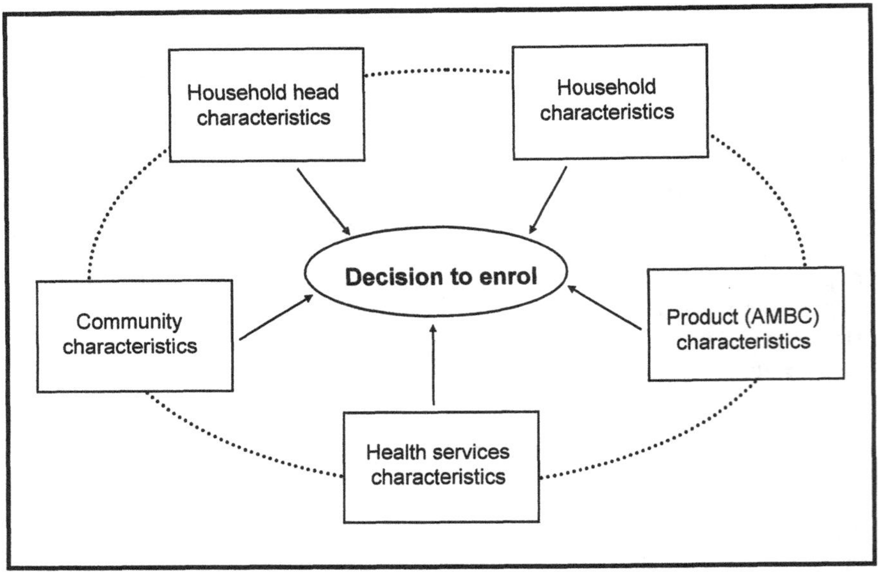

When faced with the decision of whether to enrol in the AMBC, the household head judges the product in relation to the existing alternative, i.e. access to care conditional upon the payment of fees. Depending on the health status of his family and depending on his prior experience with health service utilisation, he/she may find it more or less convenient to enrol. He/she evaluates what costs the household may expect to face because of illness during a given year. He/she will choose to enrol if such costs are perceived to be higher than the cost of enrolling.

During this evaluation process, the household head considers not only the price of the premium and the price of health services, but also the overall costs incurred by the household at enrolment as compared to the costs faced at times of illness. On the one hand, paying for care when sick entails that household may face additional costs due to the time and effort of seeking credit and/or to the grief of having to sell a considerable portion of their assets (Kahneman et al. 1991). On the other hand, if enrolling, households may face additional intangible costs due to a concern that others in their community will judge their action and/or due to fear of regretting their decision should the benefits of enrolment not match their expectations (Salkeld et al. 2000; Smith 1996). In weighing the potential costs and benefits of enrolment, household heads may use as a reference point their prior experience in other risk-sharing arrangements and make decisions accordingly.

Household socio-economic status influences the decision making process as it inevitably shapes the evaluation of costs and benefits. In a context of generalised poverty, as it is the case among many rural communities in sub-Saharan Africa, the incentive to enrol should be high as insurance allows households to protect their meagre assets against health shocks. The very poor, however, may simply be unable to enrol, even if wishing to do so, because their budget constraint does not allow them to consider anything if not the most immediate needs of their families. Their decision not to enrol may not be linked to a preference for present rather than future consumption (Schneider 2004), but rather to a contingent inability to consider future risks when preoccupied with meeting immediate necessities. On the other side of the spectrum, relatively wealthy households may not be interested in enrolment if they judge the price of health services to be trivial in relation to their income.

If the premium is set on an individual basis, then the household size also becomes an important factor mediating the effect of socio-economic status on decision to enrol. Facing a higher price, large households may be less willing to enrol, not only because of affordability *per se*, but also because of a certain resistance among rural illiterate communities towards making large payments at once (Criel and Waelkens 2003).

The product characteristics, in particular the inclusion of high-price services in the benefit package, are likely to interfere with the judgement of the potential costs and benefits of enrolment. Even wealthy households, otherwise uninterested in insurance, may decide to enrol if they feel that CHI grants access to care that would otherwise simply be unaffordable (Nyman 1999). Other product characteristics may also influence decision to enrol depending on whether they meet the preferences of the household or not. Among the product characteristics, choice of provider network is likely to be the one bearing the greatest impact on decision to enrol. Households may simply be uninterested in enrolling if they perceive facilities to be too distant or if they do not judge as adequate the quality of the care contracted by the insurance scheme (Baltussen et al. 2002; Chawla and Ellis 2000; Criel et al. 2002). Their perception of the quality of care may in turn be influenced by previous encounters with the health system as well as by the community discourse on service provision. Communities who do not value modern medical services or who are profoundly dissatisfied with the quality of services, may *a priori* not be interested in insurance as they may prefer traditional to modern biomedical care.

The age, gender, and educational attainment of the household head are also likely to shape considerations regarding the costs and benefits of enrolment. The Grossman model suggests that health depreciates with time, implying that with increasing age more health care is needed to maintain the original stock of health (Grossman 1972). One would therefore assume that older household heads, expecting to use more health services, should attribute greater value to the benefits of insurance. Evidence from the study area, pointing at the existence of an age bias privileging older people in the intra-household allocation of resources for health care (Sauerborn et al. 1994; Sauerborn et al. 1996b), would also suggest that older household heads should be more likely to enrol.

Compulsory household enrolment, however, is likely to mediate the effect of age on decision to enrol as it forces household heads to base their judgement on collective rather that individual cost-benefit considerations. In addition, counteracting the effect of age bias, is the fact that younger household heads are more likely to have been exposed to modern concepts and may therefore be more willing to engage in new initiatives, such as CHI. Likewise, individuals who have attended school and through school attendance have gained exposure to Western concepts, are also likely to value the potential costs and benefits of enrolling in CHI differently from individuals who have not attended school. Educated individuals may be both more likely to attribute greater value to modern medical services and to be more familiar with the principle and practice of formal insurance.

Although in the Nouna Health District we find no evidence of a gender bias in the intra-household allocation of resources for health care (Sauerborn et al. 1996b), one could expect women to be more reluctant than men to enrol. The local socio-cultural context may in fact constraint women from embracing new initiatives unless other men in the family or community have already done so. For instance, the willingness-to-pay study preceding the implementation of the AMBC suggested that, even after controlling for socio-economic status, women were willing to pay less than men to enrol in CHI (Dong et al. 2004b). At the same time, however, research in the study area has identified women as the main care-givers and as key decision-makers when it comes to seeking care for any member of the households (Sauerborn 1994). Therefore, enjoying greater awareness of the risks associated with being ill, female household heads could also turn out to attribute greater value to the potential benefits of enrolment than their male counterparts.

Knowledge of the insurance scheme and trust in its managerial structures are also important elements influencing the household head's decision to enrol or not to enrol in CHI (Criel et al. 2002; Derriennic et al. 2005). Considerations regarding potential costs and benefits inevitably rely on the information household heads have regarding the scheme. Availability of information is in turn affected by the marketing of the scheme and the efforts its promoters devote to the communication and sensitisation campaign. Both the content of marketing messages and the manner in which they are delivered inevitably shape community knowledge and perceptions of CHI. Communities are active interlocutors, who respond to the messages of the campaign, decode them in the light of their previous experience, and conceptualise the costs and benefits of enrolment accordingly. Collective representations of CHI are therefore very likely to influence the manner in which the individual household heads will respond to the new initiative and decide whether or not to enrol. Religion, ethnicity, socio-cultural beliefs and practices are all factors likely to shape community preferences as well as attitudes towards health, risk, and solidarity, thus mediating collective responses to CHI and subsequently also individual decision to enrol.

2.2 Adopting a mixed methodology

The review of the literature described in the previous chapter, reveals that prior studies looking at decision to enrol in CHI in sub-Saharan Africa relied exclusively on one methodological approach, either quantitative or qualitative. Researchers approaching the question within the framework of health economics have traditionally privileged quantitative methods of analysis (Jütting 2004; Osei-Akoto 2004; Schneider and Diop 2004), while researchers interested in looking at group dynamics and their impact on decision to enrol have preferred qualitative methods (Atim and Madjiguene 2000; Chee et al. 2002; Criel and Waelkens 2003). This dissertation represents an attempt to explore the research question using a mixed methodology, i.e. combining qualitative and quantitative methods of analysis.

As described in the section above, our theoretical framework is rooted in health economics. In line with economic thinking, we recognise in fact, that the decision to enrol in CHI is shaped by judgements on the costs and benefits of membership. We also recognise, however, that judgements on the costs and benefits of membership are not the exclusive product of rational decision-making aimed at maximising utility, but are also heavily influenced by the broader socio-cultural context. In the light of this consideration, we did not judge econometric modelling to be sufficient to allow us to explore all the elements considered in our conceptual framework. Given the difficulty to capture elements such as socio-cultural values and trust through means of a standardised questionnaire, it is in fact almost impossible to include them in a traditional quantitative analysis.

In recent years, a number of economists have recognised the limitations of research based exclusively on quantitative methods of analysis (Bridges 2003; Coast 1999; Ryan et al. 2001). Drawing from the teaching of Michael Q. Patton, Coast (1999) has initiated a dialogue promoting the inclusion of qualitative methods of analysis in the health economist's toolbox. She argued that qualitative methods of analysis are especially helpful when in need to make sense of complex decision-making processes, which are context-embedded and cannot easily be captured by econometric modelling. Nearly ten years earlier, Patton (1990) had already insisted on the complementary role of quantitative and qualitative methods. He argued against the epistemological debate which considers as opposite a logical-positivist approach, based on quantitative and experimental methods, and a phenomenological approach, privileging qualitative and naturalistic methods of investigation. Patton considered the strict adherence to either paradigm as a limitation to the researcher's creativity, disguising a need to abide to old methodological habits, rather than a real interest in understanding the research question. He argued that research should be guided by pragmatic considerations, rather than by disciplinary prescriptions, and that methodological appropriateness should serve as the primary criterion for evaluating the quality of a study.

Our study developed in line with Patton's *paradigm of choices* (Patton 1990), recognising that different methods of analysis are appropriate to answer different questions or to address different aspects and nuances of the same research question. If on the one hand, we recognised the limitations of econometric modelling, on the other hand, we also did not deem qualitative methods alone to be sufficient to understand decision to enrol in CHI. Qualitative methods, focusing on the analysis of a limited number of cases, permit to study selected issues in depth and details. They do not allow, however, to measure phenomena, for example the relative impact of a given factor on decision to enrol, nor to quantify casual links between variables. So, while qualitative methods may be useful to explore community dynamics, social constructs, and perceptions of CHI, they do not allow to measure if and to what extent variables such as education and socio-economic status influence the decision to enrol.

We used in-depth individual interviews to explore decision to enrol holistically, focusing on the context, asking questions such as "how?" and "why?", and attempting the grasp the point of view of the local community. We used regression modelling to explore and quantify the link between decision to enrol in CHI and a more restricted set of relevant characteristics, focusing on questions such as "how much?" and "how different?".

Figure 2.2: Quantitative and qualitative methods at a glance

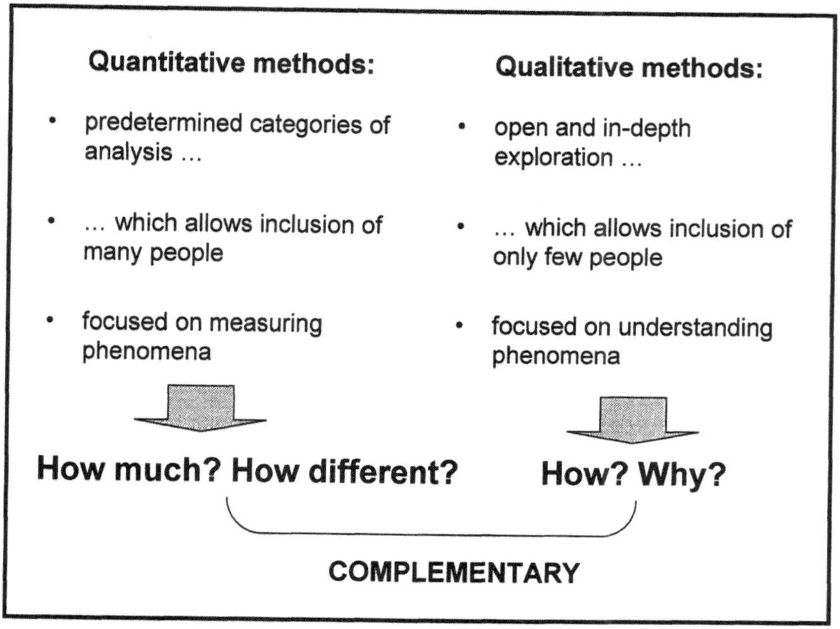

Building on the sketch presented in Figure 2.1, Figure 2.3 provides a visual illustration of how quantitative and qualitative research methods were used to explore different elements shaping the decision to enrol in CHI.

2.3 The study population

The study described in this dissertation was conducted in the Nouna Health District, specifically in the sub-portion of the district currently under demographic surveillance by the CRSN. Given the need to contextualise the emergence of the AMBC, we have already amply described the main features of the DSS area in the introductory chapter. In this section, we simply wish to remind the reader that the DSS area comprises the catchment zone of the district hospital and of six CSPS, for a total population of approximately 70,000 individuals distributed in 42 villages and in the town of Nouna.

As described in the previous chapter, the implementation of the AMBC has been set to follow a cluster-randomised step-wedge design with communities being progressively offered the opportunity to join the scheme over a three-year period. Our investigation into factors shaping decision to enrol was conducted immediately following the end of the first campaign. Therefore, it pertains exclusively to the first 12 villages and 3 town sectors being offered insurance in 2004. In February 2004, the sub-portion of the DSS area being offered insurance counted a population of 3 125 households. These households constituted the basic sampling frame for both the qualitative and the quantitative research components of our study.

Figure 2.3: Joint application of quantitative and qualitative methods
In normal script = elements explored using quantitative methods; in italics = elements explored using qualitative methods; in bold = elements explored using both quantitative and qualitative methods.

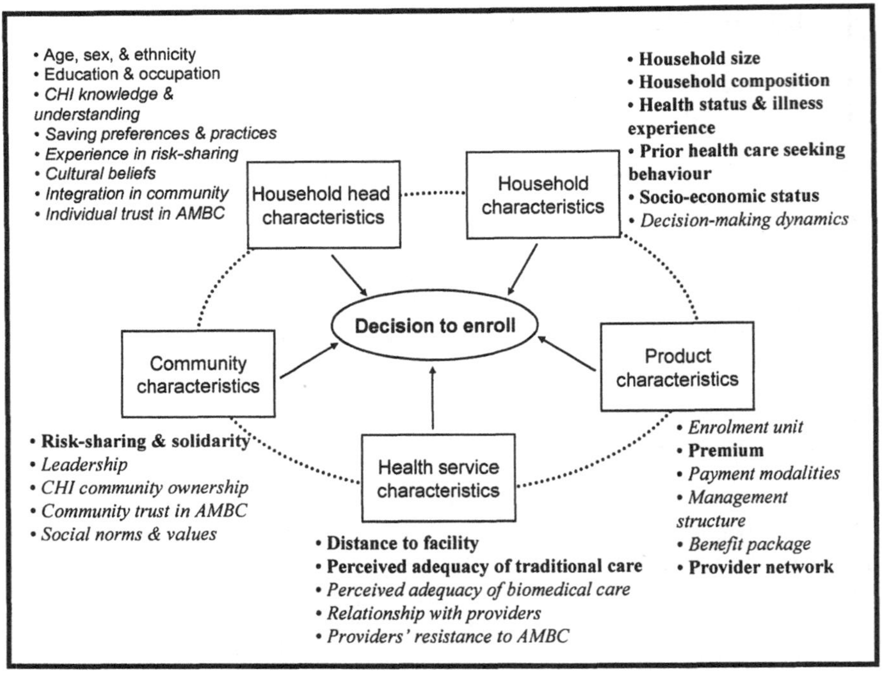

2.4 Quantitative methods

2.4.1 Sampling

Since the year 2000, a household survey is operative in area under demographic surveillance by the CRSN (Würthwein et al. 2001). The survey, known as the Nouna Health District Household Survey (NHDHS), records information on a statistically representative sample of the DSS population at regular intervals of time. Through a two-stage sampling procedure, 990 households were selected for inclusion in the survey sample. These households are proportionally distributed over the 42 villages and the 7 town sectors (Nouna town) included in the DSS. The definition of household applied to the selection of households to be included in the survey is the same as the one applied in the DSS area at large. As described in the previous chapter, the term household is used to refer to the basic socio-economic unit, within which individuals living together in a house or compound, share resources and jointly satisfy their needs under the authority of the household head. The household constitutes a social group with which the individual identifies himself/herself (Würthwein et al. 2001). Households are in turn grouped in villages or town sectors, which constitute political administrative units.

The NHDHS sample constitutes the basis for several studies conducted in the region. We were, however, unable to utilise the NHDHS sample as such given that our analysis pertained only to a sub-portion of the DSS area, i.e. those villages which received offer to insure in 2004, and that, at the end of the first campaign, the enrolment rate was extremely low with only 4.9% of the eligible population having accepted to join the AMBC.

At first, we considered conducting our analysis on the sub-sample of NHDHS households living in the 12 villages and 3 town sectors which had received offer to insure in 2004. As mentioned earlier, in February 2004, this area counted 3 125 households of which 412, corresponding to approximately 13% of the total, had been randomly selected for inclusion in the household survey. Of these 412 households, however, only 19 had accepted to enrol in the AMBC. Had we conducted our analysis on such a sample, 19 enrolled and 393 non-enrolled households, we would have faced considerable difficulties in identifying any significant associations.

Therefore, we decided to apply a case-control methodology, given that such an approach is recognised as the most effective when dealing with rare outcomes (Beaglehole et al. 1993; Kleinbaum and Klein 2002). Because of the low enrolment rate, we treated voluntary participation in the AMBC as a rare outcome. Econometricians refer to case-control studies as outcome or choice-based sampling studies (Gilbert 2000; Hills and De Stavola 2003). Exactly the same concept applies to case-control and to outcome-based sampling studies. In both instances in fact, instead of sampling subjects at random, different sampling fractions are applied to subjects with the outcome of interest (the cases) and to subjects without the outcome of interest (the controls). Given that coverage is often not high enough to allow for random sampling, differential sampling fractions have been widely used in studies exploring insurance purchase both in high-income and in low-income settings (Jowett 2003; Jütting 2004; Propper 1989; Ranson 2004).

Figure 2.4: Household survey sampling

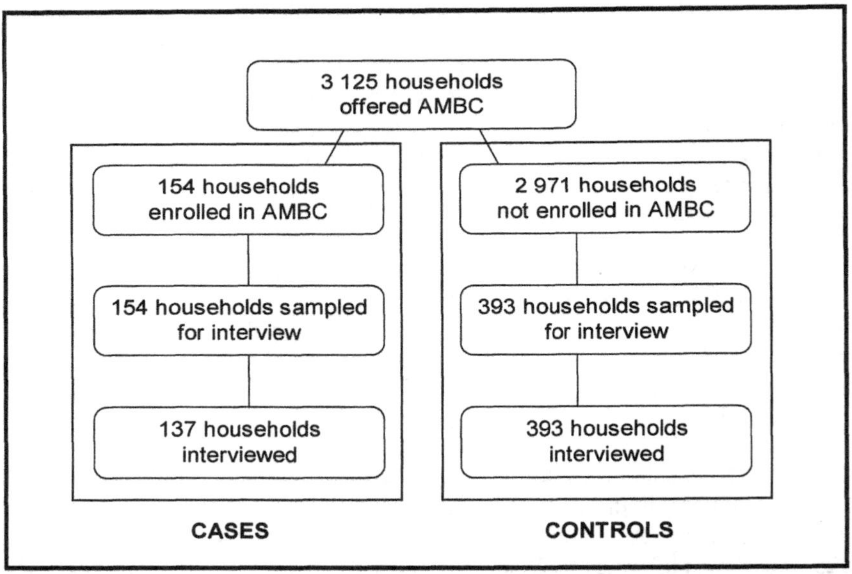

Figure 2.4 illustrates the details of the sampling procedure. By means of the DSS, we identified 3 125 households as being resident in the 12 villages and 3 town sectors which were offered insurance between February and May 2004, i.e. the months of the first enrolment campaign. From the AMBC records, we identified that out of these 3 125 households, 154 had accepted to join the scheme. We selected all these 154 households as cases. As controls, we used the 393 households not enrolled in AMBC and already part of the standard sample of the NHDHS. This corresponded to approximately 13% of all non-enrolled

households living in the area. Given that they had been chosen at random, we trusted that including those households already sampled to be part of the NHDHS would ensure that the controls be representative of the overall non-enrolled population in the area. The ratio of cases to controls was 1:2.5. Due to a mistake in field procedures, we were not able to interview 17 out of the 154 enrolled households. This means that we effectively included in the study 137 enrolled and 393 non-enrolled households for a ratio of cases to controls of 1:2.8.

2.4.2 The questionnaire

Information on both cases and controls was obtained by administering to all study participants the NHDHS questionnaire (Würthwein et al. 2001). The questionnaire is designed in a modular format, including three core modules and allowing for the introduction of additional modules depending on specific research needs. In 2004, the questionnaire included the three core modules and two additional modules, designed specifically to monitor enrolment in the AMBC (see appendix A). In addition, basic habitat (i.e. type of housing and dwelling) and socio-demographic information on all household members were collected directly as standard DSS activities. The three NHDHS core modules were:

a) the socio-economic module, collecting information on household income and expenditure;
b) the morbidity module, collecting information on self-reported morbidity and health care seeking behaviour;
c) the preventive care module, collecting information on the use of preventive care services, including family planning.

The two additional modules were:

d) the risk-sharing and quality of care module, monitoring participation in formal and semi-formal risk-sharing arrangements (other than the AMBC) and perceptions regarding the quality of care in the study area;

e) the insurance module, monitoring participation in the AMBC and reasons motivating decision to enrol or not to enrol in the scheme.

In 2004, given the addition of two modules, a reduced version of the module on preventive care was adopted in order to avoid imposing an excessive burden on the interviewed households. Other than this small change, all core modules were applied as originally developed (Würthwein et al. 2001). The two additional modules were designed in collaboration by the team working at the University of Heidelberg, including the author, and by the staff of the CRSN. The author was directly responsible, together with Mamadou Sanon, a Burkinabè anthropologist working at the CRSN, for translating and adapting the modules from English into French and for preparing the relevant manuals and training materials. Due to a mistake in field procedures, however, some questions within the two additional modules were not systematically applied to all households included in the sample as it had been originally planned. Therefore, upon conducting the analysis, only a restricted number of meaningful variables could be extracted from these two modules and incorporated in our analysis.

We collected information on each member of the household separately. Individuals below the age of 15 were classified as children. Mothers, or in their absence the closest caregiver, responded to questions regarding children.

2.4.3 Field procedures

2.4.3.1 Pre-testing the questionnaire

Before the finalisation of the four core modules, a preliminary version of the household survey questionnaire was pre-tested. In order to avoid that the same households be part of the pre-test and subsequently of the survey sample, the core modules were tested on 30 households living outside the DSS area. Ten different interviewers were involved in the pre-test phase (Würthwein et al. 2001). A similar approach is routinely adopted by the CRSN to test any additional module. The module on risk-sharing was pre-tested in March 2003, while the module on participation in the AMBC was pre-tested early in 2004.

2.4.3.2 Training and field work organisation

The questionnaire was administered by trained interviewers during the course of a face-to-face encounter with respondents. All interviewers had completed the basic cycle of secondary school, having at least ten years of education. Prior to the field activities, they received extensive training. The demographer in charge of the NHDHS, Adjima Gbangou, was responsible for the training regarding the four core modules, while Mamadou Sanon was responsible for the training on the two additional modules. Training manuals, providing methodological information as well as a comprehensive explanation of the structure of each module, were distributed to all interviewers and supervisors for further reference during field work.

Interviewers were organised in teams, each team being in charge of a given set of villages and/or town sectors. Each team reported to a supervisor, i.e. an interviewer with more extensive experience whose primary responsibility was that of checking the completeness and the coherence of the information collected. In turn, supervisors reported directly to the CRSN personnel in charge of the household survey activities, i.e. Adjima Gbangou and, for the risk-sharing and the AMBC modules, Mamadou Sanon. Group meetings, including all interviewers and all supervisors, were organised regularly to address problems arising on the field.

Interviewers received the questionnaires printed in French, but given that few people outside the town of Nouna speak French, they conducted the interviews in one of the local languages, most often Dioula, the local *lingua franca*, or Bwamu, the second most-widely spoken language. To ensure consistency in the way different interviewers posed the questions, plausible translations were developed and discussed during training. In addition, interviewers received the written translation into the main local languages of key elements, for example the list of diseases.

2.4.3.3 Data collection

Data collection lasted from May to September 2004. Each household was visited at least twice. All core modules were administered between May and June, while the two additional modules were administered between July and September. Interviewers returned to a household several times if they had not been able to reach all household members at once.

Households already included in previous rounds of the survey were accustomed to the procedure and in most instances they already knew the interviewer visiting them. Households sampled for the first time in 2004, were contacted directly by the interviewer who explained the aim of the study and sought explicit consent to proceed with the interview. No household refused the interview.

2.4.3.4 Data entry

Data entry lasted from September 2004 to January 2005. Data entry was completed by trained data entry clerks at the CRSN. All data entry clerks at the CRSN had completed secondary school and had received additional training in informatics, either in a specialised school or directly at the CRSN. Data entry clerks with extensive experience worked as trainers and supervisors.

Upon returning from the field, the completed questionnaires were turned in to the manager of the data entry service who distributed them among his data entry clerks. Data was entered in a relational database developed in Microsoft Access, which allowed for information to be stored in a set of tables that could regarded as separate entities with identifiers and attributes.

Systematic mutual checks were routinely implemented to ensure quality control during data entry. In a randomly varying sequence, one data entry clerk checked the work of the other. In addition, data entry masks contained a set of logical checks which did not allow clerks to enter numerical values in string variables, and *vice versa*, or values that lied outside a pre-defined range. The author herself checked the completeness and the consistency of the data during her most recent trip to Burkina Faso in December 2004. Following her comments on the discrepancies observed in some cases, the manager of the data entry service, Cheik Bagagnan, personally conducted an additional check on the quality of the data and gave disposition to his team to resolve all inconsistencies by referring back to the original questionnaires.

2.4.3.5 Quality control

The systematic training of both interviewers and data entry clerks, the close collaboration with supervisors, the distribution of detailed manuals, and the development of standardised procedural guidelines should ensure that the minimal amount of mistakes occur during the data collection and the data entry process. Würthwein et al. (2001) rightfully pointed out that without adequate procedures to ensure quality control, even the best designed survey may turn out to contain several mistakes which later hamper analysis.

As mentioned in an earlier section of this chapter, in spite of the great effort to control all field procedures, some questions within the two additional questionnaire modules were not systematically applied to all households included in the sample, and 17 enrolled households were not interviewed at all. The mistakes were only caught by the author in January 2005 when she received the complete database for analysis. At the time, it was discussed whether to return to the field to collect the missing and/or erroneous information or whether to proceed with analysis with the available data. After discussion with the field team, the latter option was preferred as it seemed to make little sense to return to the field asking some questions with a six-month delay and at a time when the second AMBC enrolment campaign had already started.

2.4.4 Data analysis

2.4.4.1 Variables and their measurement

Table 2.1 provides a list of the independent variables included in our regression model and a brief description of their measurement. In addition, we also describe some of these variables in greater detail given that their measurement may not be self-evident if referring exclusively to the table. We derived all variables from the household survey questionnaire described above. The only exceptions were distance to health facility, which was derived from the geographical information system, and enrolment status, which was derived directly from the AMBC records.

Preliminary results from the qualitative research suggested that different perceptions regarding the relative effectiveness of traditional versus Western care may influence decision to enrol. Therefore, we compiled a variable differentiating household heads who rated the care provided by traditional healers to be either "good" or "excellent" from household heads who rated it to be either "very poor", "poor", or "mediocre", or who said that they had no basis for judgement, never having sought treatment at a traditional healer. We assigned the label "adequate" to the first set of judgements and the label "inadequate" to the second set. Because of the incompleteness of the responses in the relevant module, we were not able to compile a variable assessing the respondent's judgement regarding the quality of care at the modern health facilities.

We assessed education in terms of exposure to institutional schooling, and not simply in terms of literacy. Therefore, we differentiated between individuals never having attended school and individuals having attended at least some years of primary or secondary school. Given the low number of individuals in either one of these last two categories, we did not differentiate between those having concluded and those not having concluded the relevant educational cycle.

As an indication of socio-economic status, we preferred expenditure to income. Given that in many low income countries, income may be subject to extreme seasonal fluctuations, expenditure is generally recognised to be a better indication of a household socio-economic status (Dercon 2002; Morduch 1995). As addressed earlier in this dissertation in fact, households tend to smooth their consumption over time, spending income accrued at a given point in time over several months. Since in 2004, only one round of the household survey was conducted, we had information on six-month, not annual, expenditure. Starting from individual-level information, we compiled an estimate of household six-month expenditure, which we later aggregated into quartiles. We assumed that the households in the lowest quartile, i.e. the ones spending the least, were the poorest and those in the highest quartile, i.e. those spending the most, were the wealthiest.

Given that the AMBC premium differentiates between adults and children, we thought it would be more meaningful to include in our analysis an estimate of the children to adult ratio rather than a simple count of the household size. Therefore, we generated a variable differentiating households where there were more children than adults (child/adult ratio > 1) from all other households (child/adult ratio <= 1).

Given the wealth of information on illness reporting and health care seeking behaviour included in the survey, we were able to construct two separate measures of adverse selection: one capturing self-reported health status and one capturing prior health service utilisation. We constructed a measure of health status by differentiating households reporting at least one chronic disease from households reporting no chronic disease. We constructed a measure of prior health service utilisation by differentiating households who reported at least one curative care contact in the 12 months preceding the interview from households who reported no curative contact.

We chose not to include in our measure of health status any indication of acute illness reporting since the questionnaire recall period for acute conditions was only one month. This made it impossible for us to distinguish households repeatedly affected by acute illnesses from households who may just happen to have suffered a malaria episode, maybe the first one in years, in the one month preceding the interview. In addition, the timing of the survey implied that several households answered questions on illness reporting only weeks after the closure of the first enrolment campaign. Hence, the information on acute illness could not be taken to be representative of the prior health status potentially influencing decision to enrol. Likewise, the recall period for any information on health spending only stretched one month prior to the time of the interview. Therefore, we also did not include information on health spending in our analysis as they pertained to the period following rather than preceding the decision to enrol in CHI.

In addition, we also constructed a measure differentiating households reporting at least one preventive care contact in the 12 months preceding the interview from households reporting no preventive care contact. This measure was not meant to capture adverse selection, but rather a certain propensity towards making investments in health. This propensity was assumed to be relevant both to the choice of seeking preventive health care and to the choice of participating in the AMBC.

Table 2.1: List of independent variables and their measurements

Variables	Measurement
Household head characteristics	
Sex	0 = female 1 = male
Age (in years)	0 = 20 to 40 1 = 41 to 60 2 = 61+
Ethnicity	0 = other ethnicity 1 = Bwaba
Education	0 = no schooling 1 = primary school 2 = secondary school
Occupation	0 = farmer 1 = other occupation
Rating of healer's care	0 = "adequate" 1 = "non adequate"
Household characteristics	
Household expenditure (quartiles)	1 = lowest quartile (poorest) 4 = highest quartile (wealthiest)
Child/adult ratio	0 = child/adult ratio <= 1 1 = child/adult ratio > 1
Chronic diseases	0 = none 1 = at least one chronic disease
Use of curative care	0 = no contact 1 = at least one contact
Use of preventive care	0 = no contact 1 = at least one contact
Community characteristics	
Distance to health facility	0 = near (<= 5 km) 1 = far (>5)
Referral facility	0 = first-line facility at Nouna Hospital 1 = any CSPS
Socio-economic equality	1 = low level of equality 2 = middle level of equality 3 = high level of equality
Participation in other risk-sharing	1 = low level of participation 2 = middle level of participation 3 = high level of participation

For each of these three variables, i.e. health status, curative health service utilisation, and preventive health service utilisation, we grouped households reporting only one chronic disease or one contact together with households reporting more than one disease or one contact. We were obliged to aggregate information in such manner because the number of households reporting several diseases or several contacts was too small to constitute a category of its own.

Given our focus on understanding how community, and not simply household head and household, characteristics mediate decision to enrol, we included in our model three novel features: socio-economic equality, community participation in risk-sharing arrangements, and referral facility.

In high-income countries, a number of studies have looked at the effect of socio-economic equality on health outcomes (Daly et al. 1998; Ross et al. 2000; Veenstra 2005). While still controlling for individual-level differences in socio-economic status, these studies have attempted to assess the extent to which the distribution of socio-economic resources within a community influences health status. To assess socio-economic equality, these studies calculated the proportion of total household income, most frequently measured in dollars, held by the poorest 50% of households. This measure, however, has been criticised as it may misrepresent socio-economic status by excluding capital gains and assets (Veenstra 2005).

As addressed earlier in this section, we trust expenditure to provide a better estimate of socio-economic status as people spend money in relation to their overall wealth and not simply in relation to their immediate income. In low-income countries especially, abundant cash is often invested in the purchase of farm animals which are progressively sold to meet the household's needs. Therefore, we decided to develop a measure of socio-economic equality based on expenditure rather than on income. To ensure consistency with the household-level estimate of socio-economic status, we used six-month expenditure to create a variable indicating the percentage of total household expenditure, measured in CFA, spent by the poorest 50% of households. Since the inclusion of the non-randomly sampled cases in the calculation could have biased the estimate, we derived socio-economic equality by taking into account only those 412 households, 393 non-enrolled and 19 enrolled in AMBC, originally sampled to be part of the NHDHS. Using tertile values as cut-off points, we aggregated estimates of the percentage of total expenditure spent by the poorest 50% of the population, i.e. our proxy for socio-economic equality, into three groups: low level of equality, middle level of equality, and high level of equality. Our assumption in wishing to include this variable in our model was that the distribution of socio-economic resources within a community influences not only health status, as reported in earlier studies, but also broader decision-making processes pertaining to health care seeking behaviour, including the decision to enrol in CHI. In addition, indicating how effective communities have been in re-distributing resources across households, we judged measures of socio-economic equality to constitute a powerful proxy to judge overall attitudes towards solidarity and risk-sharing.

Given the incompleteness of the relevant module, we could not derive individual-level information regarding participation in other formal or semi-formal risk-sharing arrangements, i.e. *tontines*, *groupements*, and associations. However, since the module on participation in risk-sharing had already been applied during the 2003 round of the household survey, it was possible for us to derive an estimate of what percentage of the adult population in each village or town sector participated in a risk-sharing arrangement other than the AMBC. We discussed with some key informants, among whom the provincial director of the ATN, the decision to include in the analysis information gathered during the previous year. We were reassured that overall participation in formal and semi-formal risk-sharing arrangements had not changed dramatically between 2003 and 2004. Using tertile values as cut-off points, we aggregated estimates of the percentage of adult population participating in risk-sharing arrangements into three groups: low level of participation, middle level of participation, and high level of participation.

It is important to clarify that the module on risk-sharing recorded exclusively participation in formal and semi-formal arrangements, institutionally similar to the AMBC. The module did not record, because impossible to quantify through means of a standardised questionnaire, risk-sharing activities which occur at the informal level, usually between people of the same family, clan, and/or gender and which permeate all aspects of African society. This explains why in order to capture overall community attitudes towards solidarity and risk-sharing, we incorporated in our model both an estimate of socio-economic equality and an estimate of participation in formal and semi-formal arrangements.

In our review of the literature on insurance purchase in sub-Saharan Africa, we have criticised previous studies for not including price and product characteristics in their models, although pooling together information on several schemes, operating at different prices and with different characteristics (Jütting 2004; Osei-Akoto 2004; Schneider and Diop 2004). In our case, the inclusion of price and product characteristics in the model would have been meaningless. Price and product characteristics were in fact constant for all households in the sample as residents of the Nouna Health District only have the option to enrol in one scheme, i.e. the AMBC, and always at exactly the same conditions. As described in the previous chapter, the premium varies exclusively as a function of the number of children and adults living within a household. Therefore, including in our model an estimate of child/adult ratio was sufficient to address possible variations due to the actual price faced by each household.

The one feature of the overall insurance package which may have differed across households was the referral facility. As described earlier in this dissertation, following the indication of the Health District, communities were assigned to a first-line facility depending on their geographical location. Given that all rural first-line facilities are equally staffed and equipped and that nurses regularly rotate across facilities, we assumed that no differential incentive to enrolment should have existed depending on the specific CSPS to which individuals were assigned. We did consider, however, that a differential incentive to enrolment may have existed for reporting directly to the first-line facility located on the premises of the district hospital in the town of Nouna, as this CSPS is somewhat better equipped and most importantly, it is much closer to second-line services. To assess possible differences in the incentive to enrol due to referral facility, we derived a variable distinguishing between households assigned to the first-line facility located directly on the district hospital premises and households assigned to any other CSPS.

2.4.4.2 Statistical methods

Given that households did not have a choice with regard to how much insurance to purchase, i.e. how many members of the family to enrol in the AMBC, we treated decision to enrol as a discrete choice problem yielding a binary outcome, enrolment vs. non-enrolment. We coded enrolment as 1 and non-enrolment as 0. Data was prepared for analysis using the software Microsoft Access (Microsoft Corporation 2002), while analysis was carried out using Stata version 8.1 (StataCorp 2003).

Before beginning our analysis, we checked that the controls were representative of the overall non-enrolled population in the DSS area. We did so by comparing the controls and the overall non-enrolled DSS population with regard to the basic socio-demographic characteristics included in the DSS database: household size, and household head's age, sex, and ethnicity.

Before developing our multivariate model, we explored univariate relationships between the outcome variable, i.e. enrolment in the AMBC, and all the household head, household, and community characteristics taken into consideration in our analysis. We used Pearson's Chi-square test to determine whether the distribution of household head, household, and community characteristics, differed significantly between cases and controls. In addition, since we had grouped continuous variables into quantiles, we tested differences between cases and controls for the continuous variables age, household expenditure, socio-economic equality, and participation in other risk-sharing arrangements. Since age of the household head was a normally distributed variable, we assessed the difference in means between cases and controls using the Student's t-test for independent samples. Since none of the other three variables were normally distributed, we assessed differences in median values between cases and controls using the Wilcoxon rank-sum test, a non-parametric analogue of the independent sample t-test (Rosner 2000).

For each of the variables included in our analysis, we calculated univariate odds ratio estimates. This provided base-line estimates against which to compare how the effect on enrolment of a given factor may change after controlling for other variables.

Given the case-control nature of the data, for our multivariate analysis, we preferred binary logistic regression to binary probit regression. Logistic regression is in fact recognised as the most suitable modelling technique when dealing with case-control studies, yielding more accurate estimates than alternative binary models (Chernick and Friis 2003; Kleinbaum and Klein 2002; Rosner 2000). Given that estimates are derived from a biased sample comprising a greater proportion of cases than the reference population, logistic regression applied to case-control studies cannot be used to predict outcome probabilities. Nevertheless, the odds ratio derived from case-control studies can be generalised to the reference population, providing a powerful insight into the strength of the association between the outcome variable and the independent variables included in the model (Kleinbaum and Klein 2002; Rosner 2000).

The conventional unconditional logistic regression model estimates the odds of being enrolled in the AMBC for the *i*th household. We denote the probability that $y_i = 1$, i.e. that the household is enrolled in the AMBC, by π_i. The logistic model can then be written as a liner function of the explanatory variables:

$$\text{logit}(\pi_i) = \beta_0 + \beta_1 X_1 + \ldots + \beta_k X_k \qquad \textbf{(2.1)}$$

which relies on the logit link function:

$$\text{logit}(\pi_i) = \log\left(\frac{\pi_i}{1-\pi_i}\right)$$

where $\pi_i/(1 - \pi_i)$ represents the odds that $y_i = 1$; β_0 is the intercept; $\beta_1 \ldots \beta_k$ are the regression coefficients; and $X_1 \ldots X_k$. are the independent variables defined at the household level. In multiple logistic regression, the odds ratio (OR) relating to the variable X_l is the exponential function of its parameter β_l ($OR_{Xl} = e^{\beta l}$). For equation (2.1) a z-test was computed to assess the significance of each parameter estimate included in the model. The overall goodness-of-fit of the model expressed by equation (2.1) was estimated using the Hosmer-Lemeshow test (Greene 1997).

In our instance, however, the application of conventional logistic regression appeared questionable. Regression modelling relies in fact on the assumption that the error terms are independent. Violations of this assumption are likely to occur when the individual observations are correlated to one another. This is likely to be the case in our analysis given that households were clustered in villages or town sectors. Households within the same village or town sector were likely to be correlated, displaying common features and thus violating the principle of independence. Therefore, applying traditional logistic regression may have proved to be inappropriate because the model would have ignored the correlation that existed across households within the same village or town sector. Ignoring such correlation may have resulted in an underestimation of the standard errors, thus overstating the statistical significance of the coefficients (Goldstein 2003; Greene 1997).

Two distinguished approaches are available to correct for clustering at the village/town sector level using Stata 8.1. The simplest approach relies on the application of Huber-White robust variance estimates to relax the assumption of independence (Greene 1997). Huber-White robust variance estimates do not affect the estimation of the coefficients, but simply that of the standard errors, allowing the researcher not to classify as significant relationships which in reality are not significant.

A more complex, although definitely more comprehensive, approach relies on the application of multilevel modelling (Goldstein 2003; Greene 1997). Multilevel modelling, also known as random-effect or hierarchical modelling, represents a recent statistical development, allowing the researcher to explicitly acknowledge the clustered nature of the data and to model simultaneously individual and community factors. Multilevel modelling allows not only to correct possible biases in the estimation of the standard errors, but it also allows to partition the residual variance across levels, teasing out community-level differences (Goldstein 2003). Having emerged primarily from the field of educational research, multilevel modelling has in recent years found broad application also within the field of health system research (Chang and Trivedi 2003; Magadi et al. 2000; Mauny et al. 2004; Veenstra 2005). Health and decision-making processes related to health care consumption are in fact largely shaped by the environmental and the social context within which individuals live. Leyland et al. (2003) argued that, because of its capacity to simultaneously capture individual and community characteristics, multilevel modelling allows public health research to be truthful to its primary objective to study the health of people in their context.

In this dissertation, we have repeatedly insisted on the importance of social context in shaping decision to enrol in CHI. Therefore, we inevitably privileged multilevel logistic regression to conventional logistic regression. The application of multilevel modelling allowed us to take into explicit account the fact that households within the same village or town sector were likely to be more similar to one other than households located in other villages. The striking differences in enrolment rates observed across villages triggered our curiosity and the search for an alternative statistical method. Our assumption was in fact that controlling exclusively for household-level variables, as done in previous research, would provide only a partial answer to questions exploring insurance purchase. The application of multilevel modelling does not entail an ability to explain all variation in the outcome variable. Nevertheless, by teasing out community-level variance, it allows to determine whether non-observed village characteristics affect decision to enrol, allowing us to make sense of the between-village heterogeneity in enrolment rates.

Previous studies on insurance purchase have at times included location into their model by creating dummy variables differentiating, for example, between towns, districts, or regions. This approach does not allow to distinguish variation due to location from possible variation due to product characteristics. In addition, this approach proves to be of limited use, because, although clearly suggesting the existence of important differences due to location, it only provides meaningful information on the very same towns, districts, or regions included in the sample. We could have chosen to follow a similar approach and include a dummy variable for each of the 15 localities, i.e. the 12 villages and 3 town sectors, being offered insurance in 2004. This approach, however, would have confirmed something that we already know, i.e. that enrolment is higher in certain villages, for example Dembéléla, than in others, for example Bankoumani. Multilevel modelling allowed us instead to treat the 15 localities as a random sample of all the villages and town sectors in the DSS area. This allowed us to make inferences about the variation among all the villages and town sectors in the region, using the sampled 15 locations as a means to an end. Given the primary interest to expand AMBC coverage to the whole DSS area and progressively to the whole Health District, this seemed to us to be a much more meaningful approach to data analysis, allowing to combine the necessity to generate statistically accurate estimates with a wish to provide answers directly relevant to policy-making.

Our model recognised two organisational levels: the household, i.e. level one, and the village or town sector where the household resides, i.e. level two. We used multilevel random-effect logistic regression to estimate the odds of being enrolled in the AMBC for the *i*th household residing in the *v*th village.

The random-effect logistic model can be also be written as a liner function of the explanatory variables:

$$\text{logit}(\pi_{iv}) = \beta_{0v} + \beta_1 X_{1iv} + \ldots + \beta X_{kv} \qquad \textbf{(2.2)}$$

which relies on the logit link function:

$$\text{logit}(\pi_{iv}) = \log\left(\frac{\pi_{iv}}{1-\pi_{iv}}\right)$$

where $\pi_{iv}/(1 - \pi_{iv})$ represents the odds that $y_{iv} = 1$, i.e. that the household *i* in village *v* is enrolled in the AMBC; $\beta_1 \ldots \beta_k$ are the regression coefficients and $X_{1iv} \ldots X_{kv}$ are the variables defined at the individual and village level. In random-effect modelling, the intercept β_{0v} consists of two terms: a fixed component β_0 and a village-specific component, the random-effect u_{0v}. Random-effect logistic regression assumes that u_{ov} follows a normal distribution with mean zero and variance σ^2_{u0}. In random-effect logistic regression, the odds ratio (OR) relating to the variable X_1 is still calculated as the exponential function of its parameter β_1 ($OR_{X1} = e^{\beta 1}$).

The key difference between conventional logistic regression and multilevel logistic regression refers to the structure of the random component of the model, i.e. the village variance estimate. From a computational point of view, random-effect modelling can be seen as a two-stage process. First, a separate individual regression is defined for each village. Then, each of the village specific coefficients is modelled as a function of village variables. Therefore, the multilevel model allows computing village-specific coefficients: a fixed part that is common to all villages and a random part varying between villages. Interative estimations are computed until the model converges (Mauny et al. 2004).

Stata 8.1 computes random-effect logistic regression using the Gauss-Hermitte quadrature approximation[7] (Greene 1997). For equation (2.2), a z-test was computed to assess the significance of each parameter estimate included in the model. A Wald test was computed to assess the overall goodness-of-fit of the model. The proportion of total variance in the outcome variable contributed by the level-two component of the model, in our case the village or town sector, is labelled as *rho*[8]. Formally, *rho* is indicated by ρ and expressed by the equation:

$$\rho = \left(\frac{\sigma_v^2}{\sigma_v^2 + 1} \right)$$

When ρ is zero, the village-level variance component is unimportant and the estimated values of the multilevel logistic regression do not differ significantly from those of the conventional logistic regression. A ρ statistically greater then zero indicates the existence of between-village heterogeneity, in our case heterogeneity in enrolment rates not explained by the variables included in the model.

---

[7] Stata 8.1 provides a test to check the numerical soundness of the quadrature approximation. The reliability of the quadrature estimation procedure can in fact be jeopardised, severely affecting the stability of the results, by two factors: large sample size and large correlations within groups. The test for the sensitivity of the quadrature estimator works by comparing the log-likelihood and the coefficient estimates of the original model with those produced after the model is re-estimated using two different numbers of quadrature points. Changes beyond 1% indicate that the quadrature approach may not be valid, discouraging the application of this modelling technique to the specific dataset. In order to verify the appropriateness of the estimation procedure with specific reference to our dataset, we run the quadrature sensitivity test. The result is presented in appendix E.

[8] To be noted that at present all statistical software packages allowing for multilevel modelling are unable to determine the exact proportion of variability attributable to the second level when the outcome variable is not continuous. Nevertheless, Stata 8.1, as well as other statistical software packages, provides a good estimation of such variance. Although not presented in this dissertation, because of limits of space, to check the consistency of the estimation techniques, we carried out our analysis also in an alternative statistical software package, MLWin, especially designed for multilevel modelling. Although MLWin applies a different estimation procedure, quasi-maximum-likelihood, we obtained very similar results to those generated in Stata 8.1. Thus, we concluded that the estimates presented in this dissertation are as accurate as one can possibly calculate given the software packages currently available.

In practice, we conducted our analysis in three subsequent steps. First, we run a multilevel model including as fixed effects exclusively household head and household characteristics. Then, in order to assess the extent to which village characteristics could explain enrolment in CHI, we included as fixed effects also a selected range of village characteristics, monitoring changes in village-level residual variance (ρ). Last, we run the complete model, including household head, household, and village characteristics, using conventional logistic regression and applying, to correct for clustering at the village level, Huber-White robust variance estimates. For each of the two multilevel random-effect models, we run a likelihood-ratio test of the *rho* to compare the panel estimator, i.e. equation (2.2), with the pooled estimator, i.e. equation (2.1). This was done to assess whether the panel and the pooled models differed significantly and thus, whether the application of multilevel logistic regression was to be preferred to that of conventional logistic regression.

Figure 2.5: Steps in statistical modelling

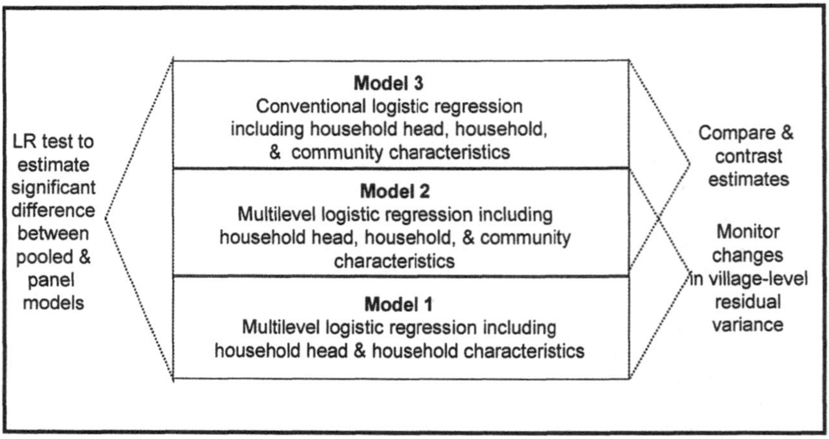

On the basis of the theoretical discussion outlined at the very beginning of this chapter and of the preliminary results emerging from the qualitative research, we formulated a hypothesis regarding the effect of the single variables on decision to enrol. Table 2.2 lists the variables and their expected sign. Given that we did not expect variables to yield different effects in the three models we run, we indicate each variable and its relevant sign only once. We expected the estimates of the multilevel model to be significantly different from those of the conventional model, with ρ being statistically different from zero.

Table 2.2: List of independent variables and their expected sign

Variable	Expected sign
Household head characteristics	
Sex	+
Age (in years)	+/-
Ethnicity	+
Education	+
Occupation	+/-
Rating of healer's care	+
Household characteristics	
Household expenditure (quartiles)	+
Child/adult ratio	+
Chronic diseases	+
Use of curative care	+
Use of preventive care	+
Community characteristics	
Distance to health facility	-
Referral facility	-
Socio-economic equality	+
Participation in other risk-sharing	+

2.5 Qualitative methods

2.5.1 Grounded theory

The methodological approach guiding the qualitative component of this dissertation is rooted in grounded theory. The phrase grounded theory refers to a methodological approach for conducting qualitative research in the social sciences which emerged out of the work of Barney Glaser and Anselm Strauss. Since the publication of their first book in 1967, the two sociologists have been working on developing and refining a methodology which allows for the inductive discovery of theory grounded in systematically analysed data (Glaser and Strauss 1967; Strauss 1987).

Grounded theory constitutes a problem-oriented approach to the conduct of social science research. Rather than being preoccupied with testing grand sociological theories, Glaser and Strauss, drawing from the extensive empirical experience of the University of Chicago, have argued in favour of research which focuses on pragmatic problems and attempts to understand social phenomena directly through the eyes of the human agent. Grounded theory is therefore concerned with the *emic* understanding of the world, i.e. the insider's perspective, conceptualising events in a manner which is meaningful to the members of a given society. The grounded theory researcher does not impose his/her point of view, but attempts to develop *etic* constructs, i.e. accounts, descriptions, and analyses expressed in terms of conceptual schemes and categories, by simply re-constructing the insider's point of view[9]. Similarly to other approaches in qualitative research, grounded theory also relies on a variety of data sources, including focus group discussions, individual interviews, and direct field observation.

Grounded theory recognises that researchers do not approach the field as *tabula rasa*, but that previous theoretical knowledge inevitably enters the formulation of the problem as well as the interpretation of the recorded information.

---

[9] The *emic* and *etic* principle was named in 1954 by the linguist Kenneth Pike, who used the terms to refer to the fact that people distinguish phon*emes* (the basic set of underlying constructs which generate the sound of language) from their phon*etic* representation (what people actually hear). In 1956, the anthropologist Ward Goodenough insisted that this principle could be borrowed from the field of linguistics and applied to areas of culture other than phonology to distinguish between the insider's, i.e. *emic*, and the outsider's, i.e. *etic*, point of view. Although ontological and epistemological debate continues to surround the exact application of *emic* and *etic*, most current anthropologists, and to a lesser extent other social scientists, continue to use the terms to distinguish between the insider's, i.e. the one being studied, and the outsider's, i.e. the researcher, conceptualisation of a given situation or event (Bernard 1990).

Explanatory models and theories are therefore generated through the systematic analysis of data patterns, which is in turn informed by previous theoretical knowledge. Grounded theory is inductive in nature and relies on the "constant comparison method", a combination of theoretical sampling procedures and systematic coding to produce meaningful data analysis useful to the development of relevant theory.

Theoretical sampling refers to selecting samples of population, events, and activities to be included in the research according to the researcher's *a priori* theoretical knowledge. This serves the aim of facilitating subsequent explicit comparisons across sub-dimensions. Systematic coding refers to the practice of grouping concepts and properties into meaningful variables, called categories. Unlike hypothetical-deductive approaches to data analysis, grounded theory argues in favour of letting categories emerge directly from the text being analysed. The grounded theory researcher starts by reading and re-reading the textual database, such as interview transcripts or field notes, to discover how a given situation is conceptualised and constructed by its very same actors. Elements are identified, named, and categorised according to how they emerge from the text. The researcher progressively focuses on identifying links between categories, building relationships between the various elements. Coding alone is in fact insufficient to produce meaningful analysis as it constitutes a fragmentation of the situation being analysed. Therefore, codes always ought to be interpreted in the light of the broader context out of which they have emerged. Glaser and Strauss argued that throughout the coding process, the ability to perceive variables and relationships is influenced by what they define as "theoretical sensitivity", i.e. the researcher's ability to conceptualise data in theoretical terms. Theoretical sensitivity is in turn influenced by the researcher's familiarity with the literature and with the broader context of his/her research (Glaser and Strauss 1967).

Given its problem-solving orientation and its focus on the insider's point of view, grounded theory, and more in general inductive approaches to qualitative data analysis derived from the work of Glaser and Strauss, have gained increasing popularity in health system research (Burnard 1991; Coast 2001; Coast et al. 2002; Litva et al. 2002; Xu et al. 2004). Given our interest in understanding how communities conceptualise CHI and why they may choose to enrol or not to enrol in a scheme, we also deemed grounded theory to be the most suitable methodological approach guiding our qualitative research. In the following sections, however, we do not refer exclusively to the work of Glaser and Strauss, but also incorporate, when appropriate, the theoretical guidance of other social scientists.

2.5.2 Sampling

In line with the principle of theoretical sampling (Strauss 1987), we selected individuals to be interviewed using a stratified purposive sampling strategy based on insurance status, distance to the health facility, and socio-economic status. In line with the grounded theory approach, enrolment status was used as the basic sampling criteria because we wished to compare and contrast enrolled and non-enrolled households to understand what factors explain the different outcome, i.e. what factors explain decision to join or not to join CHI. Distance to the health facility and socio-economic status were used as the additional sampling criteria given that the literature on sub-Saharan Africa has identified them as possible determinants of enrolment in CHI (Chee et al. 2002; Criel and Waelkens 2003; Jütting 2004; Schneider and Diop 2004). Including in our sample individuals with different experiences allowed us to capture variations across households while also investigating possible common elements and common reasons motivating decision to enrol or not to enrol in CHI (Patton 1990). In addition, given our explicit interest in exploring preferences for the single components of the insurance scheme, we wished to ensure to take into account the views of people with diverse experiences.

Figure 2.6: Stratified purposive sampling for the qualitative study

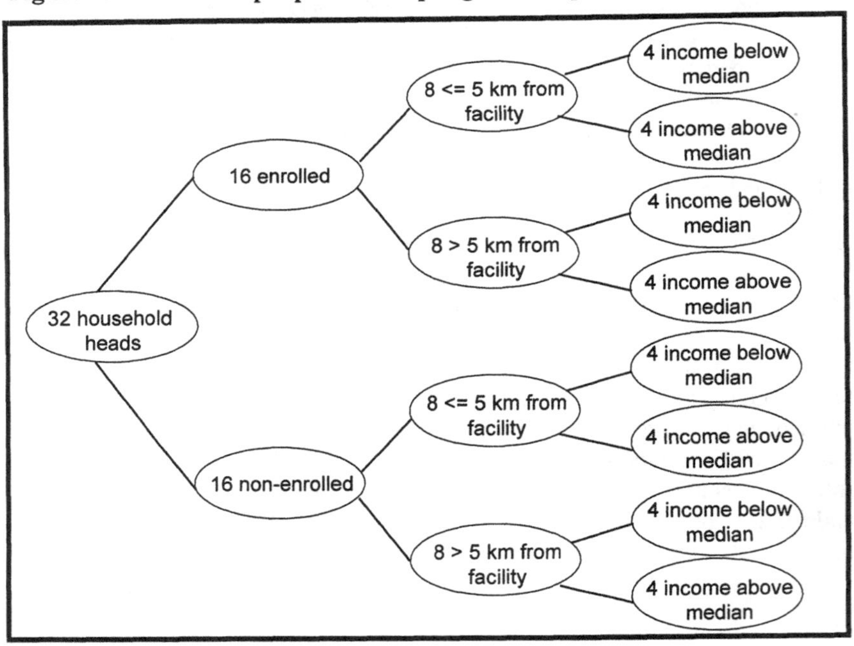

Based on the criteria described above, we selected for interview 32 household heads. As outlined in Figure 2.6, we selected 16 individuals enrolled in the AMBC and 16 individuals not enrolled in the AMBC. For each group of 16, we selected 8 individuals living within 5 km from a health facility and 8 leaving further than 5 km from a health facility. Within each group of 8, we selected 4 individuals with household income below the DSS median value and 4 with household income above the DSS median value. In order to ensure that the point of view of women be included in our analysis, we purposely selected to conduct 8 out of the 32 interviews with female households heads, who matched our stratified sampling criteria.

We interviewed each household head separately as we deemed individual in-depth interviews to be a better means of assessing determinants of enrolment, when compared to focus group discussions. Although influenced by community factors, ultimate decision to enrol in the health insurance scheme rests within the single household. Furthermore, we trusted individual interviews to be better suited to offer people who may not be particularly vocal in public settings, an opportunity to freely express their point of view without fear of being judged by others in the community (Maier et al. 1994; Ryan et al. 2001). The choice to interview exclusively household heads is due to the fact that, as described earlier in this chapter, we treated decision to enrol as a household decision given that the AMBC prescribes compulsory household enrolment. In the local context, household heads, being the ones who decide over the allocation of resources, were assumed to be the key players in determining enrolment in CHI.

2.5.3 The data collection tools

Information from respondents was collected through means of a semi-structured interview. The interview guide provided a framework within which to explore matters of interest, but allowed for thematic areas to be explored freely as they arose (see appendix B). It touched upon all of the following themes: interviewee's enrolment status and socio-demographic characteristics; knowledge and understanding of the insurance principle and in particular of the AMBC; affordability, distance, and quality of care; cultural beliefs and practices; participation in traditional risk-sharing networks; previous illness experience and health care seeking behaviour; preferences for the scheme components. Specifically, individual preferences were discussed in relation to all of the following elements: unit of enrolment; premium level and payment modalities; benefit package; health service provider network; and the AMBC managerial structures.

The author developed the interview guide and revised it in the light of the comments expressed by her supervisor, Prof. Sauerborn, and by the anthropologist Mamadou Sanon. Before piloting the instrument, she also discussed the interview guide with the AMBC management unit and with representatives of the Health District to ensure that no relevant issue was omitted. She conducted five pilot interviews, two with enrolled and three with non-enrolled individuals. Piloting served the dual purpose of ensuring that all relevant issues be included in the interview guide and of building a fluent relationship between the interviewer and her translator. All interviews were in fact conducted directly by the author with the assistance of a Burkinabè sociologist, Aline Bagayoyo, acting as her translator.

In addition to the interview guide, the author also developed an instrument to systematically record the details of the context within which each interview took place as well as her first impressions and those of the translator with regard to the interview they had just concluded (see appendix C). The instrument was also useful to record important comments that the respondents expressed while the tape-recorder was switched off. Not to intimidate nor condition the respondents in fact, neither the author nor her translator took notes during the course of the interview. During the conversation, they devoted full attention to the respondents, but promptly wrote down both any additional comment and their first impressions immediately following the end of each interview. The information recorded through means of this instrument was later matched with the text of each transcribed interview and incorporated in the database used for the analysis.

2.5.4 Field procedures

Individuals to be interviewed were identified, in the respect of the sampling criteria, by compiling information on enrolment, derived from the AMBC records, with information on distance to health facility, derived from the DSS, and information on socio-economic status, derived from the 2003 round of the NHDHS. All selected individuals were initially contacted by an employee of the CRSN and asked whether they would be willing to undergo an interview to share their knowledge and views regarding the newly implemented insurance scheme in the District. If the person expressed interest in participating in the study, the employee would set an appointment for the interview. Before conducting the interview, the author and her translator introduced themselves, explained the aim of their visit, and asked for consent to record the conversation. The author always made it explicit that the individual was free to refuse the interview or to interrupt it at any point should he/she feel uncomfortable with the questions asked. She also reassured respondents regarding the confidentiality of the information shared during the course of the interview. No one refused to be interviewed nor to have the interview recorded. One individual had to be substituted by another one with matching sampling criteria, because he had just migrated outside the study area. All interviews were conducted between May and June 2004.

All interviews were tape-recorded, fully transcribed, and translated into French by trained translators at the CRSN. Mamadou Sanon, speaking both French and the local languages, was responsible for training the transcribers. He also checked all transcriptions for accuracy. When relevant to the understanding of an individual's experience and perception of the world, expressions in the local languages were not translated. The transcription and translation process was completed by the end of July 2004.

2.5.5 Data analysis

Analysis was conducted on the French text with the support of the software Atlas.ti 5.0 (The Scientific Sotware Development 2003) and relied on a "compare and contrast" method rooted in grounded theory (Strauss 1987). Analysis began with a first reading of the transcripts to acquire familiarity with the data and clarify, with the assistance of the Burkinabè sociologist who had acted as a translator, what comments and expressions could only be understood within the specificity of the context in which they were elicited. Special attention was paid to clarifying expressions which the transcribers had chosen to leave in the local language.

In line with the grounded theory approach, we adopted *in-vivo* and open coding, meaning that categories and subcategories were developed, modified, and extended on the basis of what themes emerged as the analysis proceeded. Links between categories were progressively identified to illuminate the contextual understanding of the research question (Strauss 1987). We constantly compared and contrasted responses by different individuals to identify variations as well as common patterns. We used causal maps to facilitate the understanding of the relationships emerging from data analysis, providing a visual representation of how different elements interact with one another (Bernard 1990). We provide a complete list of all coding categories developed during the course of the analysis in appendix D.

While analysing and interpreting the text, the author also repeatedly referred to the field notes and memos that she had written during her various stays in Burkina Faso. Between September 2002 and December 2004, the author visited the study area four times, for periods ranging between three and eight weeks at a time. During each visit, in addition to research activities, she participated in community gathering and workshops related to the implementation of the AMBC. On these occasions, she interacted on an informal level with the project initiators, the health care providers, and the community at large, gaining a deeper understanding both of the local socio-cultural context and of the specific issues surrounding the implementation of the scheme. Her repeated visits to the field allowed her to gain the trust of the people she met, so that in each subsequent trip, she was able to interact at a deeper level, with people progressively incorporating her in their daily activities and being more open to freely express their opinions in her presence. In addition, the author constituted the reference point in Heidelberg for the AMBC management unit, acting as the mediator between the research and the field teams. Therefore, she was in constant touch with the concerns and problems emerging on the field. This also contributed to building her understanding of the implementation context, which proved to be extremely useful in the process of data analysis and interpretation.

Figure 2.7: Illustration of coding

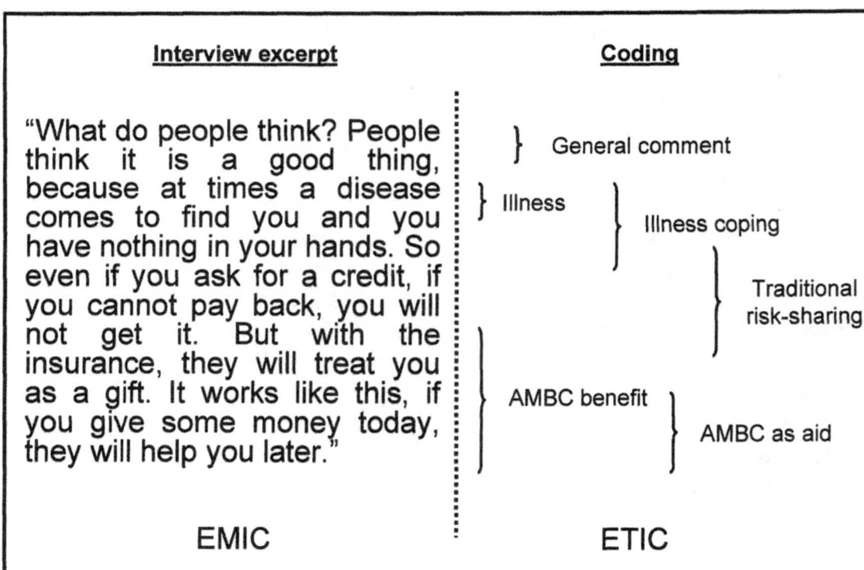

While analysing and interpreting the text, the author also repeatedly referred to the field notes and memos that she had written during her various stays in Burkina Faso. Between September 2002 and December 2004, the author visited the study area four times, for periods ranging between three and eight weeks at a time. During each visit, in addition to research activities, she participated in community gathering and workshops related to the implementation of the AMBC. On these occasions, she interacted on an informal level with the project initiators, the health care providers, and the community at large, gaining a deeper understanding both of the local socio-cultural context and of the specific issues surrounding the implementation of the scheme. Her repeated visits to the field allowed her to gain the trust of the people she met, so that in each subsequent trip, she was able to interact at a deeper level, with people progressively incorporating her in their daily activities and being more open to freely express their opinions in her presence. In addition, the author constituted the reference point in Heidelberg for the AMBC management unit, acting as the mediator between the research and the field teams. Therefore, she was in constant touch with the concerns and problems emerging on the field. This also contributed to building her understanding of the implementation context, which proved to be extremely useful in the process of data analysis and interpretation.

2.6 Triangulation

We made an explicit effort to increase the credibility of our study through a process of systematic triangulation. The term triangulation is used to refer to a process by which the researcher combines two or more methods of analysis, systematically comparing and contrasting the emerging results, with the aim of increasing the validity of a study by providing a wider evidence base (Patton 1990). The term triangulation represents a powerful metaphor taken from the field of land surveying. It refers to the fact that that knowing a single landmark only locates a person somewhere along a line in a direction from that landmark. Knowing two landmarks instead, allows an individual to take bearings in two directions and to locate himself/herself at the intersection. Similarly, in the social sciences, relying on two or more research methods allows the investigator to make sound interferences about the phenomena observed, basing his/her judgement on the "intersection", i.e. the convergence, between two or more sets of findings. The logic of triangulation is based on the premises that the adoption of multiple methods of analysis always represents a preferable research alternative, since no single method is ever sufficient to capture and explain social phenomena in their entirety.

Patton (1990) distinguished four basic types of triangulation: (1) data triangulation – the use of a variety of data sources; (2) investigator triangulation

– the use of different researchers; (3) theory triangulation – the use of multiple perspectives to interpret a single set of data; and (4) methodological triangulation – the use of multiple methods.

Within the qualitative component of our study, we applied two forms of triangulation: data and investigator triangulation.

We applied data triangulation as we systematically compared findings from the individual interviews with findings from ten focus group discussions (FGD) conducted by Mamadou Sanon to explore community perceptions and social constructions of the AMBC. Although in this dissertation we present exclusively results from the individual interviews, we cross-validated our analysis by actively discussing similarities and differences between the elements emerging from the individual interviews and those emerging from the FGD. This process of constant comparison allowed checking that the opinions/comments expressed individually were consistent with those expressed in a group. All the statements reported in this dissertation were confirmed by the findings of the FGD.

We applied investigator triangulation as both Mamadou Sanon and the author was not only engaged in independent data collection, but also later analysed data independently. As mentioned above, Mamadou Sanon facilitated the FGD while the author personally conducted the individual interviews. Although sensitive to each other's comments and suggestions, the two investigators developed the data collection tools, i.e. the interview guides, independently. Given the grounded theory emphasis on open coding, the two researchers also coded the data separately, applying different coding schemes. In line with the principle of *in-vivo* coding in fact, they generated categories independently as they progressed through the reading of the data, only comparing and converging findings at a later stage.

The process of independent data analysis was completed between July and August 2004. The two researchers met at the end of the summer of 2004 and dedicated a three-week period to the exclusive triangulation of their findings, discussing their independent analyses and resolving apparent inconsistencies by referring back to the original data.

An additional source of triangulation emerged from the opportunity to discuss directly with the community the qualitative findings. Once the qualitative analysis was completed, the author returned to the community to discuss her interpretation of the findings directly with the people involved in the implementation of the AMBC. This open discussion with community members allowed for an additional check of the accuracy, fairness, and validity of the analysis developed, ensuring that data had been adequately interpreted and no wrong inferences had been made.

In line with our aim to generate a comprehensive understanding of decision to enrol in CHI, we applied the principle of triangulation also to the systematic comparison of the quantitative and qualitative findings. In order to increase the validity of our study in fact, we compared and contrasted quantitative and qualitative findings. This process of data triangulation is at the core of our interpretation and discussion of the findings, allowing us to understand quantitative data in the light of the qualitative findings and *vice versa*. Given the focus on different aspects of the research question, reconciling qualitative and quantitative findings was at times a challenging task, which required reflecting upon and resolving apparent inconsistencies, often by going back to the original data to conduct further analysis.

An important note ought to be made with regard to the timing of the different strands of analysis, quantitative and qualitative, included in our study. Both in the methods and the results chapter, we have decided to privilege clarity by presenting first the quantitative and then the qualitative components of our research. It is important to point out, however, that this order does not reflect the timing of our scientific inquiry. As mentioned earlier in this chapter, the qualitative research preceded and informed the quantitative one. In turn, however, the quantitative findings induced us to go back to the transcribed text of the interviews to conduct further research. Therefore, the process of discovery was iterative rather than linear. First, we applied theoretical knowledge to the construction of both the qualitative and quantitative research tools. Second, we applied and confronted this theoretical knowledge with the findings emerging from the in-depth interviews. Third, we used a combination of theoretical knowledge and qualitative findings to inform the construction of the regression model. Last, we turned back to the qualitative findings to investigate in greater detail elements which had emerged from the quantitative analysis.

Just to provide one among many possible examples, descriptive statistics as well as direct contact with the field team seemed to suggest that, contrary to what observed in other settings, in the case of the Nouna Health District, distance did not constitute a major obstacle to enrolment. Thus, we decided to include distance to the health facility in our regression model to measure, other factors held equal, and its influence on the decision to enrol. Afterwards, we returned to the in-depth interviews to explain the counterintuitive finding identifying a positive rather than a negative association between distance to the health facility and enrolment. Similarly, on a different occasion, we returned to the in-depth interviews to understand why the odds of enrolment did not differ significantly between the two middle-income groups. This accurate process of iterative analysis and constant triangulation allowed us to merge two separate strands of analysis, quantitative and qualitative, into one comprehensive study.

The process of triangulating quantitative and qualitative findings was led by the author, but saw the active collaboration of the entire research team, which was called to discuss the coherence as well as the relevance of the findings. Data triangulation took place only in the spring of 2005, after both the qualitative and the quantitative analyses were completed.

2.7 Ethical considerations

This doctoral dissertation was conducted within the framework of the wider research agenda of the collaborative research project SFB 544 on the control of tropical infectious diseases, founded by the German Research Society (Deutsche Forschunsgemeinschaft). The research protocol pertaining to the insurance component of the SFB 544 obtained clearance from both the Ethical Committee of the Medical Faculty of the University of Heidelberg, Germany, and the Comité Local Etique de Nouna, Burkina Faso.

As mentioned while describing the qualitative methodology, both the author herself and the complete research team systematically shared the results of their work with the population in the Nouna Health District. Given the extreme pragmatic orientation of the research we conducted, we recognized a responsibility towards the community where we worked and deemed it to be our duty to discuss results with them. Open and active discussion was meant to inform future policy-making, but also to re-establish a balance with the researched community, granting those who were studied a right to comment and criticise the conclusions that were drawn. In addition, meeting the community represented a unique opportunity to identify future areas of research by listening directly to people's concerns, offering for once a setting where the researched could pose, rather than answer, questions.

All information gathered either through means of the household survey or through means of the in-depth interviews was treated confidentially. At no point in the presentation of the findings or in their discussion, it is possible for someone external to the research team, to identify any of the individuals who participated in the study.

3. Results

3.1. The presentation of the results

Although the ultimate aim of this dissertation is to produce a holistic understanding of decision to enrol, we have decided, for reasons of clarity, to present quantitative and qualitative findings separately. We trust that our choice best allows the reader to appreciate the richness of the single methodological components as well as the completeness of the information gathered.

In line with the sequential order adopted in the methods chapter, we first describe the quantitative results and then the qualitative ones. At the end of the chapter, before proceeding to the discussion, we briefly pull together the quantitative and the qualitative findings.

3.2 Quantitative results

3.2.1 Sample characteristics

3.2.1.1 Comparing controls and the non-enrolled population in the study area

Table 3.1 provides basic socio-demographic information for the controls included in our sample and for the complete non-enrolled population resident in the 12 villages and 3 town sectors which were offered insurance in 2004. Although potentially interesting, we did not compare socio-economic status for the two groups, because we did not have such information for the entire population of the DSS, but only for the sub-sample included in the household survey, i.e. our controls. No remarkable differences in the distribution of the household head age, sex, and ethnicity, and household size were observed between the control group and the non-enrolled population. Therefore, we concluded that the controls selected for inclusion in our study were representative of the overall non-enrolled population in the study area and proceeded with the analysis.

Table 3.1: Socio-demographic characteristics of the control group and of the non-enrolled population in the study area

Socio-demographic characteristics	Controls in our study (n = 393)	Non-enrolled population (n = 2 947)[a]
Household head age (mean)	50	48
Percentage male-headed households	87	90
Household size (mean)	8	8
Household head ethnicity (percentage)		
Dafing	33	34
Samo	14	13
Bwaba	25	25
Mossi	17	17
Peulh	8	8
Other	3	3

[a] We could ascertain complete information for 2 947 out of 2 971 non-enrolled households residing in the 12 villages and 3 town sectors which were offered insurance in 2004.

3.2.1.2 Descriptive Statistics

Table 3.2 reports information on the distribution of the factors included in the analysis across cases, i.e. households enrolled in the AMBC, and controls, i.e. households not enrolled in the AMBC. Among the individual-level characteristics, i.e. those pertaining to the household head, no remarkable differences between cases and controls were observed with regard to age and sex. The result of the Student's t-test presented in Table 3.4, however, indicated that enrolled households were on average headed by younger people, although the difference was significant only at the 10% level. Compared to non-enrolled households, enrolled households were more likely to be headed by a person of Bwaba ethnicity, with a higher education, not employed as a farmer, and with a poorer perception of the adequacy of the care provided by traditional healers.

Table 3.2: Descriptive sample characteristics
Values indicate numbers (percentages)

Variables	In AMBC (n=137)	Not in AMBC (n=393)	Chi-square p-value
Household head characteristics			
Sex			
Female	13 (9.49)	51 (12.98)	
Male	124 (90.51)	342 (87.02)	0.281
Ethnicity			
All others	63 (45.99)	288 (73.28)	
Bwaba	74 (54.01)	105 (26.72)	0.001
Education			
No schooling	77 (56.20)	335 (85.24)	
Primary school	33 (24.09)	44 (11.20)	
Secondary school	27 (19.71)	14 (3.56)	0.001
Age in years			
20 to 40	47 (34.31)	115 (29.26)	
41 to 60	66 (48.18)	184 (46.82)	
61+	24 (17.52)	94 (23.92)	0.252
Occupation			
Farmer	92 (67.15)	297 (75.57)	
Other occupation	45 (32.85)	96 (24.43)	0.056
Rating of healer's care			
"Adequate"	14 (10.22)	196 (49.87)	
"Non-adequate"	123 (89.78)	197 (50.13)	0.001
Household characteristics			
Household expenditure			
1st quartile (poorest)	15 (10.95)	118 (30.03)	
2nd quartile	25 (18.25)	107 (27.23)	
3rd quartile	37 (27.01)	96 (24.43)	
4th quartile (wealthiest)	60 (43.80)	72 (18.32)	0.001
Child/adult ratio			
<= 1	86 (62.77)	289 (73.54)	
> 1	51 (37.23)	104 (26.46)	0.017

Table 3.2: Descriptive sample characteristics (continued)
Values indicate numbers (percentages)

Variables	In AMBC (n=137)	Not in AMBC (n=393)	Chi-square p-value
Chronic diseases			
None	48 (35.04)	135 (34.35)	
At least one	89 (64.96)	258 (65.65)	0.884
Use of curative care			
No contact	81 (59.12)	303 (77.10)	
At least one contact	56 (40.88)	90 (22.90)	0.001
Use of preventive care			
No contact	102 (74.45)	306 (77.86)	
At least one contact	35 (25.55)	87 (22.14)	0.414
Village characteristics			
Distance to health facility			
Near (<= 5 km)	90 (65.69)	291 (74.05)	
Far (> 5 km)	47 (34.31)	102 (25.95)	0.061
Referral facility			
First-line facility at Nouna Hospital	57 (41.61)	189 (48.09)	
Any CSPS	80 (58.39)	204 (51.91)	0.190
Socio-economic equality			
Low level of equality	54 (39.42)	190 (48.35)	
Middle level of equality	35 (25.55)	136 (34.61)	
High level of equality	48 (35.04)	67 (17.05)	0.001
Participation in other risk-sharing			
Low level of participation	50 (36.50)	138 (35.11)	
Middle level of participation	38 (27.74)	142 (36.13)	
High level of participation	49 (35.77)	113 (28.75)	0.150

Among the household level characteristics, no remarkable differences between cases and controls were observed with regard to health status, measured in terms of chronic diseases, and with regard to the previous use of preventive health services. Households enrolled in the AMBC, however, were more likely to have used curative services in the past 12 months and to have a higher proportion of children than adults. They were also more likely to be wealthier than non-enrolled households. Median six-month expenditure was 219,400 CFA and 82,500 CFA among enrolled and non-enrolled households respectively. The result of the Wilcoxon test presented in Table 3.3 also confirmed that six-month expenditure was significantly higher among enrolled households.

Table 3.3: Test for differences between cases and controls (continuous variables) [a]

Variables	Student's t-test				Wilcoxon test			
	Mean	**SE** [b]	**|t|**	**p-value**	**rank sum**	**expected**	**|z|**	**p-value**
Age								
In AMBC	47.8	1.050			-	-	-	-
not in AMBC	50.2	0.719	1.6980	0.090	-	-	-	-
Household expenditure								
In AMBC	-	-	-	-	47303.5	36373.5		
Not in AMBC	-	-	-	-	93411.5	104341.5	-7.081	0.001
Socio-economic equality								
In AMBC	-	-	-	-	41224	36373.5		
Not in AMBC	-	-	-	-	99491	104341.5	-3.164	0.002
Participation in risk-sharing								
In AMBC	-	-	-	-	38680	36373.5		
Not in AMBC	-	-	-	-	102035	104341.5	-1.504	0.132

[a] For all tests, the number of observations was 530: 137 cases (households enrolled in the AMBC) and 393 controls (households non-enrolled in the AMBC).
[b] SE = standard error.

Of the village level characteristics, significant differences between cases and controls were observed with regard to the distance to the facility and the level of socio-economic equality within a community. Enrolled households appeared to live further away from a facility (significant at the 10% level) and in communities with higher levels of socio-economic equality. No remarkable differences between enrolled and non-enrolled households were observed with regard to the referral facility or the percentage of adults in their community participating in another formal or semi-formal risk-sharing arrangement. The results of the Wilcoxon test presented in Table 3.3 confirmed that enrolled and non-enrolled households differed with regard to the level of socio-economic equality in their community, but not with regard to the percentage of adults participating in another risk-sharing arrangement.

For completeness of information, Table 3.4 reports the mean, the minimum, and the maximum value for each quantile/group with regard to the three continuous variables - household expenditure, socio-economic equality, and participation in another risk-sharing arrangement - were aggregated.

Table 3.4: Mean, minimum, and maximum values of quantiles/groups for selected variables

Variables	Mean	Min	Max
Household expenditure (in CFA)			
1st quartile	24 638	100	48 525
2nd quartile	73 677	49 800	103 600
3rd quartile	167 457	104 050	242 000
4th quartile	714 989	242 900	9 682 400
Socio-economic equality (percentage expenditure by poorest 50% of population)			
Low level of equality	11.97	6.67	13.4
Middle level of equality	16.37	13.43	17.91
High level of equality	25.04	19.31	30.54
Participation in other risk-sharing (percentage adults in other risk-sharing)			
Low level of participation	9.82	3.95	10.55
Middle level of participation	16.21	10.64	20
High level of participation	29.31	21	52.27

3.2.2 Statistical modelling

Table 3.5 reports the results of both the univariate analysis and the multivariate analysis, for each of the three models: the multilevel logistic regression model including only household head and household characteristics (model 1); the multilevel logistic regression model including household head, household, and village characteristics (model 2)[10]; and the conventional logistic regression model including household head, household, and village characteristics (model 3). Before proceeding to describe the effect on decision to enrol of the single variables included in the models, we wish to comment on the random component of our analysis and briefly compare the three models[11].

3.2.2.1 Multilevel vs. conventional modelling

Model 1 reports ρ *(rho)* to be 0.2084. Although ρ was found to be relatively small, the likelihood-ratio test indicated that this value was statistically significant, reflecting the existence of a between-village heterogeneity in enrolment. This is to say that, after accounting for the household head and household characteristics included in the model, a statistically significant portion of the variance could be attributed to the village level, i.e. to elements that may differ between villages, but that were not included in the analysis. In addition, the significance of the likelihood-ratio test indicated that in this instance, the application of multilevel modelling was to be preferred to that of conventional logistic regression, since there was significant heterogeneity in enrolment across villages which would have not been captured by conventional modelling techniques.

---

[10] As described in detail in the methods chapter, we tested the sensitivity of the quadrature estimator used by Stata 8.1 to compute multilevel random-effect logistic regression models. The results are provided in appendix E. The test showed that the coefficient estimates did not change in relation to the number of quadrature points applied to compute the model, thus confirming that the quadrature estimator was stable when applied to our dataset.

[11] Compared to conventional logistic regression, the Stata output for the random-effect logistic model also includes an estimation of the standard deviation σ_{u0} for the random effect u_{0v}. We omit, however, to report the value of σ_{u0} as its interpretation is only relevant in relation to the coefficient of the intercept. Given the case-control structure of our data, we focus exclusively on the presentation and interpretation of the odds ratio estimates, disregarding any discussion of the intercept. Therefore, we prefer to present and discuss exclusively the values of *rho*. This estimate in fact, provides, also in case-control studies, a powerful means of assessing heterogeneity across groups, in our specific case heterogeneity in enrolment across villages.

Table 3.5: Odds ratio estimates - univariate and multivariate analysis
OR = odds ratio; SE = standard error

Variables	**Univariate**		**Model 1**		**Model 2**		**Model 3**	
Fixed effects	**OR**	**SE**	**OR**	**SE**	**OR**	**SE**	**OR**	**SE**
Household head characteristics								
Sex								
Female	1.00		1.00		1.00		1.00	
Male	1.42	0.47	1.09	0.47	0.98	0.43	0.98	0.23
Ethnicity								
All others	1.00		1.00		1.00		1.00	
Bwaba	3.22[1]	0.66	3.15[3]	1.08	2.06[2]	0.65	2.06[2]	0.59
Education								
No schooling	1.00		1.00		1.00		1.00	
Primary school	3.26[1]	0.86	2.96[2]	1.09	3.86[1]	1.43	3.86[1]	1.29
Secondary school	8.39[1]	2.96	6.40[2]	3.80	7.45[1]	4.06	7.45[1]	3.96
Age in years								
20 to 40	1.00		1.00		1.00		1.00	
41 to 60	0.88	0.20	1.27	0.39	1.21	0.37	1.21	0.28
61+	0.62[3]	0.18	1.25	0.52	1.18	0.49	1.18	0.71
Occupation								
Farmer	1.00		1.00		1.00		1.00	
Other occupation	1.51[3]	0.33	0.82	0.28	0.87	0.30	0.87	0.27
Rating of healer's care								
"Adequate"	1.00		1.00		1.00		1.00	
"Non-adequate"	8.74[1]	2.62	12.37[1]	4.53	13.4[1]	4.79	13.4[1]	6.77
Household characteristics								
Household expenditure								
1st quartile (poorest)	1.00		1.00		1.00		1.00	
2nd quartile	1.84[3]	0.65	2.86[2]	1.27	3.44[2]	1.55	3.44[2]	1.7
3rd quartile	3.03[1]	1.02	3.07[2]	1.36	3.47[2]	1.56	3.47[2]	1.90
4th quartile (wealthiest)	6.56[1]	2.13	7.32[3]	3.36	7.67[1]	3.55	7.67[1]	3.50
Child/adult ratio								
<= 1	1.00		1.00		1.00		1.00	
> 1	1.65[2]	0.35	2.02[2]	0.61	1.76[3]	0.53	1.76[3]	0.50
Chronic diseases								
None	1.00		1.00		1.00		1.00	
At least one	0.97	0.20	1.06	0.30	1.03	0.29	1.03	0.20
Use of curative care								
No contact	1.00		1.00		1.00		1.00	
At least one contact	2.33[1]	0.49	1.28	0.39	1.28	0.37	1.28	0.30
Use of preventive care								
No contact	1.00		1.00		1.00		1.00	
At least one contact	1.21	0.28	1.31	0.49	1.38	0.47	1.38	0.30

Table 3.5: Odds ratio estimates - univariate and multivariate analysis (cont.)
OR = odds ratio; SE = standard error

Variables	Univariate		Model 1		Model 2		Model 3	
Fixed effects	**OR**	**SE**	**OR**	**SE**	**OR**	**SE**	**OR**	**SE**
Village characteristics								
Distance to health facility								
Near (<= 5 km)	1.00		-	-	1.00		1.00	
Far (> 5 km)	1.49[3]	0.32	-	-	4.51[1]	1.97	4.51[1]	1.83
Referral facility								
First-line facility at Nouna Hospital	1.00		-	-	1.00		1.00	
Any CSPS	1.30	0.26	-	-	0.38	0.23	0.38	0.20
Socio-economic equality								
Low level of equality	1.00		-	-	1.00		1.00	
Middle level of equality	0.91	0.22	-	-	1.25	0.47	1.25	0.36
High level of equality	2.52[1]	0.62	-	-	7.54[1]	3.37	7.54[1]	3.10
Participation in other risk-sharing								
Low level of participation	1.00		-	-	1.00			
Middle level of participation	0.74	0.18	-	-	0.81	0.35	0.81	0.26
High level of participation	1.20	0.28	-	-	1.55	0.81	1.55	0.74
Random effects								
rho - coefficient; SE	-		0.2084; 0.1064		<0.001; <0.001		-	
Model diagnostics								
Log-likelihood	-		-205.1783		-193.33686		-193.33685	
Wald chi2(df); p>chi2	-		98.54; <0.001		118.02; <0.001		-	
Likelihood-ratio test of *rho* - (Chibar2(01); p>=chibar2)	-		12.73; <0.001		<0.001; 1.000		-	
Chi square (df); p>chi2	-		-		-		219.09; <0.001	
Pseudo R-square	-		-		-		0.3617	
Hosmer-Lemeshow test – chi2(10); p>chi2	-		-		-		12.27; 0.268	
Observations	530		530		530		530	

[1] significant at the 1% level; [2] significant at the 5% level; [3] significant at the 10% level.

Once we added village-level characteristics to our model, as we did in model 2, the value of *rho* decreased to <0.001, indicating that there was no longer any village-level variance to be detected. This means that the village characteristics selected for inclusion in model 2 were sufficient to explain the village level variance previously observed in model 1. The result of the likelihood-ratio test of the *rho* confirmed that this value was no longer statistically significant and that the estimates produced by the random-effect logistic regression model were no longer statistically different from those produced by a conventional logistic regression model including the same set of variables. Therefore, once we included in the model this specific set of village-level characteristics, we no longer had any reason to prefer multilevel above conventional modelling.

The simple comparison of the results between model 2 and model 3 provided further evidence of the fact that estimates did not differ remarkably between the multilevel and the conventional model. The odd ratio estimates derived in the two models were exactly the same. One of the arguments in favour of multilevel modelling when compared to conventional modelling concerns the accurateness of the estimation of the standard errors. Multilevel modelling in fact, takes into account intra-cluster correlation, i.e. the fact that observations may differ across but not within groups, thus avoiding that non-significant relationships are incorrectly identified as significant. In the case presented in this dissertation, however, applying Huber-White robust variance correction to conventional logistic regression was sufficient to produce significance levels that matched exactly those of the multilevel model.

The standard errors did differ slightly between the two models, i.e. model 2 and model 3, but these differences were not sufficient to produce any changes in the significance level of the z-test for the variables included in the analysis. The significance of the z-test, measured at the 10%, 5%, and 1% level, was in fact identical in the two models.

Given that the point estimates and the significance levels for model 2 and model 3 were identical, we will no longer differentiate between the two when presenting the results concerning the effect of the single variables on decision to enrol. Hereafter, we will simply differentiate between estimates generated by the univariate analysis, by the model including exclusively household head and household characteristics, and by the model including household head, household, and community characteristics (in this last instance, we will refer to the standard error estimates from model 2). For reasons of clarity, although always referring to Table 3.5, we will present results by grouping them according to household head, household, and community characteristics.

3.2.2.2 Household head characteristics

As shown in Table 3.5, the univariate analysis revealed that enrolled households were more likely to be headed by people of Bwaba ethnicity, with a higher educational level, not employed as farmers, and rating the care provided by traditional healers as "non-adequate". The univariate analysis also suggested that the oldest household heads, those in the age group 61 and above, were the least likely to enrol. The odds ratio estimate of 1.42 suggesting that men might have been more likely than women to enrol their households was far from being statistically significant, thus indicating no effect of the sex of the household head on the decision to enrol.

The results of the multivariate analysis confirmed the impact on decision to enrol of Bwaba ethnicity, educational attainment, and poor perceptions of the adequacy of the care delivered by traditional healers. The direction of the association remained stable whether taking into account the model including only household head and household characteristics (model 1) or the model including also community characteristics (model 2). The strength of the association between Bwaba ethnicity and enrolment status progressively decreased as more variables were added to the model, declining from the original univariate point estimate of 3.22 to the point estimate of 2.06 in the final model including community characteristics. The opposite was true for the variable measuring the perceived adequacy of the care provided by traditional healers. In this case, the odds ratio estimates progressively increased as we added variables to the regression model. In the final model (model 2), we noted a particularly strong association between enrolment status and rating the care provided by traditional healers as "non-adequate" (OR = 13.4; SE = 4.79). Controlling for other household head, household, and community variables altered the univariate estimates regarding education in a mixed manner. The odds ratio estimate measuring the association between enrolment status and having attended primary school increased from an initial 3.26 (univariate) to a final 3.86 (model 2), while the estimate concerning secondary school decreased from 8.39 (univariate) to 7.45 (model 2).

Multivariate analysis also confirmed the observation that the sex of the household head did not influence decision to enrol. It disproved instead, the association observed in the univariate analysis between enrolment status and the age and the occupation of the household head. In both instance, the direction of the estimated association was reversed and far from being statistically significant. This shift in direction and loss of significance occurred as soon as we controlled for other household head and household characteristics, and remained true also once we included community characteristics in our model.

3.2.2.3 Household characteristics

As shown in Table 3.5, the univariate analysis suggested that enrolled households were more likely to be wealthier, to have a higher proportion of children, and to have used curative services in the 12 months preceding the interview. The univariate analysis further suggested that there was no association between enrolment and health status, measured as the presence of any chronic diseases in the household. Likewise, the univariate analysis reported a very small, and not statistically significant, effect of the use of preventive health care services on the decision to enrol.

The multivariate analysis confirmed the existence of a strong positive association between enrolment and socio-economic status. The strength of the association between enrolment and socio-economic status increased as we included more variables in the model. The final regression model indicated that the effect of socio-economic status on the decision to enrol was consistent across quantiles: the higher the socio-economic status, the higher the odds of being enrolled. The odds of being enrolled, however, did not differ dramatically between the second and third socio-economic quartiles (OR = 3.44 and OR = 3.47 respectively), while they were obviously much higher for the wealthiest socio-economic quartile (OR = 7.67). Likewise, the multivariate analysis also confirmed that enrolled households were more likely to have a higher proportion of children. Before the inclusion of community characteristics in the model, the odds ratio estimates capturing the effect of the child/adult ratio increased compared to the univariate estimates. In the final model, however, they returned closer to their initial value (OR = 1.76; SE = 0.53) and were significant only at the 10% level.

The multivariate analysis disproved the existence of a positive association between enrolment status and the previous use of curative services. In the final model, the odds ratio estimate declined from 2.33 (univariate) to 1.28 (model 2) and was no longer statistically significant. Multivariate analysis also confirmed that health status and the previous use of preventive care services were not associated with enrolment. The lack of association between enrolment and both health status and the previous use of curative services suggested that there was no adverse selection into the scheme.

3.2.2.4 Village characteristics

Table 3.5 shows that out of the four village characteristics included in our model, only two, distance to the referral facility and socio-economic equality, were associated with the decision to enrol in the AMBC. Living further away from a facility, 5 km and beyond, and living in a community with higher levels of socio-economic equality were both positively associated with the decision to enrol. In both instances, the strength of the association increased substantially as we moved from the univariate to the multivariate analysis. In the case of distance, the significance of the association also increased remarkably when comparing univariate with multivariate estimates. To be noted how the association between enrolment status and the level of socio-economic equality in a community was only particularly strong and significant for the group living in communities with the most equality (OR = 7.54; SE = 3.37). No remarkable differences were observed between communities with low and middle levels of socio-economic equality.

The multivariate analysis confirmed that the percentage of adults within a community already engaged in another risk-sharing arrangement and the referral facility to which communities were assigned were not associated with enrolment status.

3.3 Qualitative results

3.3.1 Basic information on the interviews and on the interviewees

Most of the interviews, 24, were carried out in Dioula, the local *lingua franca*; 6 interviews were carried out in Bwamu, and 2 interviews were carried out directly in French. Interviews lasted between 30 min and 1 h 30 min.

Table 3.6 illustrates the basic socio-demographic characteristics of the interviewees. The table reports information set *a priori* as sampling criteria and additional socio-demographic information collected at the time of the interview. We interviewed people with very diverse experiences, reaching individuals with different ethnicities, occupations, household sizes, and educational levels. Without having planned it in advance, we conducted 4 out of 32 interviews with individuals who had been elected as local AMBC representatives and who were able to share with us particular insights on the community response to the implementation to the scheme. Appendix F provides complete socio-demographic information for all interviewees[12].

---

[12] We trust that appendix F does not break our obligation to treat all material confidentially. In order to protect individual identity in fact, we omit to indicate the name and the village of origin of the interviewees. Providing only generic socio-demographic information makes it impossible for anyone not directly involved in the data collection process to identify the single respondents.

Table 3.6: Interviewees' socio-demographic characteristics

Socio-demographic characteristic	n = *32*
Number of females	8
Enrolled in AMBC	16
Above-median income	16
Living within 5 km from the health facility	16
Median age	42 (23-72)
Residency:	
Urban	10
Rural	22
Ethnicity:	
Dafing	14
Bwaba	8
Mossi	2
Peulh	2
Samo	6
Religion:	
Catholic	10
Muslim	20
Animist	2
Marital status:	
Monogamous	15
Polygamous	10
Not in marriage [a]	7
Educational level:	
No schooling	22
Primary school	7
Secondary school	3
Occupation [b]:	
Farmer/livestock keeper	24
Small scale revenue-generating activity	10
Civil servant	3
Household size:	
Up to 10 people	22
Between 11 and 15 people	7
16 people or more	3
Resident in village with:	
Less than 4% of target population enrolled	14
Between 4% and 10% of target population enrolled	10
More than 10% of target population enrolled	8

[a] Not in marriage refers to being widowed or never having been married

[b] Numbers concerning occupation sum up to more than 32 because some farmers also run small scale revenue-generating activities.

3.3.2 General remarks

Before presenting the findings, we wish to note that women were more reluctant than men to express their opinions freely. In spite of their initial difficulty to speak unreservedly, we observed no remarkable differences between women and men with regard to the discussion of the factors influencing the decision to enrol in the AMBC. Similarly, in general, we observed no striking differences across different ethnic and/or age groups. In the description of the findings, we do report explicitly on any difference noted across people with different occupations as well as different educational and/or socio-economic statuses. It needs to be pointed out, however, that we do so exclusively with the aim of highlighting how perceptions of the schemes and reasons motivating or discouraging enrolment may differ across people with different experiences. We never report differences with the aim of measuring quantitatively the impact of any socio-demographic characteristic (socio-economic status, occupation, and education) on the decision to enrol.

We also wish to report on how we checked the adequacy of our sampling strategy. As described in the previous chapter in fact, we chose to interview exclusively household heads as we assumed them to be the key decision-makers with regard to the choice of whether to enrol or not to enrol in the AMBC. During the interview, we asked respondents to describe how the household had reached the decision to enrol or not to enrol. Specifically, probing respondents with several questions, we explored the extent to which household heads had discussed the decision with other adult family members. Other than the three civil servants interviewed in Nouna, none of the respondents reported having discussed the decision either with their spouse(s) or with any other adult family member. Respondents repeatedly reinforced how the responsibility over the allocation of household resources rests on the household head. Some respondents were even taken aback by our questions regarding the decision-making process and, especially in the rural areas, forcefully stressed the strict division of roles within the family.

> *It is up to the owner of the court* (the household head) *to take charge of his family. Once you have taken a woman as a spouse, then you are responsible for her and all the children. You cannot ask her to make decisions in your place.* (Interview 10)

> *Since I am the head of this kitchen (household), when an expense comes, it is me who has to deal with it. It was in my own thoughts that this is a good thing, so I went to enrol my entire family. The other people in my family do not even know about it yet ... because when they are sick, it is me who needs to pay for the care.* (Interview 20)

3.3.3 Findings

The presentation of the qualitative findings is organized in six sections which represent a further clustering of the elements presented in Figure 2.3 into major thematic areas. These six sections do not simply reflect the broad grouping which we presented as the core of our theoretical framework (Figure 2.1). Although such grouping was essential for the construction of the data collection tools as well as for the analysis, we judged it not to be adequate to constitute the basic structure for the presentation of the findings. We preferred instead, to adopt a structure which, drawing on the elements described in Figure 2.3, also explicitly highlights the interactions that exist between different sets of characteristics.

The first section explores knowledge and understanding of the insurance concept and of the specific elements of the AMBC. The second section looks at issues of affordability. The third section reports on how perceptions surrounding health care provider network have influenced decision to enrol. The fourth section investigates previous illness experience and health care seeking behaviour in relation to enrolment. The fifth section looks at the influence of cultural beliefs and practices, and finally the sixth section examines questions of scepticism and trust. The presentation of findings concerning people's preferences for the specific elements of the scheme is included within these six sections. Findings are elucidated using verbatim quotations from the interviews, translated into English by the author. For each quotation, we indicate the respondent's socio-demographic characteristics which were used as the sampling criteria. Table 3.7 illustrates the abbreviations used.

Table 3.7: Abbreviations for the interviewees' characteristics

Socio-demographic characteristic	Abbreviation
Enrolled	E
Non-enrolled	NE
Within 5 km from health facility	5-
Further than 5 km from health facility	>5
Income above median (rich)	R
Income below median (poor)	P
Male	M
Female	F

3.3.3.1 Knowledge and understanding

The vast majority of respondents, 29 out of 32, had heard of the AMBC. Whether enrolled or not enrolled, respondents mentioned the village/town sector meeting organized by the AMBC management team as their main source of information on the scheme. Respondents were generally very pleased with the way the discussion was conducted during these sessions. Several interviewees appreciated the fact that people from the town of Nouna had moved to the rural areas to share information with them.

> *Their way of explaining was really good. The child* (the young man) *who came to our village was very understanding. He explained to us what this was all about. He came here three times to explain this, then the fourth time, people took their money and joined the scheme.*
> (Interview 2 - E, >5, R, M)

> *They have come all the way here to talk with us. This is a good thing.*
> (Interview 4 - NE, <5, R, M)

Nine people mentioned having heard of the AMBC on the radio, but they referred to this broadcasting only as a complementary source of information.

> *We heard this woman who had come to our village talk on the radio from Dedougou. We all sat to listen again and to understand well what she was saying.* (Interview 10 - E, >5, R, M)

We found three people who had never heard of the AMBC, two women living in the rural areas and one wealthy man living in the town of Nouna. The sensitization campaign took place during the dry season, a time of the year when people, not working in the fields, travel to visit family and friends in other localities, possibly outside the DSS area. All three people claimed having been away from home at the time of the communication and sensitization campaign. In addition, the two women attributed to their status of *griottes*[13], the fact that they had not being informed of the new initiative following their return.

---

[13] A particular feature of Burkinabè society is the existence of two castes, i.e. groups of people who have traditionally been in charge of specific functions within the community. The *forgéron* or *numu* are the traditional smiths, while the *griots* or *jeli* are the traditional musicians. In spite of increasing urbanisation and modernisation, both the *forgéron* and the *griots* are still identified as separate groups among many communities. People generally recognise and respect the particular role of the *forgérons* and the *griots*, but still treat them with a certain distance. Marriage between a *griot* or a *forgéron* and someone outside the caste, for example, is rare and still looked upon by the rest of society.

> *I am a griotte. When there is a meeting of men, women cannot attend. But even when it is a meeting for women also, I am often not informed unless I hear about it by chance and then go there out of my own will. But nobody tells me. They are all informed other than me. This is why I do not know about this insurance you are talking about.* (Interview 6 - NE, <5, P, F)

The communication and sensitization campaign rested on the assumption that the local AMBC representatives and the three *animateurs villageois* employed for the campaign by the Steering Committee would follow up the work initiated by the AMBC Management Unit during the village gatherings. Their task was to promote knowledge and understanding of the new initiative through informal discussion at the community level. We found, however, that in hardly any village, the local AMBC representatives and the *animateurs villageois* had really complied with their task. Out of 32 respondents, 6 reported, only once probed, having discussed the AMBC with either the local representatives or the *animateurs villageois*. Only in the village of Boron, all the four people we interviewed reported having been encouraged to enrol directly by the President of the local AMBC committee.

> *The people who are at the front of this initiative* (the local AMBC representatives) *have organized this meeting with the people from Nouna. They have told us it was good to join. But after that meeting, we did not talk to them again.* (Interview 17 - NE, <5, R, M)

> *The three people who have been elected in our village* (Boron) *have travelled to Nouna to learn more about the insurance. When they came back, they informed all of us on what they had learned ... the délégué also intervened in the discussion and told people that he thought this is a good thing and that we should all try to join.* (Interview 31 - E, >5, P, M)

Although most people had heard of the AMBC, knowledge of the specific scheme elements was overall very poor. When probed to describe the main features of the scheme, only seven enrolees and three non-enrolees could accurately do so, the only exceptions being the level of the premium, the membership fee, and the enrolment unit, elements recalled correctly by all interviewees aware of the AMBC.

Knowledge of the benefit package was imprecise and incomplete both among enrolled and non-enrolled respondents. Most people defined the AMBC benefit package in terms of the "*prise en charge de la maladie*", literally the "taking charge of illness". Respondents did not conceptualise the benefit package in terms of a specific set of services provided free of charge at point of delivery, but rather in terms of complete free provision of care in case of illness or in terms of the inclusion and exclusion of diseases.

They have said that if you fall sick, they will take charge of caring for you. If you fall sick or if you are injured and you are in the insurance, you go to the facility, you show your card, and they will take charge of your illness thanks to the insurance. But if you are not in the insurance, they cannot take charge of your illness. (Interview 10 - E, >5, R, M)

I cannot remember them anymore, but I know some diseases are included and some are excluded. (Interview 26 - E, <5, R, F)

There are some diseases that they treat and some diseases that they do not treat. (Interview 18 - E, <5, R, M)

In spite of their poor accurate knowledge, most respondents claimed to appreciate the benefit package, recognising the impossibility to include coverage of all services, or all diseases, given the limited premium. Although none of the non-enrolees attributed his/her choice not to enrol to the benefit package, the comments expressed by a few people show how the erroneous belief regarding the exclusion of some diseases may in some instances have discouraged enrolment.

Some diseases are included and some are excluded. They have excluded some diseases because the money would not be enough to pay for them. I would like it if one day, they could cover all diseases, but today it is good as it is, so that the insurance can have money till the end of the year. (Interview 23 - E, <5, P, M)

Even if the insurance can only take charge of some diseases, this is already much better than no insurance at all. (Interview 28 - E, <5, R, M)

The insurance is not really taking charge of illness. You cannot claim that you are taking charge of illness unless you include all diseases ... a disease is a disease, can you really know in advance what disease will get you? (Interview 18 - E, <5, R, M)

In particular, it is possible that the erroneous belief that HIV positive people would be excluded from the scheme, and not simply treatment for HIV as it is in reality, discouraged some people from enrolling. No interviewee drew a link between the exclusion of HIV cases and his/her decision not to enrol. Several respondents, however, commented on the exclusion of HIV positive individuals from the scheme and expressed the belief that in order to ensure compliance, the insurance may in the future impose HIV testing before granting enrolment. If reported during the interviews, this is likely to have been a topic of discussion among the community, indicating a certain fear of compulsory testing which probably discouraged some households from enrolling.

> *The insurance people have said that they cannot take charge of AIDS, of people who have AIDS. We think that maybe they will test all the people ... maybe when you arrive at the facility and you cough, they will tell you that before taking charge of your illness, you have to do the test ...*
> *(Interview 28 - E, <5, R, M)*

Although they could not recall the entire benefit package with precision, respondents were often able to recall the elements which had caught their attention the most. Appreciation was shown in particular for the coverage of all essential drugs and of emergency transport.

> *If a disease falls on your household, they will treat you for free. They will give you medications for free.* (Interview 14 - NE, >5, P, M)

> *We can walk or take a bike to reach Dara. But if our disease cannot be treated in Dara, they will look for an ambulance and take us to Nouna.* (Interview 29 - E, >5, R, F)

In spite of a generalised inability to recall the specific elements of the benefit package, other than one enrolee convinced that the AMBC also offers coverage of services outside the Nouna Health District, all other interviewees recognised that the scheme activity is limited to the District health service network. Likewise, no interviewee expected the AMBC to reimburse the cost of medications purchased on the market and/or at private pharmacies nor the cost of treatment provided by traditional healers. While almost all non-enrolees could not recall the modalities of access to care, 14 out of 16 enrolees could correctly do so and were aware that they ought to seek care first at the local CSPS and then, only upon referral, at the Nouna Hospital. They were also aware that no co-payment fees apply to the services included in the benefit package.

> *Once you are in the insurance, you first go to the CSPS in the village. If you see that you do not get better, you ask for the authorisation to go to the Hospital in Nouna.* (Interview 5 - E, <5, P, F)

> *You do not have to pay anything when you are sick. You show your card to the nurses in Dara and the insurance will take care of reimbursing the cost of the treatment.* (Interview 20 - E, <5, R, M)

Respondents' knowledge of the specific elements of the AMBC managerial structure was also very poor. With very few exceptions, mainly the four people who were directly involved in the scheme management, interviewees could not accurately describe the different levels of management nor locate the specific responsibilities assigned to each level. Although a clear indication of weak community ownership, respondents themselves did not perceive their poor knowledge as a limitation to enrolment. When probed on the matter, respondents expressed their opinion regarding the management structure confidently, focusing on the elements which they knew best.

The two elements that were clear to most interviewees, irrespective of enrolment and socio-economic status, were the existence of AMBC representatives in each village/town sector and the fact that overall supervision of insurance activities, including the management of funds, rests in Nouna. Although they could not identify the specific functions of the local AMBC representatives, respondents appreciated that the scheme management relies on members of their own community. Setting a management committee in each village was perceived as a guarantee for the well-functioning of the scheme and was judged to be socially and culturally appropriate given the overall hierarchical structure of local communities and the custom to organise any activity around a leader.

> *In each village, they have chosen some people as leaders so that the work of the insurance proceeds well. No activity can be good if there is no chief.* (Interview 8 - E, >5, P, M)

> *The work of the local leaders? Their work is to be serious and to look that things proceed well with this new activity.* (Interview 5 - E, <5, P, F)

> *They have taken people in all villages ... some people in each village ... to be the people at the front* (the leaders) *of the insurance.* (Interview 14 - NE, >5, P, M)

Only the four interviewees directly involved in the scheme management and two well-educated enrolees in Nouna could recall that the AMBC funds are kept in a bank and that the Steering Committee and the AMBC management unit are directly liable to the community in case of fraud. All other respondents simply recalled that the money is kept somewhere in Nouna. No objection was raised either by enrolled or non-enrolled individuals against this decision. People felt rather reassured to know that money is not kept nor managed at the level of each village or town sector. Respondents residing in the rural areas especially appreciated the decision to manage all funds in the District capital because they did not trust members of their own community to carry out the work adequately.

> *We have joined the insurance because we know that the money is in a safe place where it is good ... but I do not know exactly where this is.* (Interview 20 - E, <5, R, M)

> *... in our village? I do not think it would be a good idea to keep the money in our village. Here? In the hands of farmers? Better give it to those who know how to care for it.* (Interview 11 - NE, >5, R, M)

> *This thing should not be changed. Since the leaders are in Nouna, the money should also be in Nouna. Since it is the money that will do all the work, then it is good that the money is at their side. So, if they need to spend something, they can just take the money and pay in the name of all the people. It would never be good to keep the money in a small village.* (Interview 12 - E, >5, R, M)

In spite of the poor knowledge of the specific scheme elements, respondents, irrespective of enrolment and socio-economic status, showed appreciation for the new initiative. Both enrolees and non-enrolees conceptualised the benefit of the AMBC in terms of the unrestricted access to care it grants people throughout the year. All respondents recognised that the cost of care constitutes an important obstacle to access and that seasonal cash fluctuations render seeking treatment particularly difficult during certain times of the year. Therefore, they clearly appreciated the AMBC as an attempt to facilitate access to care, by removing the barrier of payment at point of delivery, while at the same time offering protection of their meagre assets. Respondents repeatedly affirmed that the AMBC can reduce the *wariko*, i.e. the burden, on the household head by taking charge of the payment for health care.

> *At times, the disease arrives and you have nothing in your hands ... you look for credit, but you cannot get it. If you are in the insurance, you show your card, and the doctor will treat you. This is the advantage of the insurance.* (Interview 7 - NE, >5, R, M)

> *If a disease gets you and you have no money, you are forced to sell your animals, to look for credit ... some people have to sell their bikes to pay for drugs.* (Interview 12 - E, >5, R, M)

> *The benefit of the insurance is first of all for the household head, then for his woman, then for the household as a whole ... the insurance helps reduce the wariko* (the burden) *for the household head, so he finds peace and when he is in peace, the wife is also in peace and the whole family is in peace.* (Interview 16 - E, >5, P, M)

When asked to describe what the AMBC is about, all interviewees aware of the existence of the scheme repeatedly used the word "*aide*", i.e. aid, and the verb "*aider*", i.e. to help. Respondents, irrespective of their enrolment and socio-economic status, recognised the AMBC as an external form of aid rather than as a self-help organisation endogenous to the community. This notion of aid was directly linked to a discourse attributing to an external agent, either the government of Burkina Faso, the CRSN, or an unidentified European person, the initiative for the foundation of the scheme.

The insurance is an aid ... an aid that comes from our Country to make the life of the people easier. (Interview 19 - NE, <5, R, M)

The insurance is an aid to make it easier for us to get treatment when we are sick. I think it comes from the Prapass (old name of the CRSN). (Interview 24 - NE, <5, P, M)

The insurance has come to be an aid for the farmers.
(Interview 10 - E, >5, R, M)

The insurance is an aid for the poor people ... it comes from the Toubabou (the white people). (Interview 16 - E, >5, P, M)

Although both enrolled and non-enrolled respondents identified in the AMBC a form of aid, a deeper investigation showed very different conceptualisations of the basic principles of insurance, i.e. pooling and risk-sharing. Both enrolees and non-enrolees referred to the fact that, once insured, "*on va te soigner cadeau*", i.e. "you get treated for free".

They say you pay something today and they will treat you as a gift (for free) *when you are sick.* (Interview 7 - NE, >5, R, M)

We have found the courage to join because we know that when a child is sick, they will treat him for free at the hospital. (Interview 29 - E, >5, R, F)

Unlike non-enrolees, however, enrolees also clearly acknowledged that receiving care free of charge is possible only because of the pooling and risk-sharing the insurance entails. Although often referring to the concept of being treated for free and to the original initiative of an external agent, enrolees mentioned the community as the ultimate owner of the scheme much more often than non-enrolees did. Although this terminology was not adopted during the communication and sensitisation campaign, enrolees often referred to the AMBC as a *groupement* or *tontine*, founded on the same principle of risk-sharing as similar formal and semi-formal arrangements in the region, but intervening in a different field.

These people from Nouna came and talked about the good of the insurance ... they counselled our village on the insurance ...but the insurance does not belong to them. The insurance, how can I say it, does not belong to one person. It is the people grouped together that make up the insurance, so the insurance belongs to all the people. (Interview 16 - E, >5, P, M)

You know, the insurance is like a groupement. Even if you in your corner do not fall sick, the other people may fall sick. So the money everyone has paid is taken to care for the sick.(Interview 10 - E, >5, R, M)

The insurance is about people helping people. (Interview 32 - E, >5, P, F)

You cannot get the money of the premium back even if you do not fall sick, because it is this money you have paid that is put together to cure the others. (Interview 26 - E, <5, R, F)

Enrolled and non-enrolled respondents also differed in their conceptualisation of the benefit of participation, measured in terms of return to investment. Considering the possibility of not falling sick for one or more years, non-enrolled respondents tended to define the payment of a premium as somewhat of a waste of resources.

You may have to pay 10 000 CFA for your family for one year. And then, if you do not fall sick, you still cannot recuperate this 10 000 CFA you have spent ... and next year you still have to pay again.
(Interview 4 - NE, <5, R, M)

Enrolled individuals instead, stressed the unpredictability of disease and the fact that in case of illness, the cost of care may easily be higher than the total premium paid to the insurance. Likewise, they expressed no concern regarding the fact that they may not fall sick for one or more years. In some instances, they even added that payment of the premium may in fact act as a way of keeping God's blessing, protecting them from falling sick.

In my family, if you count all together, we have paid 9 000 CFA. Now, even if just one of us falls severely sick and the care costs 10 000 CFA and the insurance pays, then the other people will look at us and understand the good of the insurance. (Interview 18 - E, <5, R, M)

You should not ask for your money back from the insurance because it is God who has helped you not to fall sick ... it is as if the money you have paid has protected you from all diseases. (Interview 31 - E, >5, P, M)

3.3.3.2 Affordability

All interviewees mentioned lack of financial means as a concrete barrier to enrolment. Among non-enrolled individuals, regardless of the socio-economic status of the household, lack of means was identified, often even before a probing question, as the primary reason for not having joined the scheme.

I wanted to enrol, but I did not find the means. Maybe next year ...
(Interview 24 - NE, <5, P, M)

Why have I not joined the scheme? It is because of a problem of money. The times are hard and we do not have enough money.
(Interview 17 - NE, <5, R, M)

Enrolled individuals, however, frequently questioned the use of this explanation to justify the non-enrolment of other households in their community. They made a distinction between people who truly lack the means to pay the premium and people who hide behind this justification not to adduce the real reasons for not enrolling.

... many people see that the price they would have to pay to enrol is too much for their means. They simply do not have the money. But others who do have the money are afraid of spending it. They just do not like the insurance and this is why they have stayed at the side without enrolling.
(Interview 2 - E, >5, R, M)

Many people cannot enrol because they are poor, but for many people who have the means, it is a problem of comprehension. They say they have no money, but this is not the truth. (Interview 3 - E, <5, P, M)

Asking interviewees to comment on the premium level, the enrolment unit, the modalities of payment, and the timing of the enrolment campaign allowed us to explore further limitations to a household's ability to pay, decomposing and better understanding the concept of affordability.

Other than five individuals who rated the premium to be too high, all interviewees agreed that given the benefits to which AMBC members are entitled, the premium is fair. Similarly, not one single interviewee raised any objection against the payment of the membership fee. People in the region are in fact accustomed to pay an *una tantum* membership fee upon joining any associative organisation.

1 500 CFA, if you look at it as the price for the single person, you understand it is affordable ... you may fall sick and easily spend more than 1 500 CFA. (Interview 18 - E, <5, R, M)

I think 500 CFA to care for a child is really nothing ... you know how often children can fall sick? And what could you do with only 500 CFA?
(Interview 29 - E, >5, R, F)

To write my name in the insurance, I paid 200 CFA. That's all.
(Interview 12 - E, >5, R, M)

Respondents, irrespective of socio-economic status, appreciated the fact that the AMBC differentiates between the adult and the child premium. Allowing parents to comply with their responsibility to cover the cost of their children's premium by lowering its level, was judged to be socially and culturally appropriate, given the local value system of reciprocal obligations binding people across generations.

> *It is a good thing to have a lower premium for the children. Since they cannot work, it is their parents who help them, who take care of them. It is for this reason that the insurance has a lower premium for the children, so that in the future, when they are older, children will help their parents.* (Interview 8 - E, >5, P, M)

In spite of the overall appreciation for the premium level, almost all respondents unanimously recognised that the current enrolment unit poses an obstacle to enrolment, especially for large households. Whether enrolled or non-enrolled in the scheme, respondents amply criticised the definition of household currently applied by the scheme. As described in the introductory chapter of this dissertation, the AMBC relies on the DSS classification, which defines a household as a group of people living together in a house or compound, sharing resources, and constituting a social group with which the individual identifies himself/herself. Respondents recognised that while socially valid overall, this definition of household does not adequately reflect all decision-making processes in their everyday life. They affirmed that several adults, usually siblings, often co-habit with their wives and children within the same household, but can decide independently over the allocation of some economic resources available specifically to themselves and their direct dependents. Respondents asked that the AMBC modifies the definition of household guiding its enrolment policy to allow smaller family units to join the scheme. Interestingly, this proposition was put forward equally frequently by members of large households, who felt directly affected and limited by the current definition of household, and by members of small households, who recognised household size as a possible obstacle to enrolment, even if not directly relevant to themselves.

> *It is necessary to divide households, to allow a man to join with his wife and his children, so that those who have understood the good of the insurance and have the will to do so, may enter ... if you do it like this, many people will enter.* (Interview 8 - E, >5, P, M)

Although actively proposing a modification in the definition of household guiding enrolment, 26 out of 32 respondents openly acknowledged the value of group enrolment and clearly recognised the possible limitations of a system which allows individual enrolment. They conceptualised these limitations not in terms of a possible adverse selection effect, but rather in relation to the equity impact and the completeness of financial protection that only household enrolment can secure.

> *I think the enrolment of the whole family is a good thing, otherwise there would be people preferring some children and some wives over all the others and this would create segregation within the family.* (Interview 23 - E, <5, P, M)

> *If you only register yourself and leave the rest of your family behind, if a disease catches someone else in your family, then it is still your problem to pay for the care.* (Interview 17 - NE, <5, R, M)

> *A family is together day and night ... if you only register one person, who tells you this is the person who will fall sick? Better register the whole family.* (Interview 28 - E, <5, R, M)

Respondents also unanimously recognised in current payment modalities and in the timing of the first enrolment campaign two important barriers to enrolment. Whether enrolled or non-enrolled, respondents identified as a problem, if not for themselves definitely for others in their community, the fact that the premium ought to be paid all at once. This was especially true for large households and for civil servants. While wealthier than many other people in the society, both large households and civil servants faced the difficulty of mobilising large amounts of cash all at once, and therefore asked that provisions be made to allow households to dilute payment over a longer period of time. Although not facing the problem themselves, small households were aware of the needs of others in their community and often put forward the same suggestion. Respondents also reported that lack of access to credit constitutes a further barrier to enrolment.

> *In our case, we did all we could to pay the premium. We looked for the money and we managed to find it. But for large families, this is very hard. It would be better if they could pay little by little. So, when they have some money, they turn that in. Then, when they find the rest, they pay again.* (Interview 23 - E, <5, P, M)

> *... if the AMBC people had said that I could divide the whole amount in parts, I would have managed to enrol.* (Interview 1 - NE, >5, R, M)

> *There was a colleague of mine* (a civil servant employed at city hall) *who really wanted to join. But they are twelve people. He did all he could to gather the money during the three months of the enrolment campaign, but he did not manage. When they told him that the campaign was closing, he felt very discouraged.* (Interview 26 - E, <5, R, F)

> *You will not manage to get a credit. Nobody will lend you money if you say that it is for joining the insurance. If you are really sick, people may pity you and some may lend you money. But not for the insurance ... it is impossible to get money to enter the insurance.*
> (Interview 30 - NE, >5, P, M)

Since most households in the region rely on agriculture, respondents asked that the timing of the enrolment campaign be anticipated to better match seasonal revenue fluctuations. Specifically, they asked that the campaign starts in December, right after closure of the harvest season. A few interviewees, recognising how different economic activities may produce income at different times of the year, suggested opening enrolment throughout the year.

> *Out here in the countryside, the availability of money poses a problem ... we, the farmers, have money after the harvest, but by the time the rainy season arrives, we have nothing left in our hand and out here you cannot find where to borrow money.* (Interview 11 - NE, >5, R, M)

> *You need to give everyone a moment to enrol ... the farmer has the money in December ... and in this moment you allow him to enter. But the one who does not have the means at this time, he wants to enter as well, and a moment will arrive when he can have his money, and he will enrol his family.* (Interview 18 - E, <5, R, M)

> *You need to proceed softly ... well, the ideal period is after the harvest season ... for some people, the time of the sale of sesame, for others, the time of the sale of cotton.* (Interview 17 - NE, <5, R, M)

3.3.3.3 Health care provider network

As described in detail in the introductory chapter, the AMBC contracts services exclusively with the district hospital and with the six CSPS located within the DSS area. During the interview, we explored the extent to which different characteristics of this health care provider network may have affected the decision to enrol. Specifically, we looked at how distance to the health facility, perceptions of the quality of care, and the imposition of a strict gate-keeping system might have conditioned the decision to enrol.

None of the interviewees mentioned upfront distance to the health facility as a factor hampering enrolment. Out of 18 individuals interviewed in villages with no CSPS, only 5 individuals recognized, once probed, distance as a direct obstacle to enrolment.

> *... if there was a doctor in our village, more people would enrol ... to have a doctor right at your ankle* (side) *would encourage many to enter.* (Interview 7 - NE, >5, R, M)

The other 13 interviewees recognised distance as a barrier to access to care, but did not link it directly to the decision not to enrol in the scheme. Enrolees unanimously recognised the absence of a CSPS in their own village as an obstacle to enrolment only insofar as it limited the visibility of the benefits of the scheme.

> *Of course it would be nice to have a CSPS here ... but look at me, I have joined this scheme even if I have to travel to Dara ... if the people of this village really want their own CSPS, they need to work for it little by little, but this has nothing to do with the insurance.* (Interview 10 - E, >5, R, M)

> *If the doctor was in our village, our hearts would be lighter ... still some people would not enrol. The problem is money, not distance.* (Interview 2 - E, >5, R, M)

> *If there was a hospital here, those waiting to be treated would see that the insured people are treated fast ... people would be envious, would think that the same could be true for them if they joined the scheme ... everyone would enrol.* (Interview 8 - E, >5, P, M)

Given the additional burden imposed by travelling and given that none of the CSPS suffers from frequent drug shortages, respondents found no reason to object to the gate-keeping system. Seeking care at the district hospital only in case of severe conditions reflects in fact their common practice. Likewise, surprisingly, no respondent objected to the imposition of a three-month window period. Enrolees consistently identified in this window period a means to screen entrance in the scheme, clearly protecting its financial assets.

> *These three months are good otherwise some people would join the insurance only when they are sick ... then the insurance would soon have no money left ...* (Interview 12 - E, >5, R, M)

What respondents did not appreciate was the fact that, following the District guidelines, the AMBC assigns entire villages to one specific CSPS and restricts access to services accordingly. Respondents argued that this decision may have discouraged many households from enrolling as people would rather be asked where they wish to seek care, given that the facility to which the AMBC assigns them may not match their preference. They justified their reluctance to accept the facility imposed by the AMBC mainly in terms of the overall social relations between their village and the village where the facility is located. Respondents, especially if satisfied with the care they have received so far at a specific facility, were clearly not willing to trade their preference for a given CSPS for the benefits associated with insurance membership. Interestingly, it was often the ones already in the scheme who put forward the request for a modification that may allow others in their community to enrol as well.

> *There are two health facilities not far from our village* (Sobon), *Dara and Toni. They have told us to go to Dara, but many people prefer to go to Toni. It is not only the quality, it is also that we have many of our people there in the village, so when you arrive there, you know you will always find some help. More people would have enrolled if the insurance people had said that we could also go to Toni.* (Interview 16 - E, >5, P, M)

> *I have enrolled, but many people have not enrolled because the insurance has told that they have to go to Dara. And many of us from Pâ do not like to go to Dara. Our people argued with the people of Dara, so even if the quality of care is good, we do not like to go there.*
> (Interview 10 - E, >5, R, M)

No interviewee identified upfront the quality of health care services as the reason discouraging enrolment. Once probed, however, 16 respondents expressed dissatisfaction with the quality of the services available at the district facilities. Although they enjoy closer access to a better equipped facility, respondents living in the town of Nouna were the ones who expressed the most dissatisfaction with the quality of services. All 10 people interviewed in Nouna, irrespective of enrolment status, sharply criticised the quality of care. Criticisms, across all locations, consistently focused on three aspects of care: long waiting times, excessive prescribing, and differential treatment depending on a patient's socio-economic status. No interviewee questioned the ability of providers to treat patients adequately nor complained about drug shortages.

> *Sometimes you go and you have to wait for a long time, you suffer and you feel they are neglecting you ... but once they treat me, I am satisfied.* (Interview 30 - NE, >5, P, M)

> *Some people are satisfied, others are not. Many people complain that they prescribe too many drugs, so you cannot pay for all of them ... and then you are also not sure what they are all for.* (Interview 18 - E, <5, R, M)

> *It is hard to speak about the quality of care, there are times when you get there and they do not treat you well, but if you arrive and the nurse knows you ,if you are well known in town, then he treats you well.*
> (Interview 26 - E, <5, R, F)

The analysis of the comments expressed with regard to the quality of care also revealed that both enrolled and non-enrolled individuals felt disempowered when facing the providers and did not know how to alter the *status quo* to improve health service provision.

> *Today if you go to the health facility, if the nurses like it, they take care of you, if not, they leave you, they take your money and tell you to go back home, and you can say nothing about it ... even if your heart cries, you take your sick person back home ... even if he is going to die in your arms.* (Interview 19 - NE, <5, R, M)

> *Taking good care of the sick people has become rarer and rarer ... if you are poor, you cannot even get close to the hospital ... they will not even look at you and what can you do? We are people with no education, can we really tell these nurses anything?* (Interview 21 - E, <5, P, M)

Both enrolled and non-enrolled interviewees reported having heard during the sensitization campaign that the AMBC will help solve what problems patients currently face when seeking care. While non-enrolees seemed reluctant to fully trust that the AMBC will induce a change in providers' attitudes, enrolees were trustful that this is true and joined the scheme to see their wish realised. Enrolees referred to the insurance as an opportunity to gain a voice *vis-à-vis* the providers. They trusted that the AMBC will effectively solicit providers to improve the quality of their work. Especially among urban residents, this hope was nourished by the knowledge that the CRSN is among the project initiators and will therefore actively take part in monitoring the providers' performance.

> *The people of the insurance have said that they will tell the doctors to treat you well and fast, so that you can be happy ... but they* (the providers) *won't do it ... the insurance alone cannot change the behaviour of Adam's sons* (human beings). (Interview 22 - NE, <5, R, M)

> *We cannot trust the doctors ... we do not know them, if you do not know someone, you do not understand his work, you cannot trust him ... we trust the health insurance ... if the health insurance could talk to the doctors so that they can treat us well, so that if we are sick and arrive at the facility, they treat us well ...* (Interview 28 - E, <5, R, M)

> *With the insurance, there will be more security, because they* (the CRSN) *will run a survey to make sure that people are treated well ... they will ask you who looked after you and how, and are you satisfied with the treatment you received ... they will monitor it all the time ... but if you go to the hospital today with no insurance, they treat you with no respect.* (Interview 19 - NE, <5, R, M)

3.3.3.4 Illness experience and health care seeking behaviour

Without attempting to measure the effect of health status and previous health service utilisation on the decision to enrol, the interviews offered us an opportunity to explore the community illness experience and their perceptions regarding Western medical services. In the section above, we have described how product characteristics, for example assigning members to a given CSPS, and perceptions of the quality of care available at district facilities shaped the decision to enrol. In this section, we rather focus on how the broader conceptualisation of the illness experience and the perceived adequacy of modern medical care influenced people's construction of the benefit of health insurance and thus their choice to enrol or not to enrol in the AMBC.

The vast majority of respondents were reluctant to report recent illness episodes unless they pertained to someone having suffered from a severe condition. Once explicitly probed, all respondents mentioned how someone in the family, most often children, had suffered, in the months just preceding the interview, from common diseases, usually either uncomplicated malaria, respiratory-tract infections, or skin rushes. Unless the disease had been severe, respondents tended to attribute little importance to it, quickly dropping the topic from the conversation.

> Respondent: *Last year, there were no diseases in my family.*
> Interviewer: *Not even a simple case of soumaya* (fever/malaria)*?*
> Respondent: *Well, I do have a child ... we call it the founou bana, the disease that makes your body swell ... this disease caught him. I bought the drugs for him and he got better. That's all ... nothing else that I can say.* (Interview 1 - NE, >5, R, M)

If someone in the family had suffered from a severe condition, the respondents spared no detail, accurately describing both the illness experience and the health care seeking behaviour.

> *My daughter was sick. We did not know what she had. So, we took her to the nurse in Bourasso ... we did not have the nurses here yet ... but nothing, she did not get better. We took her to Nouna, but still she did not get better. So, we took the child to Dedougou. We paid the medications they told us to buy for 10 000 CFA. I took the child back home, but she still did not get better. So, I took my child again and brought her to the Sisters* (the Catholic nuns in the town of Nouna). *They found the right medication and my daughter finally got better.* (Interview 5 - E, <5, P, F)

Irrespective of their education, their enrolment, and their socio-economic status, all respondents conceptualised falling sick as an unpredictable event. In Dioula, the unpredictability of disease is summarised by the expression, "*I ti là nay é, I ti tile nay ế*", translated as "when you go to sleep, you do not know whether you will fall sick; during the day, you do not know whether you will fall sick". Even those who reported never having suffered from a severe condition insisted on the fact that a person can never know if and when a disease will strike someone in the family. Across interviews, we consistently observed how it is always the disease that catches the person and never the other way round. Only highly educated people, the three civil servants interviewed in the town of Nouna and the treasurer of the AMBC interviewed in Bankoumani, talked of falling sick rather than being caught by a disease. As mentioned in an earlier section of this chapter, respondents, especially among the enrolees, often drew a link between the unpredictability of disease and the benefit of enrolling in the AMBC.

> *Apart from the soumaya* (fever/malaria), *diseases do not have the habit to catch the people in my family.* (Interview 25 - NE, <5, R, M)

> *Do you see that child over there? That's the only one that the soumaya* (fever/malaria) *has the habit to catch.* (Interview 27 - NE, <5, P, F)

> *I have never gone to a health facility ... my children have never been so sick to need to go there ... I treat them with the leaves. But I have enrolled because one can never tell when a severe disease will get you.*
> (Interview 32 - E, >5, P, F)

> *We have enrolled because you really never know when a disease will catch you.* (Interview 28 - E, <5, R, M)

With the exception of two women claiming that they had never visited a health facility, all interviewees reported at least one contact, in some cases only because of a delivery or a vaccination campaign, with modern health care services. Irrespective of their enrolment status and of the distance to the health facility, interviewees reported using alternatively traditional and Western medicine to treat common conditions. They explained this dualism in terms of affordability. Both enrolled and non-enrolled respondents indicated that traditional remedies are used when an illness is perceived not to be severe enough to justify the cost of seeking formal care and when such remedies are perceived to be sufficiently effective to treat a given condition. Alternatively, although it would not be the preferred treatment choice, traditional medicine is used as a substitute to Western medicine when, after seeking care at the facility, the family lacks the financial means to pay for the medications. To be noted that respondents referred to traditional medicine mainly to indicate folk remedies which are delivered at home, and not necessarily to indicate that they sought the assistance of a traditional healer.

If the disease is severe, we take the person to the health facility. If the disease is not severe, we boil some leaves and wash the person with those. (Interview 2 - E, >5, R, M)

Often if you find that you cannot pay for the prescription, you come back to look for the medicines of the Fara Fin (the African people). (Interview 19 - NE, <5, R, M)

Only one woman explicitly reported having sought the assistance of a traditional healer for a severe condition affecting her daughter, locally known as *urine de cheval*, i.e. jaundice, as she believed that the illness could not be treated by Western medicine.

It is the medicines of the Bwaba that I used ... people do sacrifices on the streets and if you walk on this, you get a disease called urine de cheval ... this disease cannot be treated by the nurses, so I took my daughter to a traditional doctor. (Interview 6 - NE, <5, P, F)

Given the high cost of care, respondents, irrespective of enrolment status, often reported waiting for days before seeking care at a facility, hoping that the disease may pass alone and taking time to gather the money necessary to pay for the treatment.

Last year, the disease came to find me. I waited, then on the third day I went to Dara. The nurses gave me medications and I came home that night. It was the first day it rained. I should have worked, but I was too sick and it took fifteen days before I could work again well. (Interview 8 - E, >5, P, M)

When one of our children is really sick, we go to Dara. We leave with what money we have, we pay, and then we come back here. We look round and round till we find the money to pay for more treatment. (Interview 14 - NE, >5, P, M)

Ten out of 32 respondents mentioned having incurred in recent times in a health care expenditure which they considered to be very high in relation to their income. All of them were people enrolled in the AMBC, who spontaneously drew a link between their decision to enrol and their awareness of how expensive medical care can be in case of severe conditions.

Sometimes, when someone is sick, we can pay as much as 6 500 CFA or even more, 7 500 CFA ... the nurses know us, so if we do not have the money, they let us gather it and then come back to pay ... but it is still not easy ... the insurance will help us to solve this problem. (Interview 3 - E, <5, P, M)

> *Just at the time when I was thinking of enrolling in the insurance, one of my wives fell sick. I had to take her to Dara. They kept her there three days. It cost me 30 000 CFA ... and just for one person! And this is without counting the cost to get there and back ... 30 000 CFA just for the medications.* (Interview 12 - E, >5, R, M)

When probed on the matter, 13 out of 16 enrolled respondents claimed that in spite of their insurance status, they will continue the dual use of traditional and Western medicine. They did consider seeking care faster than in the past, but still only in case of real necessity. They explained their choice in terms of adequacy of treatment as well as in terms of the additional burden, measured in terms of direct and indirect costs, imposed by the direct and indirect cost of travelling to the health facility.

> *If the disease is not too severe, I will not go to the health facility ... I will use the leaves from the plants ... you have to take into account to walk there and back, you lose all the time from your work.*
> (Interview 19 - NE, <5, R, M)

> *From now on, I will not hesitate to go to the facility when sick. Well, only for the diseases which we fear of course* (diseases that are severe). *For the others it is not worthwhile. Too much travelling ... You can tell which ones are the severe diseases, they are the diseases that don't hide and tire you.*
> (Interview 2 - E, >5, R, M)

> *It is just not worthwhile to go to the hospital for something that you can treat with our tradition* (traditional folk remedies).
> (Interview 29 - E, >5, R, F)

3.3.3.5 Cultural beliefs and saving practices

Interviewees, irrespective of socio-economic status, were reluctant to justify decision to enrol or not to enrol in relation to cultural beliefs and practices. When probed on the matter, both enrolled and non-enrolled individuals acknowledged the fact that setting money aside for health care may be perceived as attracting diseases, but they were always very careful to attribute this belief to others in their community and never to members of their own household.

> *It is the old people who say that if you keep an idea in your head, this thing will happen, but nowadays we do not think like this anymore.*
> (Interview 3 - E, <5, P, M)

> *People who believe that saving for illness is bad live in a lie. It is like closing your eyes to the reality. But some people still think that.* (Interview 28 - E, <5, R, M)

When asked to describe saving practices, all interviewees reported setting something aside to take care of future expenses, smoothing their consumption over periods of high and low income related to seasonal cash flows. In Dioula, respondents consistently referred to saving as *bolo koro sigui*, literally translated as "keeping something near your hand". All respondents, however, irrespective of insurance and socio-economic status, expressed a general resistance towards setting cash aside to face future expenses. Their answers unanimously portray a preference towards investments in kind, usually purchasing cattle or some other small farm animal that can easily be sold in times of need. Only 3 urban respondents, the three civil servants, reported depositing savings in a bank.

> *If we have something left over, we invest it in the purchase of a cow or of a goat ... if something arrives, you take your animal and sell it. Cows can be used for some needs and goats for others. Even selling a chicken, which is not much, can help you take care of some needs at times.*
> (Interview 7 - NE, >5, R, M)

> *You cannot keep cash aside, because then every day you will want to take out some money ... 100 CFA today, 100 CFA tomorrow ... better to buy animals ... you know, this is the problem of the poor people.*
> (Interview 8 - E, >5, P, M)

In spite of a common resistance towards setting aside cash, enrolled and non-enrolled interviewees provided very different answers to questions exploring what use they make out of their savings. Recognising many competing needs and the availability of only very scarce resources, both enrolees and non-enrolees reported a tendency not to earmark savings towards the consumption of a fixed set of goods. However, when discussing the function of savings, enrolled individuals referred upfront to the unpredictability of disease and the high cost of medical care while non-enrolled individuals first listed other expenses, such as attendance of social events, purchase of farming tools, and school fees.

> *There is always a problem in deciding where the money of the bolo koro sigui* (savings) *should go ... so many different needs ... food, funerals, the working instruments, schooling, health ...* (Interview 24 - NE, <5, P, M)

> *When we can, we set something aside to meet the family needs ...first of all, health. When someone falls sick, we have enough to treat them ...then comes the schooling of the children.* (Interview 23 - E, <5, P, M)

> *Every year, we have so many expenses. Between the condiments* (food that is not produced directly by the household), *the cost of the schooling, and the small family celebrations, we spend most of our savings ... even 150 000 CFA in one year.* (Interview 19 - NE, <5, R, M)

When asked to explain the preference they stated for future consumption of goods, several non-enrolled individuals, who had previously denied the belief that saving for illness may attract negative fate, referred to the fact that while in good health, one should not think of the possibility of falling sick.

> *When we save, we do not talk of diseases. One does not say that he keeps this one animal for a case of illness. It is not good to keep diseases in your mouth* (to talk about diseases) ... *of course, if we need to, then we will use animals also to pay for care, but you cannot say it in advance.*
> (Interview 4 - NE, <5, R, M)

Enrolled individuals instead, often even recalled some simple form of self-insurance, e.g. purchasing drugs before being sick to ensure the availability of treatment in times of need. They also repeatedly referred to the fact that, in spite of their efforts, savings are not always sufficient to meet the cost of medical care as other pressing needs may force them to employ resources destined to health.

> *When I have some money, I spend it to buy some drugs before the money is gone to pay for something else. I buy some drugs, look at the expiry date, and keep them in my house ... so when someone is sick, if the doctor prescribes something, I first see if I already have it at home ... plus we always have paracetamol and chloroquine in our home.*
> (Interview 20 - E, <5, R, M)

> *I have joined the insurance because I save to have money for when the disease arrives ... but it is always difficult ... usually, when the disease comes, the cost of the treatment is often higher than what is left of our savings.* (Interview 31 - E, >5, P, M)

3.3.3.6 Scepticism and trust

All enrolled respondents spontaneously constructed a link between their choice to enrol and the trust they have in the management of the AMBC. In spite of the novelty of the initiative, the unconditional trust that its members grant the scheme was consistently justified in relation to five factors: (1) the completeness of the information shared during the communication and sensitisation campaign; (2) the release of documents, including insurance contracts and photo ID cards;

(3) the election of local representatives in each village; (4) the support of the CRSN; and (5) the overall village attitude towards the new project.

> *If we must trust one another, we must first of all trust those who have brought the insurance to our village. I trust them because I appreciate their work and what they have said. One can gain confidence in another person because of the way this person speaks.* (Interview 8 - E, >5, P, M)

> *We trust those people because they have given us papers to keep.* (Interview 3 - E, <5, P, M)

> *I trust the people who have come from Nouna to talk about the insurance because our local representative trusts them. We have elected one of our children* (one of the young men in the village) *as the local representative. We all trust him.* (Interview 2 - E, >5, R, M)

> *The Prapass* (old name of the CRSN) *has talked with us about insurance for a long time. They are also in it ... this work is done like the work of Toubabou* (white people) *... can you imagine the Prapass people running away with money?... and you know if this was the work of one person, I would not trust ... but this is the work of many people, of a whole community.* (Interview 16 - E, >5, P, M)

> *We trust the people who have come from Nouna because we, the local representatives, have joined them in their work. Out of many ideas, we are making out one big idea only ... one for all of us in our village ... and in doing so, we have become each other's witnesses.* (Interview 28 - E, <5, R, M)

Non-enrolled respondents also claimed trust in the AMBC. Their discourse, however, was often filled with comments hinting at sentiments of scepticism. Non-enrolees articulated no reason to distrust the scheme, especially because of its close link to the CRSN, but just appeared doubtful that its promises will be realisable in practice. Non-enrolees most often expressed their scepticism by attributing this sentiment not to themselves, but to others in their community and by referring to how they may consider enrolment only in the following years.

> *If you see that people doubt, it is because it is a new thing. It is something new, so we cannot say that it is bad, but we can also not say that it is good. If it gains strength, it is good. If it does not gain strength, that's it ... if we find the means, we may join next year.* (Interview 1 - NE, >5, R, M)

> *It is difficult to join something before you have seen its advantages ... some people say that it is impossible to treat people for free ... that the insurance is cheating the villagers ... that care for free is simply impossible.* (Interview 4 - NE, <5, R, M)

> *Now that this campaign is over, we have time to reflect. And if the insurance continues and we find the money, we will join next year.* (Interview 17 - NE, <5, R, M)

All respondents, irrespective of enrolment and socio-economic status, explained sentiments of scepticism among their communities in relation primarily to three factors: (1) the health providers' negative attitude towards the scheme; (2) previous disappointing experiences with other risk-sharing arrangements or development projects brought to the area; and (3) lack of adequate knowledge and understanding regarding the AMBC. To be noted that frequently, especially in villages with a CSPS, interviewees revealed that the very same health care providers had actively discouraged them from enrolling, claiming that the contracting arrangements with the AMBC were insufficient to cover the cost of care. Interestingly though, these comments were most often deliberately made only once the tape-recorder was switched off. Respondents admitted feeling discouraged by the providers' comments, although unable to understand their argument, especially with regard to the implication of capitation payments.

> *One day, I passed at the hospital and heard the nurses complain about the insurance. They were sceptical ... they did not want to sign the contract ... when people hear this, they do not enrol.* (Interview 23 - E, <5, P, M)

> *Some time ago people formed a groupement and they put together money, but some of them took this money and this is not good ... it is because of them that it all failed ... this is why now some people believe it when the nurses say that even if you fall sick, the insurance cannot help you ... that the insurance is stealing all the money ... people have not understood well.* (Interview 10 - E, >5, R, M)

> *Even if these people from Nouna have come many times to explain what this is all about, many people still do not understand. You don't know how it is in the countryside ... we are all with no education ... even if they explain, we cannot understand and remember everything.* (Interview 11 - NE, >5, R, M)

In a previous section of this chapter, we have extensively described weaknesses in the knowledge and understanding level, especially among non-enrolees. It is therefore plausible to assume that, in several instances, the link people draw between scepticism and poor knowledge and understanding is real. As shown in the last comment reported above, respondents, irrespective of enrolment status, often drew a link between their difficulty in understanding and retaining the details of the new initiative and their lack of education. They perceived their own lack of education and the lack of education of others in their community as a concrete obstacle to enrolment, making it difficult for them to fully comprehend and appreciate the benefit of new initiatives.

> *I did not attend school. If you have not gone to school, can you easily understand the new things that come to your village?*
> (Interview 1 - NE, >5, R, M)

> *It is because of illiteracy that people do not understand well. It is because of this that people cannot understand and appreciate something new quickly. People think that you want to take advantage of them, put them under the soil ... it is hard to understand when someone really wants to help you if you have no education.* (Interview 16 - E, >5, P, M)

We found, however, that among communities where leaders have taken an active role in promoting the AMBC, poor knowledge of the specific elements of the scheme no longer constituted an obstacle. In the village of Boron, for example, we found a young single mother, who could hardly recall any information on the organisation of the scheme, but who had proudly enrolled because her leaders had encouraged everyone in the community to do so.

> *I trust it because it is a collective affair. It is because people in my village have joined that I trust the insurance. I know it is something serious ... The délégué has told us many times that this is something good.*
> (Interview 32 - E, >5, P, F)

Similarly, people bypassed their limited knowledge and granted trust to the new initiative if they felt personally linked to any one of the AMBC leaders.

> *We trust the people of the insurance, because one of our sisters, Mèma, is among them*[14]*. Can a relative of yours cheat you and make you believe something that is not true?* (Interview 11 - NE, >5, R, M)

---

[14] At the time of the study, Mèma was the communication specialist working for the AMBC management unit. She is a Dafing whose family is originally from the village of Pâ. Although she was born and raised in Nouna, the predominantly Dafing community in Pâ, like the man expressing this comment, still recognised her as a sister.

> *I trust the insurance because I know these people very well ... we were all in school together.* (Interview 26 - E, <5, R, F)

3.4 Bridging the link between the quantitative and the qualitative results

As mentioned at the very beginning of this chapter, the ultimate aim of this study is to produce a holistic understanding of decision to enrol in CHI. Therefore, we considered it useful to bridge the link between the quantitative and the qualitative research by presenting a brief summary which combines findings from the two strands of analysis applied. This process of triangulation served the purpose of cross-validating our findings while at the same time facilitating the identification of the main areas of interest emerging from our analysis and deserving to be discussed in detail in the following chapter.

Findings from the regression model describing the existence of a strong positive association between enrolment and socio-economic status confirmed and allowed to quantify people's claim that lack of means constituted one of the main obstacles to enrolment, at least for large portions of the population. The interviews allowed to further decompose the concept of affordability to identify additional obstacles to enrolment. They drew attention to the fact that affordability was largely a function of the scheme's ability to adequately meet community preferences for specific elements of the AMBC institutional set-up. Qualitative findings highlighted that institutional rigidities, such as a stringent enrolment unit, a fixed enrolment period, and inflexible payment modalities, substantially limited the ability to pay of large and middle-class households. Likewise, both the quantitative and the qualitative findings identified a few institutional attributes that, by meeting community preferences, actively facilitated enrolment. For instance, both analyses confirmed that the adoption of a differential premium for adults and children was widely recognised as a valuable asset of the scheme, effectively favouring the enrolment of families with a high proportion of children.

The quantitative and the qualitative findings also provided consistent evidence on the role of education in shaping the decision to enrol. People's claim that lack of formal education made it difficult for them to comprehend the concept of insurance and retain details regarding the various elements of the scheme appeared to be confirmed by the quantitative findings, indicating that the higher the household head's education, the higher the odds of being enrolled.

Similarly, both the interviews and the regression model indicated that perceptions regarding the adequacy of traditional medical remedies, i.e. a potential substitute for the biomedical services reimbursed by the AMBC, played an important role in shaping the decision to enrol. On one hand, the quantitative analysis measured the strength of the association between enrolment and the perceived adequacy of the treatment delivered by traditional healers. It highlighted that those having expressed a negative judgement were most likely to enrol in the AMBC. On the other hand, the qualitative analysis allowed us to explore the matter in further depth, explaining how health care provider choices are the product of a complex decision-making process, made in the light of judgements on the severity of the disease, the relative effectiveness of substitute treatments, and the resources available to the household. The qualitative interviews suggested that communities most often resorted to traditional remedies not as the preferred treatment, but rather as a substitute to biomedicine given the high cost of seeking care at modern facilities.

Gaps in the completeness of the quantitative data made it impossible for us to quantify the link between enrolment and the perception of the quality of care available at the district facilities. The results of the qualitative analysis, however, suggested that, although not fully satisfied with health service provision, concerns about the quality of care available did not constitute a major element of discouragement for those wishing to enrol in the AMBC. In general in fact, respondents appeared to trust the competency of health professionals, but were profoundly disappointed with the behavioural component of the provider-patient encounter. The expectation that the AMBC would intervene to improve health service provision, mainly by allowing patients to gain respect *vis à vis* the providers, was found to constitute an important element motivating enrolment.

The interviews suggested that individuals who were aware of the high cost of medical treatment, mainly because of a recent severe illness experience, were also more likely to think that the benefits of membership in the AMBC outweighed the costs. Due to lack of meaningful retrospective data on health spending, however, we could not use regression modelling to confirm and quantify this link. We were able though, to measure the link between enrolment and both household health status and previous use of curative health services, finding no evidence of adverse selection. Likewise, we found no association between enrolment and previous use of preventive health services.

The fact that distance to the referral facility was not identified in the interviews as a major obstacle to enrolment was confirmed by the quantitative analysis, indicating that households living further away from a facility were in fact more likely to have enrolled in the AMBC. Qualitative findings detecting a wide-spread appreciation for the completeness of the benefit package, including highly valued services such as emergency transport, were useful to understand the counterintuitive finding of the effect of distance on decision to enrol. Also contrary to expectations, the quantitative analysis detected no differential incentive to enrol depending on being assigned either to one of six CSPS or directly to the first-line facility located on the premises of the district hospital. The qualitative analysis, having identified no objection to the gate-keeping system or to being assigned to a rural facility, supported this finding. In addition, however, qualitative findings highlighted how assignment to a specific facility may have deterred enrolment, not because of objective considerations regarding quality of care, but mainly because of the broader social context, favouring family and kin relationships and influencing choices regarding health care seeking behaviour.

Both the qualitative and quantitative findings pointed at the importance on decision to enrol of contextual elements pertaining to life within a specific community. On the one hand, the quantitative findings detected a positive association between enrolment and high levels of socio-economic equality within a community, indicating that decision to join the AMBC was shaped by pre-existing attitudes towards risk-sharing and solidarity. On the other hand, the interviews revealed that enrolment was higher among communities where the *délégué* and the key village leaders had actively invested in the promotion of the scheme. Knowledge and perceptions of the scheme as well as trust in its managerial structures could only be explored in the qualitative analysis. The interviews showed that in spite of the fact that the overall perception of the scheme was positive both among enrolees and non-enrolees, the two groups differed remarkably with regard to the specific knowledge and comprehension of the scheme elements. Substantial differences in knowledge levels were observed across villages. Interviewees were found to understand the principle of insurance and trust the scheme structure much more in communities where leaders had taken an active stand in favour of the AMBC. The interviews also showed in fact, that knowledge and comprehension inevitably influenced trust levels, affecting one's decision to enrol. In several instances, we observed that trust could also be positively influenced by the ability to identify links between the newly emerged scheme and well-established existing institutions, such as the CRSN.

The qualitative analysis alone provided insight into the influence of cultural beliefs and practices on decision to enrol, detecting a certain resistance on the part of rural communities to earmark savings, especially towards the future consumption of health care benefits. Although not directly exploring cultural beliefs and practices, the quantitative analysis also contributed to the understanding that social norms and values must have played an important role in shaping decision to enrol. The regression model in fact, identified a positive significant association between enrolment and Bwaba ethnicity, providing quantitative evidence in favour of the claim that specific socio-cultural elements did influence considerations on the costs and benefits of membership in the AMBC and subsequently, also the decision to enrol.

4. Discussion

4.1 Methodological considerations

4.1.1 The mixed methodology approach

The study presented in this dissertation represents an attempt towards constructing a holistic understanding of household decision to enrol in CHI. As described in the introductory chapter, previous studies exploring the decision to enrol in CHI have employed alternatively either qualitative or quantitative methods, thus limiting their analysis to a constrained set of relevant issues. Building on the specific strengths of each methodological approach, we were able to explore the decision to enrol in CHI in a more comprehensive manner, considering at once a wider set of issues relevant to the research question. As mentioned earlier in this dissertation, our decision to employ jointly qualitative and quantitative methods of analysis stemmed out of a desire to answer pragmatic concerns about the implementation of CHI schemes in sub-Saharan Africa.

Patton (1990) discussed how the methodological status hierarchy in science ranks quantitative methods above qualitative ones, yielding the former "hard data" and the latter "soft data". He argued against this simplistic definition and highlighted how the specific strengths of each methodological approach may successfully be employed towards the understanding of different research questions or different aspects of the same research question. In the case presented in this dissertation, the combined application of qualitative and quantitative methods allowed us to explore aspects which would have escaped our analysis had we employed exclusively one research method. A known limitation of household surveys, for example, is their focus on the outcome of a decision, in our case enrolment in CHI, rather than on the process through which the decision is made. So, on the one hand, qualitative methods of analysis allowed us to compensate for this limitation, by listening to the thoughts and considerations which shaped the process of reaching the final decision to enrol or not to enrol in the AMBC. On the other hand, regression modelling allowed quantifying the influence that a constrained set of household head, household, and community characteristics had on the decision, in a manner which would have simply been unfeasible had we relied exclusively on qualitative methods of analysis.

4.1.2 The timing of the study

A potential criticism of our study could be directed against the decision to carry out the research immediately following the end of the first enrolment campaign. One could in fact argue that a comprehensive exploration of the decision to enrol should only take place a few years after the implementation of a scheme, observing how households move in and out of CHI over time. However, as described in the introductory chapter, field experience across sub-Saharan Africa suggests that many schemes do not survive beyond one or two years because they never manage to overcome the basic problem of low enrolment faced at their very onset. With the exception of the study by Criel and Waelkens in Guinea-Conakry (2003), previous research consistently looked at the experience of schemes already in place since a few years (Atim and Madjiguene 2000; Chee et al. 2002; Jütting 2004; Osei-Akoto 2004; Schneider and Diop 2004). This choice inevitably introduced a source of bias since it focused on understanding motivation to enrol or not to enrol in CHI only among relatively successful schemes.

Our choice to carry out this study right after the end of the first campaign stemmed out of the pragmatic consideration that in order to adequately advise policy-makers on the implementation of CHI in sub-Saharan Africa, we ought to understand what motivates or discourages enrolment when a scheme is first set up in a rural or semi-rural community. The very survival of the scheme largely depends on its ability to secure adequate coverage levels already during its initial years. Having said this, we do agree that continuous monitoring of reasons motivating and/or discouraging enrolment should accompany the long-term implementation of any CHI scheme as the barriers identified at the very onset may, through adequate policies, be overcome, but new ones, linked to changing political, social, and economic conditions, may come into place.

4.1.3 Strengths and weaknesses of the quantitative study

The household survey analysis presented in this dissertation focused exclusively on the question of enrolment in CHI. With the exception of Osei-Akoto's analysis of enrolment in Ghana (2004), previous quantitative research conducted in sub-Saharan Africa explored demand for voluntary health insurance only within the framework of broader studies, primarily focused on measuring the impact of insurance status on health service utilisation and out-of-pocket health spending (Jütting 2004; Schneider and Diop 2004). The exclusive focus on the decision to enrol in CHI allowed us to include in the regression model a wider range of relevant variables, such as perception of traditional care and socio-economic inequality, which had been omitted in earlier studies. This was possible both because of the reflection informed by the qualitative analysis on possible reasons motivating or discouraging enrolment, and because we had the opportunity to rely on *ad hoc* instruments for data collection, i.e. the two additional modules included in the household survey questionnaire exclusively to monitor enrolment behaviour. As mentioned earlier in this dissertation, however, the incomplete compilation of some questionnaire modules, due to difficulties encountered on the field, limited our capacity to model all the factors which we had originally planned to include in our analysis.

We also explicitly attempted to model community characteristics and their impact on the decision to enrol in CHI. As described in the review of the literature, previous quantitative studies both in sub-Saharan Africa and in high income countries, explored the role of community characteristics only marginally, often including no more than a dummy variable indicating distance to the health facility and/or the district/region of residence[15]. This trend is probably attributable to two factors: the difficulty to compile relevant data and an exclusive focus on the individual as the rational decision-maker, typical of the field of economics (Folland et al. 2001), the discipline which has dominated much of the theoretical and empirical literature on insurance purchase. Although our analysis drew heavily from the field of health economics, our public health orientation led us to acknowledge the limit of focusing exclusively on individual or household level characteristics. In the light of the qualitative findings, we had to recognise that the decision to enrol was heavily shaped by the context within which it took place. Although other authors have previously stressed the central role of context (Criel et al. 2004; Waelkens and Criel 2004), we are not aware of any attempt to explicitly include contextual elements in a quantitative analysis, modelling, as we did, the effect of community characteristics on the decision to enrol.

In line with our wish to devote much attention to the contextual nature of the decision-making process, we adopted an innovative statistical approach, i.e. the multilevel modelling. As described in the methods chapter, multilevel analysis is widely recognised as the most suitable technique when attempting to model jointly household and community characteristics. Contrary to our expectation, however, after inclusion of all household head, household, and community characteristics, the model no longer identified the existence of village-level residual variance due to differences between localities and did not yield results statistically different from those of the conventional logistic regression model.

---

[15] The recent work by Propper (1999) represents the first and unique attempt to explicitly model the impact of contextual factors on demand for health insurance. As described in the review of the literature, her recent models of demand for health insurance in the UK included variables measuring institutional elements, such as the quality of health services.

This finding disproved our original hypothesis according to which we would have expected to find significant residual variance attributable to the village-level (ρ), reflecting heterogeneity in enrolment across localities. We had assumed ρ to remain significant even after accounting for community characteristics because we had assumed that village heterogeneity could not be fully captured by the variables included in the model.

Methodologically, although initially disconcerting, the result of our final random-effect model (model 2) could be explained in relation to two factors. On the one hand, the inclusion of highly relevant community characteristics could have explained the entire village-level variance previously detected in model 1. On the other hand, the small number of communities (15) included in the analysis could have limited the power to ascertain a village-level effect (Goldstein 2003). The fact that our final model did not identify any residual heterogeneity in enrolment across villages is an indication of the fact that, given our sample size, the household head, household, and community characteristics included in the model were sufficient to explain the variation in enrolment rates we had originally observed across the 15 localities included in our study.

Given the unexpected result, we checked our model construction and discussed its results directly with Harvey Goldstein, professor of statistics at the University of London and one of the fathers of multilevel modelling[16] (personal communication, April 2005). Goldstein confirmed our interpretation of the quantitative findings, linking the ability to explain all village-level variation to the inclusion of pertinent variables in the model. He suggested that the higher enrolment observed in some localities might have simply been due to a higher concentration of a specific set of household-level characteristics, for example higher socio-economic status and/or Bwaba ethnicity, among certain communities. As expected, he also invited us to reflect upon the fact that random-effect modelling treats the number of level-two observations as a random sample taken from a population. In the case presented in this dissertation, it is as if we had sampled 15 localities to represent all localities in the DSS area. This is obviously too small a sample, which would allow to detect village-level variation only if such variation was of considerable size. After controlling for household head, household, and community characteristics, the residual variation across villages became of negligible size, hence it could no longer be detected in a model based exclusively on 15 level-two observations. It needs to be considered, however, that our sampling was constrained by the fact that only 15 localities were offered the opportunity to join the AMBC in 2004.

---

[16] The author had the opportunity to discuss the analysis directly with Prof. Harvey Goldstein on the occasion of a course on multilevel modelling held at the University of Bristol in April 2005.

We would not have been able to increase our level-two sample size even if we had wished to do so.

The problem of small sample size pertains also to the selection of household-level observations, with a total of only 530 households included in our study. Small sample size inevitably affected the power of the study, making it difficult to identify weaker associations between enrolment status and independent variables. The small sample size also made it impossible for us to conduct any analysis by sub-group, differentiating for example according to the sex or the ethnicity of the household head. The size of our sample, however, is comparable to that of similar studies conducted in sub-Saharan Africa (Jütting 2004; Osei-Akoto 2004). Small sample size constitutes a common problem across studies on insurance purchase conducted in low income countries and is most likely attributable to two factors: the lack of extensive insurance coverage and the lack of systematic data collection processes. The former factor imposes an obvious constraint on sample selection as there may simply be not enough schemes, and, within schemes, not enough enrolled people to be included in studies. The latter factor indirectly affects sample size as it forces researchers to rely almost exclusively on data collected *ad hoc* for the study, considerably increasing the financial costs of the research and thus inevitably imposing a trade-off between the quantity and the quality of the information to be gathered.

In our case, the selection of the sample was clearly constrained by the number of households having accepted to enrol in the AMBC in 2004. In spite of the small sample size, we trust that we complied with the most stringent requirements of sample selection, attempting to minimise selection bias. We trust that, having included as controls 13% of all non-enrolled households and having checked for socio-demographic consistency between the two groups (i.e. controls and the overall non-enrolled population in the study area), we adequately represented the households not participating in the AMBC. Likewise, we judge the proportion of cases to controls, set at a ratio of 1: 2.8, to be adequate and in line with the literature on case-control studies (Beaglehole et al. 1993). We do recognise, however, as a potential source of bias the fact that we were not able to interview 17 enrolled households. We cannot exclude the possibility that the 17 enrolled households not interviewed differed in some significant manner from the ones interviewed. Given the absence of information on these households, we cannot estimate the direction of the bias. To be noted, however, that securing the participation of nearly 90% of all people presenting the outcome of interest is well above the standard of case-control studies conducted in high-income countries (Boeing et al. 1991; Martinez et al. 2005; Steindorf et al. 2003; Xu et al. 2004).

A comprehensive evaluation of the methodology guiding our quantitative analysis requires that we also take a critical look at the instrument used for data collection, i.e. the household survey questionnaire. Given the extensive work at the root of the development of the four core modules (Würthwein et al. 2001), we trust that measurement bias was reduced to a minimum and that the questions asked realistically captured information on the households' socio-economic status, illness experience, and health care seeking behaviour. Given the operational difficulties encountered on the field and the subsequent incompleteness in the two additional survey modules, those on risk-sharing and on insurance, we cannot make any conclusive statement on the ability of these instruments to adequately measure the dimensions for which they had originally been designed. In the light of the incompleteness of these two modules, we could have chosen to use what information we had to impute values to the missing observations. We preferred instead to exclude from our analysis any variable for which we did not have complete information or for which responses appeared inconsistent, indicating answers which were not in line with what we had originally wished to know. We preferred to limit the extent of our analysis, by disregarding some of the variables in which we had originally been interested, rather than to compromise its validity, by including variables whose measurement we judged to be uncertain.

The incompleteness in the data collection process induced the research team, both in Heidelberg and at the CRSN, to reflect upon the procedures accompanying the introduction of additional modules in the survey. It is possible that the training and the quality checks routinely in place are not sufficient to ensure that new modules are compiled correctly, especially when they entail a certain degree of complexity. In the light of these considerations, the research team decided to revise both the structure of some questions and the relevant field procedures. It is anticipated that the difficulties and limitations encountered in 2004 will be solved in the following wave of the household survey. This should allow subsequent analyses of enrolment to include the wider range of variables which we had originally envisioned.

Pokhrel (2004) discussed the ability of household surveys in low income countries to truly capture illness experience and health care seeking behaviour. He argued that illness reporting may be lower than in affluent societies due to lower socio-economic status and lower educational levels. In our study, the level of illness reporting, measured exclusively in terms of chronic diseases, was relatively high, but comparable to that of previous waves of the household survey conducted in the Nouna Health District (Dong et al. 2004a). Higher values of illness reporting than those usually observed in the literature are most likely due to the fact that information was aggregated at the household level and not treated at the individual level, as generally done in most studies on illness reporting and health service utilisation (Chang and Trivedi 2003; Hjortsberg 2003; Magadi et al. 2000; Pokhrel and Sauerborn 2004). It is impossible to discern whether the higher proportion of enrolled households reporting use of curative services in the 12 months preceding the interview represented the reality or constituted a source of recall bias. Even if the latter option were true, results would be biased towards an overestimation of the association between enrolment status and previous use of curative services. Therefore, the bias would not alter our conclusive finding, which detected, after controlling for other household characteristics, no significant association between enrolment status and previous curative health service utilisation.

In our study, we included several variables measuring health status and previous health service utilisation. We trust that this allowed us to capture a large proportion of the variation in enrolment due to health status and health service utilisation. In the qualitative interviews, however, several enrolled households drew a link between their decision to enrol and a recent high spending on health care. As described in the methods chapter, given the absence of retrospective data on health expenditure beyond the questionnaire one month recall period, we were unable to measure the link, identified by interviewees, between their decision to enrol and prior substantial health care spending. Likewise, also given the timing of the survey and the limited recall period, we were unable to include any measure of acute illness reporting. Therefore, we cannot exclude the possibility that either one of these two variable would have bore an impact on the decision to join the AMBC.

The apparent inconsistency between the qualitative and the quantitative findings indicates that to rule out the existence of adverse selection, quantitative analyses of demand for health insurance ought to comprise accurate measurements of all dimensions relevant to quantify health status and previous health service utilisation, including spending. For instance, a study conducted in 1991 in the United States showed that insurance purchase was associated with previous health expenditure, but not with health status (Wolfe and Goddeeris 1991). However, we must consider that the analytical need to include several dimensions of health status and health care seeking behaviour ought to be balanced against pragmatic recall considerations. It is often very difficult for respondents, especially among rural illiterate communities, to report with accuracy events which occurred several months before the interview. The challenge for future surveys is to identify ways to measure all relevant parameters in such a way as to reconcile analytical needs with the natural constraints of recall. An alternative to such an approach is to administer the household survey questionnaire twice, once immediately before and once immediately after the enrolment campaign. In order not to overburden households, a possibility would be to split the survey, recording information relevant to quantify adverse selection prior to the enrolment period and information on enrolment behaviour only afterwards.

4.1.4 Strengths and weaknesses of the qualitative study

The literature recognises that the validity and credibility of qualitative research rests upon two main elements: the competence of the researcher conducting the study, and the application of rigorous techniques and well-documented methods for data collection and analysis (Bernard 1990; Glesne and Peshkin 1992; Patton 1990).

Patton (1990) argued that in qualitative research, the investigator becomes the direct instrument through which data is collected and analysed. Therefore, the investigator has to be adequately trained to handle qualitative analysis as the level of direct interaction with field situations and the people affected by a programme is much higher than for quantitative researchers. The author, having studied Sociology, received systematic training in the conduct of qualitative research and, before working in Nouna, had already gathered experience in the field. In addition, as described in the methods chapter, she did not conduct the work alone, but in close collaboration with other two people, Professor Sauerborn and Mamadou Sanon, who, enjoying an extensive experience in qualitative research, were able to provide continuous advice and support.

Patton (1990) recognised that, whether conducting qualitative or quantitative research, the researcher's approach to data collection and analysis will inevitably be shaped, and thus biased, by his/her thoughts, values, opinions, and experiences. Close interaction with the community being studied may induce changes in the researcher's way of thinking, continuously re-shaping his/her interpretation of the situation. In the light of these considerations, Patton (1990) argued in favour of disclosing any personal and professional information which may affect the collection, analysis, and interpretation of the data. In line with his suggestion, we have described in the methods chapter the role of the author with regard to the implementation of the AMBC. The author, however, recognises as an element of strength, rather than a weakness, her close link to the community in the District and her frequent trips to the field, as those proved to be the essential element, together with an accurate review of the literature, which allowed her first to frame the research question and then to interpret, in a meaningful manner, the information collected. She recognises that, had she simply conducted her research from a distance sitting at her desk in Heidelberg, she would have never been able to understand reasons motivating or discouraging enrolment in the AMBC to the same extent. In all instances, she attempted to abide to what Patton (1990) described as "empathic neutrality" – showing care and interest in the experience of the people, while at the same time remaining neutral with regard to the findings, managing the impact of her *self* on the research.

An obvious limitation of the author is her extremely limited knowledge of the local language Dioula. Throughout this dissertation, we have insisted on the importance of understanding the insider's view, i.e. the *emic* perspective. It is apparent, however, that one cannot fully understand another person's view unless he/she first understands the other person's language. Language represents in fact a way of organising the world, shaping the manner in which communities frame situations and experiences. Not being able to understand the local language, the author is likely to have missed out on the interpretation of some concepts, which, read in the French transcription, might have lost at least some of the significance they expressed in Dioula. Similarly, during the interviews, the author might have missed the opportunity to probe respondents on some interesting comments because of the inability to catch nuances of meaning once their responses were translated back to her in French.

Systematic efforts, however, were made to minimise the risk that important information and concepts be lost in the process of translation. As described in the methods chapter, the author and her translator worked together on the interview guide and on five pilot interviews to achieve a fluent relationship that allowed both of them to be comfortable with translation during the data collection process. Similarly, the staff transcribing and translating the interviews was trained to produce verbatim translations, carefully reporting in French the original text of the conversation without summarising concepts with the aim of making them more easily comprehensible. The staff was also advised to leave in the original language particular words and expressions that could not easily be translated into French, such as idiomatic sentences and proverbs. As described in the methods chapter, the author and her translator carefully worked through the transcripts to clear the understanding of Dioula expressions and of sentences which, reproducing exactly the original structure of the local language, could not easily be understood in French. The presentation of the findings, drawing heavily from local expressions and words, is a clear indication of this systematic effort on the part of the author to overcome the limitation imposed by her very limited knowledge of the local language.

Rigorous techniques and methods were applied to all aspects of the research, and not simply to the transcription and translation process. The adoption of theoretical sampling, the development of a well-structured interview guide, the accurate transcription of all the interviews, and a detailed process of coding are all steps in data collection and analysis that served the purpose of ensuring abidance to high standards of qualitative inquiry, increasing the validity and credibility of the findings. In addition, the application of three parallel triangulation approaches (analyst, data, and community feedback) ensured the development of a coherent and meaningful interpretation, even before the final process of triangulating the qualitative and the quantitative findings.

Our study differentiates itself from most previous qualitative investigations of enrolment in CHI. As described in the review of the literature in fact, with the exception of the study by Criel and Waelkens (2003), previous qualitative investigations of enrolment in CHI were conducted within the framework of consultancy reports (Atim and Madjiguene 2000; Chee et al. 2002). These reports inevitably focused more on the evaluation of one specific programme than on the development of broader scientific knowledge on CHI. Although we were also interested in informing the implementation of the specific scheme operative in the Nouna Health District, our primary objective was to generate scientific knowledge on the reasons motivating or discouraging enrolment in CHI beyond the boundary of the setting where the study was conducted. Different objectives and focuses rest at the core of different approaches to the application of qualitative methods (Patton 1990), marking the clear departure of our scientific study from previous programme evaluations of other CHI experiences in sub-Saharan Africa.

One could argue that an important limitation of our study is associated with the fact that we interviewed exclusively household heads, failing to listen to the opinion of other household members. Previous qualitative research on CHI in sub-Saharan Africa included a wider spectrum of respondents (Atim and Madjiguene 2000; Chee et al. 2002; Criel et al. 2002). These studies, however, had as their primary objective the exploration of community perceptions of CHI. In the study presented in this dissertation, instead, we purposely focused exclusively on understanding the decision to enrol at the household level. In line with previous research conducted in the study area to explore household coping mechanisms given illness (Sauerborn 1994), we assumed the household head to be the key player in deciding whether to enrol or not to enrol in CHI, since participation in the scheme entails a decision over the allocation of the family resources. As described in the results chapter, field evidence largely supported our initial assumption, justifying both the choice to sample exclusively household heads for the interviews and the choice to include in the regression model individual level characteristics only insofar as they pertained to the household head. This is not to say, however, that further investigations accompanying the implementation of the AMBC or of any another CHI scheme, should not consider to focus on wider community constituencies. The choice of the sample in fact, depends exclusively on the specific research question to be answered (Glaser and Strauss 1967; Patton 1990).

One further criticism could be directed against the choice to adopt an interview guide, rather than simply conducting informal conversational interviews, relying entirely on the spontaneous generation of questions. As described in the methods section, however, we preferred the former to the latter because we trusted the tool to be better suited to address the same set of issues in all interviews. Still, we made a systematic effort to adapt to the specific conditions of each interviewee, quickly assessing the person and the setting in which the interview took place, to decide in which order and in which manner best to approach the various themes. Likewise, we never cut off interviewees when they reported information and/or experiences which diverted from the interview guide, as it was often through those very free comments which we learned the most about a person's decision to enrol or not to enrol in the AMBC. Also to be noted how in the results chapter, we made an explicit effort to report verbatim quotations from all interviewees. Our choice is representative of our constant attempt not to allow the breath and the depth of the information collected during some interviews – those of people who spoke most freely and most extensively – influence the overall analysis and interpretation of the data.

4.1.5 The generalizability of the results

The generalizability of the results emerging from a study is a central concern of both quantitative and qualitative research.

A common simplification of the discussion attributes to the application of rigorous sampling and statistical tests, the generalizability of quantitative findings. While this assumption may hold true for studies exploring biological and chemical mechanisms, it is unlikely to hold true for studies focusing on understanding human behaviour. Even if measured with the highest degree of accuracy, the socio-economic characteristics which constitute the focus of much social science research are likely to play out in very different manners depending on the context under analysis. Therefore, a comprehensive evaluation of the concept of generalizability cannot be based exclusively on "the law of statistics", but also needs to rely on the researcher's interpretation and judgement of the findings. In turn, the latter are informed by the researcher's knowledge of the problem at stake and the context within which the problem is inscribed (Rothman and Greenland 1998). The essential element is to distinguish conditions that are relevant from conditions that are irrelevant to generalization. While statistical testing may be sufficient to generalise results to the source population, the researcher's and the reader's judgement are necessary to generalise results beyond the source population, discussing their relevance in other settings.

Similarly, qualitative researchers refer to the relevance of their findings beyond the study population more in terms of extrapolation than generalization. They generally refute the idea that the relevance of a given set of findings can be defined exclusively in terms of statistical and probabilistic considerations, and rather prefer to rely on their judgement of whether findings may be applicable under similar, although not identical, situations (Patton 1990). In their discussion of grounded theory, Glaser and Strauss (1967) argued that the applicability of rigorous scientific methods, first among all theoretical sampling, enhances the researcher's ability to develop theoretical knowledge starting from empirical data, allowing for a discussion of the relevance of the findings beyond the study population.

In the light of this discussion, we trust that our findings are relevant to understanding the decision to enrol in CHI in similar rural and semi-rural settings both within and beyond the boundary of Burkina Faso. Our approach to consider enrolment in CHI as a household decision is coherent both with previous research (Atim and Madjiguene 2000; Chee et al. 2002; Criel and Waelkens 2003; Jütting 2004; Osei-Akoto 2004; Schneider and Diop 2004) and with the reality of most sub-Saharan settings, where the allocation of economic resources is decided at the household rather than at the individual level (Sauerborn 1994). Likewise, we trust that in most African societies, the household head remains the person in charge of making most decisions on behalf of his/her household. We leave it to the reader, however, to judge whether our household approach is relevant to the specific setting where he/she may be working. We acknowledge the possibility that our analysis of the decision to enrol in CHI may not be relevant to understanding social behaviour in relation to schemes which do not target whole households, but only a sub-portion of the population (such as schemes open exclusively to micro-credit holders, to cotton producers, and/or to women working in the informal sector).

We trust that the results of our study can be generalised beyond the specific context since the Nouna Health District is not dissimilar from many other rural and semi-rural health districts in sub-Saharan Africa. While the specific conditions of health service provision may differ across districts, it is true that in Burkina Faso, like in many other sub-Saharan countries, government facilities remain the exclusive providers of health services in many remote rural areas. In addition, we can assume that rural populations across the continent rely on the very same subsistence agriculture which constitutes the main economic activity in the Kossi Province. Likewise, in most instances, as documented extensively in the literature, rural populations across Africa suffer from the same diseases and face similar problems of access to care (Ensor and Cooper 2004; Hjortsberg 2003; Hutton 2004; Korte et al. 1992; Sauerborn 1994; Stierle et al. 1999; Wagstaff 2002). The religious and ethnic composition clearly differs across provinces and across countries, making it difficult to generalise the higher enrolment of the Bwaba recorded in the Nouna Health District. Our findings on the impact of ethnicity, however, represent a warning sign, encouraging policy-makers across the continent to be aware of how responses to a new health initiative may not be homogenous even within a restricted region. Similar differences, due to ethnicity, religion, and culture, are likely to emerge elsewhere and need to be adequately addressed in policy-making.

One of our essential duties as researchers is to provide the reader with all the details necessary to understand the context within which we conducted our researcher. We leave it to the reader to judge whether certain elements of our context make it possible to generalise our findings also to urban areas and to low and middle income countries beyond the African continent.

4.2 The discussion of the results

The discussion of the findings jointly draws from the quantitative and the qualitative analysis. We have organised the discussion of the findings in such a way as to reflect the themes addressed in the conceptual framework presented at the very beginning of the methods chapter. The strict division which guided the presentation of the results in the previous chapter will be abandoned in favour of an approach which facilitates meaningful discussion by integrating findings that emerged at different points during the analytical process. The interpretation of our findings is in fact possible only if we consider all relevant elements at once, balancing quantitative and qualitative results in the light of the broader context within which our research was set. In order to facilitate the contextual understanding of our analysis, we will often refer to the case of specific communities. This will help elucidate the interaction between individual, household and community characteristics.

4.2.1 The contextual nature of the decision making process

The very first statement we make in our conceptual framework regards the contextual nature of the decision-making process concerning membership in CHI. We argue that households deciding whether or not to enrol in CHI weigh costs and benefits of membership not only in terms of total expected utility, but also in the light of the wider socio-cultural circumstances within which the decision-making process takes place. The argument which constitutes the point of departure of our theoretical framework, recognises that the estimation of utility is shaped by social and cultural factors beyond those traditionally identified by analyses of demand for health insurance grounded exclusively on expended utility theory (Hopkins and Kidd 1996; Liu and Chen 2002; Manning and Marquis 1996; Marquis and Long 1995; Propper 1989; Propper 1993; Wolfe and Goddeeris 1991). Findings from both the quantitative and the qualitative analysis provided empirical evidence in support of our theoretical argument.

4.2.1.1 Leadership

In the in-depth interviews, respondents repeatedly referred to the role of leaders in shaping community perceptions regarding the benefits of the newly implemented scheme, often attributing their choice to enrol to the encouragement received by their *délégué*. The respondents' comments, described in detail in the previous chapter, were strengthened by the simple observation that the highest enrolment rates were registered in the four communities where the *délégué* had joined the scheme at the very beginning of the enrolled campaign: Labarani, Lékuy, Dembéléla, and Boron.

The link identified between the decision to enrol and the explicit commitment of community leaders may at first be difficult to understand if one does not consider the collective orientation of communities in sub-Saharan Africa (Wladarsch 2003). Research on insurance purchase in high-income countries has never reflected on the role of leadership, because it assumes that individuals make decisions independently without holding as an example the choice of their mayor or of their prime minister. This view, however, fails to recognise that the enrolment of the village leader reproduces an effect similar to the one produced by advertisement in wealthier societies. In high income countries, commercials broadcasted on television make frequent use of "testimonials", well-known people who claim to like and use a certain product. The public is induced to purchase the given product because it transfers to the manufacturer of the product the trust granted to the testimonial. Alternatively, the public is induced to buy the product simply out of a desire to imitate the behaviour of a person who, possessing the attributes many wish to possess, has become a role model. In the African context, the enrolled leader, in our specific case the *délégué,* becomes the "testimonial" of the new initiative. The hierarchical structure of traditional African societies and the closely knitted nature of social interactions further enhance the symbolic value of the enrolment of leaders. Feeling the authority of the leader, trusting that he can better judge new initiatives, and wishing to imitate his behaviour are all elements likely to encourage many households in the community to enrol.

Our findings indicate that the positive domino effect which follows the enrolment of community leaders is further advanced if, in addition to simply being enrolled, leaders also become active in promoting the new initiative. In this case in fact, given the respect due to their leaders, households may also feel the additional pressure to comply with the advice received and choose to enrol in CHI. In the village if Boron, for example, people indicated having joined the scheme following the advice of their leader. As described in the previous chapter, trusting the leader's judgement allowed people to immediately trust the insurance scheme.

4.2.1.2 Knowledge

Communities where leaders enrolled and showed interest in the new initiatives were also the communities where people experienced the most conducive environment to the acquisition of adequate knowledge on the scheme. We have already noted in the results chapter, how all interviewees in the villages of Lékuy and Boron reported having received information on the scheme directly by their leaders. Villages where the leaders themselves were sceptical of CHI experienced exactly the opposite conditions. In the village of Koro, for example, we happened to interview as a non-enrolee the *délégué*. In spite of his attempt not to display his resistance to the scheme overtly, it was obvious from his comments as well as from his overall attitude that he was very sceptical of the scheme and that he had shared his opinion with others in the community. We later learned from the AMBC management unit that the *délégué* in Koro had actively discouraged his community from participating in the sensitisation activities organised to promote awareness of the scheme. The four communication and sensitisation events organised in Koro were the most poorly attended in the whole region. This explains why, weeks later while conducting our research, we recorded in Koro some of the lowest knowledge levels observed in the region. Interestingly, the enrolled households in Koro were not indigenous to the village, but were Bwaba families having moved to a predominately Dafing village for reasons of work. Thus, they most probably enrolled in the AMBC because they did not intimately recognise the authority of the local *délégué* nor necessarily identified themselves with the attitudes of the wider community.

Our results also indicate that even in villages where the leaders take an active stand in promoting enrolment, traditionally discriminated groups, in our specific case the *griots*, may still not be involved in the village activities to the extent necessary to secure the acquisition of adequate knowledge on CHI. Both *griotte* women claiming that they had not been informed of the new initiative came in fact from villages, Lékuy and Sobon, with some of the highest enrolment rates and where community leaders had actively promoted the AMBC. From the comments generated during a FGD conducted in the village of Lékuy, we also learned that leaders may privilege the distribution of information among their own ethnic group rather than among the village at large. Respondents reported that in Lékuy, the activism of the *délégué*, who was also elected to be the president of the local AMBC committee, focused on the Bwaba, largely neglecting promotion of the scheme among the Mossi minority. Given that African societies are often not homogenous, similar circumstance are likely to be reproduced across settings, considerably hampering enrolment.

Our extended discussion of the role of leaders in promoting knowledge rests on the assumption, also outlined in our theoretical framework, that knowledge of the scheme operations and entitlements constitutes an essential element for the informed estimation of the costs and benefits of membership. Consistent with prior research (Criel and Waelkens 2003), our study reveals that poorly informed respondents tend to focus on the cost of enrolment, rather than to balance this cost against the future benefit of accessing care free of charge and of protecting their assets from potentially catastrophic health spending. In spite of understanding the general concept of insurance, respondents could often not assess the benefit of membership because they had incomplete, and at times even erroneous, information on the specific elements of the scheme (e.g. benefit package, managerial structure, providers' network). Given the collective orientation of traditional societies, we recognise as essential the role of leaders in promoting an environment conducive to the transfer of knowledge across people.

We recognise, however, that the acquisition of adequate knowledge is obviously not only a function of the social context, and specifically of the leaders' activism, but also a function of the tools developed to market the scheme and promote enrolment. It is plausible to assume that the generalised poor knowledge we witnessed regarding the specific elements of the AMBC may also be partly attributable to the use of promotion and marketing tools, which, in spite of the much care with which they were designed, might have not been sufficient to capture the attention of the community and allow households to retain the information needed. We have, however, no element to discuss critically the tools employed during the first communication and sensitisation campaign. The evaluation of the tools was not explicitly addressed during our interviews, since it constituted the focus of a separate study. In addition, the respondents did not mention any overt criticism regarding the conduct of the sensitisation campaign, making it impossible for us to provide any scientific evidence on the link between the tools used and the resulting level of knowledge.

The link between poor knowledge and decision not to enrol in CHI has been discussed before in the literature. Prior discussion, however, attributed lack of interest in CHI to an information deficit which was defined as the complete unawareness of CHI and its functioning (Meessen et al. 2002). Our findings indicate that the concept of information deficit needs to be expanded to include incomplete knowledge of a scheme components. Other than an attempt by Chee et al. (2002), previous research in sub-Saharan Africa did not systematically explore the link between enrolment in CHI and the specific knowledge of the scheme benefits. Similarly, the theme has also not been widely addressed in the literature on insurance purchase in high income settings. McCall's analysis of demand for long-term care insurance in the United States represents a unique attempt to model the effect of knowledge of long-term care on the decision to purchase the relevant insurance coverage (McCall et al. 1997; McCall et al.

1998). Her model identified a positive association between knowledge of benefits and insurance purchase. Although derived exclusively from qualitative analysis, our findings seem to confirm that knowledge of benefits is an important element shaping the decision to enrol. In addition, our findings indicate that the leaders play a key role in promoting knowledge. Although Criel and Waelkens (2003) rightfully point out that knowledge alone does not secure enrolment, our study clearly suggests that access to information remains an essential empowering tool, the only one securing that households can reach an informed decision, adequately balancing the costs and benefits of CHI membership.

4.2.1.3 Scepticism and trust

As interviewees themselves reported, poor knowledge of the scheme components may foster sentiments of scepticism. In line with previous research (Atim and Madjiguene 2000; Criel and Waelkens 2003), we found that scepticism discourages enrolment in CHI. Similarly to what Criel and Waelkens observed in Guinea-Conakry (2003), scepticism in our study was expressed in terms of a generalised feeling that the AMBC may not be able to secure the benefits it promises to deliver. Households that do not fully understand the concept and function of pooling, may have comprehensible difficulties to trust the prospect of free health care provision. Unlike Atim's findings in the Nkoranza District (2000), our results highlight that scepticism is not necessarily linked to the belief that a third agent is purposely profiting from the insurance scheme. In some instances, such as in the case of the Nouna Health District, scepticism is rather nurtured by a generalised disbelief, in turn nurtured by a poor understanding of the concept of risk pooling, that the insurance management will have the capacity to purchase free access to care with the limited resources gathered through the payment of the individual premium.

Also in line with the research by Criel and Waelkens (2003), our findings suggest that scepticism is fostered not only by poor knowledge of the institutional set up of the scheme, but also by previous bad experiences with collective arrangements. Rural societies are likely to mistrust new initiatives because they doubt their institutional capacity to follow through in case of fraud (Meessen et al. 2002) and are therefore reluctant to invest their limited resources unless they have proof of a concrete return. Our findings clearly indicate that the comparison between the insurance scheme and previous failed collective arrangements discourages households from enrolling. The "sit and wait" attitude displayed by many interviewees can be explained in the light of regret theory (Salkeld et al. 2000; Smith 1996). The choice to join the scheme may prove not to match the expectations of the household, causing the household head to experience additional intangible costs linked to later regretting the decision made. In addition, the choice not to enrol may be induced by the fear that, should the insurance fail, enrolled households will face the scorn of more prudent households among their community.

The interviewees' responses indicated that in the case of the Nouna Health District sentiments of scepticism were also fostered by the providers, who channelled their resistance to the implementation of the scheme towards actively discouraging communities from enrolling. As described in the introduction, although initially resistant to signing the contract with the AMBC, providers, under the pressure of higher health authorities, signed the agreement with the insurance scheme and accepted to be paid on a capitation basis. The interviewees' responses, however, clearly indicated that beyond the appearance of a peaceful collaboration with the scheme, providers actively attempted to boycott the new initiative. Given the generalised low literacy level, negative comments on the part of a few educated people in a community can easily influence opinions on a newly emerging scheme and subsequently, the decision to enrol. Across sub-Saharan Africa in fact, nurses are often perceived as authorities within the community. Although people frequently criticise the nurses' work, they still respect their views which, in the light of a higher educational status, they often judge to be superior to their own. In addition, it is plausible to assume that when facing overt providers' resistance to a scheme, people may prefer not to enrol out of fear of not receiving adequate treatment should they later fall sick.

At first sight, the fact that overt resistance on the part of providers has not been documented in earlier analyses of enrolment in CHI appears surprising. One must consider though, that with the exception of the Maliando scheme in Guinea-Conakry (Criel and Waelkens 2003), all research on enrolment in CHI has so far primarily focused on the experience of provider-based schemes (Atim and Madjiguene 2000; Moens 1990; Osei-Akoto 2004) or schemes initiated within the framework of wider government re-structuring policies (Chee et al. 2002; Schneider and Diop 2004). In spite of the different ownership of the intervention, however, it is hardly possible to believe that no conflict has ever emerged even within provider-based schemes. It is easy to imagine that even within one single health facility, some providers may have been in favour of CHI, while others may have feared and actively resisted its implementation, exactly in the same manner as what observed in the Nouna Health District. In the light of this straightforward consideration, we can safely postulate the hypothesis that what conflict has emerged within provider-based schemes has always been resolved within the health team. Providers, maybe fearful of constituting the target of research, might have also been careful enough not to let information about potential conflicts leak out to the scientific community.

On the other hand, the scientific community, including our own research team, seems to have devoted only marginal attention to the study of providers. This may also not be the result of an explicit decision, but rather the product of a generalised attitude towards locating the problem of low enrolment only at the level of the community. The scientific focus has rested on understanding community attitudes towards CHI and household determinants of enrolment. This approach ignores the fact that providers are themselves stakeholders of an insurance scheme, and fails to capture the influence of their behaviour on the decision to enrol. In addition, given their comparatively high education and their social standing, granting them authority over other people, they constitute a very special constituency within the community. Understanding their attitudes and their behaviours is therefore central to understanding factors shaping the decision to enrol or not to enrol in CHI in the community at large.

Yet another explanation for the little attention paid to the study of providers' attitudes and behaviours may be linked to the fact that, although witnessing overt resistance, communities may simply be unwilling to discuss it openly. Thus, it may be difficult to even notice the problem. We were startled by the fact that comments regarding the providers' boycott of the scheme were the only ones that respondents wished to report once the tape-recorder was switched off. Although respondents recognised that there existed no direct link between the interviewers and the providers, their choice seems to suggest that they feared to suffer negative consequences because of their comments. It is not possible to judge with certainty what the respondents might have feared. Still, their wish to make sure that no recording existed of their remarks on the nurses' boycott appears to be an indication of their disempowerment *vis à vis* the providers. We will return to the discussion of empowerment later in this chapter, when addressing issues pertaining to the perceived quality of the services available at the local health facilities.

In spite of much evidence in favour of the existence of a generalised sentiment of scepticism towards the new initiative, our findings also identified a core group of enrolled people who unconditionally trusted the insurance scheme. The trust granted by these people to the scheme was so strong that it could not be corroded by previous negative experiences with other collective arrangements nor by the providers' explicit resistance. We found the link that was drawn between the CRSN and the newly emerged scheme to be particularly interesting to understand unconditional trust. Although during the enrolment campaign, the AMBC Management Unit had not made explicit its relationship to the CRSN, many people spontaneously identified the existence of a collaboration between the two institutions by simply linking the previous research conducted in the area to the implementation of the scheme. Thus, they easily transferred the trust which the CRSN has gained over the years to the newly born initiative. In particular, respondents confided in the fact that the CRSN will monitor both the work of the insurance and that of providers, ensuring that the interests of the community are protected. Our finding is consistent with previous research, having identified the importance of the "transfer of trust" within the medical profession, both in sub-Saharan Africa (Criel 1998b; Criel et al. 1998a) and in high-income settings (Mechanic 1998). Across the world, people appear to be more trustworthy of new initiatives if they can link these initiatives to well-established and recognised institutions. Our findings suggest that CHI schemes may secure higher enrolment rates by explicitly acknowledging, rather than concealing, a link to existing respected institutions.

4.2.1.4 Social norms and values

The positive association detected between Bwaba ethnicity and enrolment may also be taken to be an indication of the influence of context on the decision to enrol. The higher enrolment of the Bwaba in fact, can be interpreted as the expression of a community which promoted the AMBC more actively. Although interaction across groups is frequent, ethnicity in the study area still represents an important element of differentiation between people. The literature on the role of ethnicity in Burkina Faso describes the existence of important differences in the social norms and values regulating life within each ethnic group (Kevane and Wydick 2001). The Bwaba have consistently been found to be more open towards modernisation, with women enjoying greater emancipation than among other Burkinabè groups (Kevane and Wydick 2001). A recent study conducted specifically in the Nouna Health District found that the Bwaba were more aware of the risk of contracting HIV and more willing to accept the introduction of health interventions aimed at reducing HIV transmission in their community (Sarker et al. 2005). The greater openness of the Bwaba towards new health initiatives has traditionally been explained in terms of their education. The majority of Bwaba are in fact Christian[17] and thus, a greater proportion of their population has attended school,[18] in particular schools managed by missionaries. In our regression model, however, we controlled for the effect of education on decision to enrol. This allowed us to detect an independent effect of ethnicity, which can only be explained in terms of the different social norms and values shaping attitudes and regulating behaviour within the Bwaba community. We assume that these norms and values created an environment which was more

[17] As described in the methods chapter, we did not include religion in our regression model because of collinearity with ethnicity. More than 80% of all Bwaba included in our sample in fact, were Christian.

[18] In our sample, 35% of all Bwaba people had attended at least primary school compared to 16% of people among all other ethnic groups.

conducive to the discussion of the benefits of membership, subsequently encouraging enrolment.

Our finding detecting an independent effect of ethnicity on the decision to enrol confirms what previously observed in Senegal, where being Wolof was found to be positively associated with the probability of purchasing voluntary health insurance (Jütting 2004). Jütting, however, did not discuss the relevance of this finding in relation to the broader social norms that regulate behaviour within the community. He acknowledged the positive effect on enrolment of being Wolof, but did not postulate any reason to explain the finding. Neither Schneider (2004) nor Osei-Akoto (2004) explored the role of ethnicity or religion in shaping enrolment. In both instances, however, one could deduce that the observed effect of location on enrolment captures, at least partially, socio-cultural differences due to ethnic and/or religious identity. Similarly, Chee (2002) also justified the different enrolment rates observed across zones in the Hanang District in Tanzania at least partially in terms of socio-cultural variability in the target populations.

It is difficult to conceptualise the potential reasons for the higher enrolment of one group compared to others, which has consistently emerged across studies. One possible explanation may be linked to the level of exposure of that particular group to Western concepts and ideas. In the introductory chapter, we have described how the concept of insurance represents a departure from the African tradition of risk-sharing. Insurance requires people to pool resources across communities, bridging the gap of kin and ethnicity, and asking people to relax the assumption of reciprocity implicit in more traditional arrangements (Meessen et al. 2002; Platteau 1997; Sommerfeld et al. 2002a). It is plausible to assume that within a region, the group which has been the most exposed to Western concepts is also the group most readily willing to accept new initiatives, such as HIV testing and CHI. Through repeated exposure to Western institutions, communities may come to value the costs and benefits of such institutions differently from the rest of their community. Thus, they may be more willing to participate once such an institution, in our case health insurance, is set up in their own region.

In addition, previous exposure to the Western concept of insurance may shape risk perceptions among a community. This increases the likelihood that a community will progressively become more risk-averse and thus be more open to insurance purchase. Previous studies in the Nouna Health District have identified a greater preference for present above future consumption that what commonly observed in Western countries (Gbangou et al. 2005; Wladarsch 2003). It is plausible to assume, however, that among communities exposed to Western concepts, preferences progressively shift to become more similar to those of Europeans and North-Americans. In turn, this is likely to induce a shift in people's behaviour, encouraging investments in initiatives that require sacrificing current resources to protect households from future risks.

An alternative explanation for the higher enrolment of one group compared to all others could be linked to different conceptualisations of illness and different attitudes towards health care seeking behaviour. Discussion with the AMBC team induced us to reflect upon the fact that Christians for example, are often actively discouraged by their religious leaders from seeking the advice of traditional healers. The estimation of the costs and benefits of membership in CHI may therefore also be influenced by a religious constraint against the use of traditional care, which cannot even be considered as an alternative to Western medicine.

Understanding why a certain group may be more willing than another to enrol requires a deeper understanding of how conceptualisations of illness, perceptions of risk and vulnerability, and attitudes towards health care seeking behaviour differ across ethic and/or religious groups. Given its focus on the decision to enrol rather than specifically on any of the three above themes, our qualitative investigation was insufficient to fully illuminate our understanding of differences in enrolment due to ethnicity. One must consider that at the time when we conducted the in-depth interviews, we had no awareness of the higher odds of enrolment for the Bwaba. Therefore, we did not explicitly probe respondents to explain differences due to ethnic and/or religious identity. Similarly, prior research carried out in the study area on risk perceptions (Sommerfeld et al. 2002b) and health care seeking behaviour (Sauerborn 1994; Dong et al. 2004a) explored overall community beliefs and attitudes, without narrowing its focus exclusively on the influence of ethnicity. Therefore, given our inability to discuss our findings in the light of previous research, we can only advance hypotheses to explain the higher enrolment of one group compared to all others, but we cannot make any conclusive statement to this regard.

4.2.1.5 Cultural beliefs and saving practices

In spite of the existence of differences in social norms and values across ethnicities, our findings identified rather homogeneous saving practices and beliefs regarding saving for illness. Although the importance of cultural beliefs in relation to enrolment in CHI has been discussed extensively in the literature (Arhin 1995; Criel 1998a; Meessen et al. 2002; Platteau 1997), our study represents the first attempt to explore this link in practice. Therefore, we cannot rely on any comparison with previous qualitative or quantitative investigations of demand for health insurance in low income countries. In high-income countries, where research has been dominated by econometric modelling, no study has systematically investigated the link between cultural beliefs and the decision to purchase health insurance. Our study suggests that, across communities, cultural beliefs and current saving practices may at times constitute an important barrier to enrolment.

Our findings identified a generalised resistance towards earmarking a consistent portion of the household resources towards the exclusive consumption of one good. In the vast majority of instances, however, CHI schemes in sub-Saharan Africa offer protection exclusively against health risks. Thus, they force households to choose between enrolling and earmarking funds, and non-enrolling to maintain a certain degree of flexibility should the family face a non-health problem. It is plausible to assume that, given scarcity of resources and a common reliance on subsistence agriculture, resistance towards earmarking funds represents a common element across rural societies in sub-Saharan Africa. When weighing costs and benefits of membership, households cannot help considering that enrolment entails diverting a consistent proportion of their resources from potentially competing needs (Kahneman et al. 1991). Again, households may fear the prospect of regret should they later realise that the resources devoted to the insurance could have been spent to meet a different, but equally pressing need (Smith 1996).

In addition, we found that some people may be reluctant to enrol because of a belief that seeking to prevent illness may attract bad fate, leading to the very same illness one is attempting to prevent. Findings from the qualitative interviews draw attention to the fact that some people may erroneously perceive health insurance to be an attempt to prevent illness rather than a means of facilitating access to care given the unpredictability of illness. The belief that seeking to prevent illness may attract bad fate was observed before in the study area and explained in relation to the local etiological discourse, recognising disease as the result of a combination of physical, social, and spiritual factors (Sommerfeld et al. 2002a; Sommerfeld et al. 2002b). Sommerfeld et al. discussed how this broad conceptualisation of the causes of illness leads communities to believe that one's ability to prevent disease is limited. Attempts to overcome this limit are assumed to challenge supernatural forces and thus, they are judged to be highly inappropriate and bound to attract negative fate against the person. By highlighting the existence of a link between cultural beliefs on illness causation and the decision not to enrol, our research expands on the relevance of prior findings.

In spite of the concrete barrier to enrolment imposed by the belief that investments towards future health care consumption may attract bad fate, an encouraging element emerged from the comments of people indicating a progressive shift from old to new habits. Even rural communities in the most remote areas of sub-Saharan Africa are inevitably constantly exposed to new concepts and called, through such exposure, to reconsider practices, which do not favour financial protection and economic development. This progressive shift was obvious in the comments of several interviewees, who recognised the need to abandon ancient beliefs impeding them to earmark savings for illness and who eagerly welcomed the new initiative. History teaches us that throughout the centuries, social change and progress have most often been initiated by small groups of individuals, who have dared to divert from ancient norms to plunge into the new. It is through the initial deviation from the social norm of a small group of individuals that entire societies are brought to reconsider dominant beliefs and practices, progressively abandoning traditions that are no longer suitable to secure their successful survival in favour of new ones.

In addition, in spite of a generalised resistance towards making advanced investments for future health care consumption, communities in sub-Saharan Africa have consistently been found to recognise themselves at risk of falling sick and to be aware that the price of care represents a potential source of catastrophic spending (Atim and Madjiguene 2000; Criel et al. 1998; Sommerfeld et al. 2002b; Criel and Waelkens 2003; Meessen et al. 2003). This awareness represents an encouraging element for the successful expansion of CHI. It marks the first step towards recognising the potential benefit of health insurance and thus, to move beyond traditional saving practices and cultural beliefs on illness causation to accept enrolment in CHI.

4.2.1.6 Solidarity and risk-sharing

As discussed in the section addressing methodological considerations, our study represents an attempt to model the effect on enrolment of community characteristics, meant to capture overall attitudes towards solidarity and risk-sharing. Our findings indicated no effect on enrolment of the proportion of adult population already engaged in another formal or semi-formal risk-sharing arrangement. They did indicate, however, that the higher the socio-economic equality within a community, the higher the odds that a single household will choose to enrol in CHI. Interestingly, the strength of the observed association increased substantially after controlling for household head and household characteristics, which confounded the true value of the community effect. The results of the regression model were reflected in the simple observation that the three villages with the highest levels of socio-economic equality, Lékuy, Boron, and Dembéléla, were also the three villages where enrolment was the most successful, with rates indicating that 17% to 25% of the target population had chosen to enrol in the scheme. To be noted that the overall level of wealth differed remarkably across these three communities, so it is not to say that the villages experiencing the lowest level of socio-economic inequality were also the wealthiest. For instance, median household six-month expenditure was 26 600 CFA in Boron, 72 700 CFA in Lékuy, and 656 649 CFA in Dembéléla.

Previous investigations of demand for voluntary health insurance did not consider the role of socio-economic inequality on the decision to enrol. There is, however, a wealth of literature having explored the impact of socio-economic inequality on health status. These studies usually explain the link between socio-economic inequality and health status in relation mainly to two factors (Daly et al. 1998; Ross et al. 2000; Veenstra 2005). First, an equitable distribution of resources across a community may be due to a set of institutional processes which are representative of a political interest to promote the well-being of all people, also through direct investment in health-related infrastructures. Second, an equitable distribution of resources may influence a person's view of the social environment, affecting social cohesion and perceptions of fairness, elements which in turn hold a positive effect on health.

Much of the wisdom which has emerged from previous research linking socio-economic inequality and health status can be applied to understanding the observed link between socio-economic inequality and enrolment in CHI. Given our focus on the micro-level, however, it is unlikely that we can attribute equitable distribution of resources to political and institutional processes measured, as commonly done, at the national or regional level. All the 15 locations included in our study in fact, were subject to the same political jurisdiction, with no institutional differences in the investments made across communities.

It is plausible to assume, however, that although unable to influence wider political and institutional processes linked to the establishment of health infrastructures, the leaders of the single communities are generally able to influence village activities and subsequently, the distribution of resources within their community. Linking our current argument with what previously discussed concerning the role of leaders, we note that the three villages with the lowest levels of socio-economic inequality all had leaders who promptly joined the AMBC and who actively promoted enrolment among others in their community. The leadership they assumed on the occasion of the launch of the CHI scheme is likely to be the same leadership they assumed in previous occasions while coordinating village activities, always fostering risk-sharing and equitable distribution of resources among their community. In turn, prior experience with sharing resources to achieve lower levels of inequality is likely to forge social cohesion and long-term perceptions of fairness, creating an environment which is more conducive to the introduction of new risk-sharing arrangements, among which CHI. It is reasonable to assume that households living in communities which are more used to sharing resources, are simply more willing to easily welcome a new initiative that favours additional risk-sharing.

The fact that we did not observe an effect on enrolment of the percentage of adults in other formal or semi-formal risk-sharing arrangements is an indication of the fact that communities which achieve low levels of socio-economic inequality, do not necessarily do so through the establishment of formal and semi-formal arrangements. It is plausible to assume that communities that achieve low levels of socio-economic inequality do so through informal mechanisms linked to the ancient African tradition of risk-sharing (Besley 1995; Dercon 2002; Platteau 1997; Sommerfeld et al. 2002a; Weinberger 2000) rather than through institutionalised arrangements. Therefore, contrary to our original hypothesis, our findings suggest that it is not necessarily previous experience with institutionalised risk-sharing arrangements that favours enrolment in CHI, but rather a more generalised attitude towards sharing resources with others in the community, which is *per se* an expression of social cohesion and solidarity. In line with findings from previous research (Criel and Waelkens 2003), the comments collected during the in-depth interviews suggested, as discussed earlier in this chapter, that personal experience with institutionalised collective arrangements may discourage rather than promote enrolment in CHI, by eroding trust in such arrangements.

It is important to note here that two previous studies identified a link between membership in another risk-sharing arrangement and the decision to join CHI (Jowett 2003; Jütting 2004). Differences between our findings and prior research are probably attributable to the fact that while we measured participation in other risk-sharing arrangements at the group level, prior studies measured it at the individual level. Different measurements entail shifts in the focus of the analysis and capture different effects. Group measurements allow to derive a proxy of overall community attitudes towards risk-sharing and solidarity, while individual measurements capture the influence of the prior risk-sharing experience of the single household head. Ideally, given that different measurements describe different effects, models of demand for health insurance in low-income settings should include both individual-level and group-level indicators of participation in risk-sharing. In our case, however, given the incompleteness of the relevant module, we were unable to derive individual level estimates. Therefore, we cannot exclude the possibility that, if measured at the individual level, we would have also observed an effect of participation in another risk-sharing arrangement on the decision to enrol.

The contribution of our findings to the literature reaches beyond the already relevant finding of detecting an effect of socio-economic inequality on the decision to enrol in CHI. On the one hand in fact, previous research on socio-economic inequality and health status did not attempt to explain the link between the two in terms of the role that the former may have in mediating decisions about health care consumption (Daly et al. 1998; Ross et al. 2000; Veenstra 2005). On the other hand, both in high and low income settings, studies on health care seeking behaviour have not investigated the effect of socio-economic inequality on health service utilisation, restricting the analysis exclusively to individual and household level socio-economic indicators (Cameron et al. 1988; Chang and Trivedi 2003; Dong et al. 2004a; Harmon and Nolan 2001; Hjortsberg 2003; Magadi et al. 2000; Pokhrel and Sauerborn 2004). Our study indicates instead, that the level of socio-economic inequality influences household decisions concerning health care consumption. As described in the introductory chapter, health insurance is not desired *per se*, but rather as a means of securing access to health services (Arrow 1963). Therefore, there is reason to believe that socio-economic inequality is likely to influence decision to enrol in CHI not only because it captures overall attitudes towards risk-sharing and solidarity, as described above, but also because of its underlying influence on decisions concerning health care consumption. Low levels of socio-economic inequality can be treated to be an expression of social capital, defined in terms of social cohesion, which is likely to facilitate access to services, through active sharing of both information and resources. Unfortunately, given the lack of empirical data on the relationship between socio-economic inequality and demand for health care, we cannot confirm the veracity of our argument. If our assumption proved to be true, however, we could expand current theoretical arguments on the role of socio-economic inequality to explain the observed impact on health status also in terms of increased access to health services.

4.2.2 Health status and health care seeking behaviour

4.2.2.1 Adverse selection

In our theoretical framework, we postulate that the household head weighs costs and benefits of enrolment against the illness experience and prior health care seeking behaviour of his/her household. In practice, the qualitative interviews suggested that people having faced a recent high health care spending were more prone to enrol in the AMBC. The quantitative analysis, however, did not confirm this finding as it detected no evidence of adverse selection in the scheme. The regression model in fact, identified no association between enrolment and health status nor prior health service utilisation. The association between enrolment and health status identified in the univariate analysis disappeared as soon as we controlled for socio-economic status, indicating that the former was confounded by the latter. Likewise, the regression model identified no association between enrolment and previous use of preventive health services.

In the section on methodological considerations, we have already addressed how the apparent inconsistency between the qualitative and the quantitative findings may be partly due to the adopted measurements, as in the household survey we did not include a suitable indicator of health spending. It is also plausible, however, to assume that what adverse selection could potentially have taken place at the individual level was effectively counteracted by compulsory household enrolment. During an in-depth interview, enrolled individuals, feeling that they had to justify their decision to join the scheme, might have been more likely to easily recall recent events of severe illness and high health care spending. In the regression model, however, aggregating information on health status and health service utilisation at the household level allowed the individual illness experience to be balanced against that of the entire family, proving that no adverse selection took place at the household level. In addition, regression modelling allowed to control for socio-economic status. This was obviously impossible when analysing the transcribed text of the in-depth interviews.

Our findings are consistent with previous research conducted in sub-Saharan Africa (Jütting 2004; Osei-Akoto 2004; Schneider and Diop 2004). Although the notion of adverse selection receives extensive attention in the theoretical discussion on insurance (Folland et al. 2001), there is paucity of evidence in favour of its existence emerging from applied research both in low and in high income settings. Our review of the literature identified only three studies having detected evidence of adverse selection (Phelps 1973; Browne 1992; Hopkins and Kidd 1996). Only the earliest of the three studies (Phelps 1973), however, included in its model a measure of health status as such. The other two studies justified their claim in favour of the existence of adverse selection either in relation to the timing of the last contact with a physician (Hopkins and Kidd 1996) or in relation to modelling projections indicating that low-risk individuals buy more insurance coverage in group-markets than they would otherwise demand in individual-markets (Browne 1992). All other studies explicitly including in their models a direct measure of health status detected no effect or a negative effect of health status on health insurance purchase (Cameron et al. 1988; Ettner 1997; McCall et al. 1998; Propper 1989; Propper 1993; Shmueli 1998; Wilcox-Gok and Rubin 1994; Wolfe and Goddeeris 1991).

Across studies in high income settings, the absence of adverse selection is generally attributed to underwriting practices that effectively limit insurance purchase on the part of the very sick. Our findings indicate that, even in contexts with limited managerial capacity to design and handle complex underwriting procedures, simple measures, such as household enrolment and the imposition of a waiting period, can successfully be employed to limit adverse selection. The experience of the Nkoranza scheme, however, clearly indicates that without rigorous checks, families can easily bypass the imposition of household enrolment (Atim and Madjiguene 2000; Osei-Akoto 2004). In the case of the

Nouna Health District, compliance with household enrolment was secured by the existence of DSS records, which allowed the AMBC team to perform systematic checks on the number of members enrolled within a household. In schemes which are confined to a small community, compliance with household enrolment can be secured through active social control (Fonteneau 2000). The difficulty, as shown by the Ghanaian experience, is to secure compliance with household enrolment for schemes that address entire districts, but that cannot rely on continuously updated extensive demographic information, such as those provided by a DSS.

4.2.2.2 Perceived effectiveness of modern health services and traditional care

An encouraging element emerging from our research is the overall appreciation for the effectiveness of modern medical care. Low demand for CHI in sub-Saharan Africa could simplistically be attributed to a preference for traditional rather than modern medical services. In line with previous findings both in the study area (Dong et al. 2004a; Mugisha et al. 2002b), and elsewhere in the continent (Gilson 1997; Gilson et al. 2000; Hutton 2004), our findings indicate that, for common conditions such as malaria and respiratory-tract infections, most people prefer modern medical services. Because of lack of means, however, they often resort to alternative treatment options. In line with previous research (Criel et al. 1998; Criel and Waelkens 2003), our findings indicate that communities in sub-Saharan are potentially receptive to the implementation of CHI, valued to be a means of facilitating access to the preferred health care provider. This propensity to appreciate CHI and the medical services to which CHI grants access represents an important element encouraging enrolment.

A generalised preference for modern medical services does not imply that communities do not value the indigenous healing tradition. The in-depth interviews revealed in fact that people, across communities, trust traditional folk remedies and have a clear sense of the extent of their effectiveness. In addition, they tend to make a distinction between the conditions that can be treated by biomedicine and those that can be treated by a healer. The identification of this distinction re-occurs in the literature on health care seeking behaviour across the continent and is often explained in relation to socio-cultural constructions on the aetiology of diseases (Mariko and Cisse 2000; Oberlander and Elverdan 2000; Samuelsen 2004; Sommerfeld et al. 2002b). Prior research in the study area indicated that people trust biomedicine to be effective in treating: (1) symptomatic disorders, such as bodily aches, cough, diarrhoea, fever; (2) widely known diseases, such as *soumaya* (malaria) and schistosomiasis; and (3) problems needing surgical intervention, such as hernia and wounds. Conditions that also entail a psychological component or are believed to be the product of supernatural forces, are more likely to be reported to a traditional healer (Sommerfeld et al. 2002b). Therefore, the marketing of CHI is likely to be most effective insofar as it builds on local theories of causation, primarily offering coverage of those conditions that communities expect biomedicine to be able to treat. Offering coverage for conditions that the population does not traditionally report to a modern health facility is unlikely to motivate enrolment.

The results of the regression model indicated the existence of important differences between enrolees and non-enrolees with regard to the judgment on the adequacy of the care provided by substitute providers, i.e. traditional healers. The association between enrolment and this judgement was the strongest detected in our model. This finding clearly suggests that prior considerations about the adequacy of treatment by substitute health care providers can significantly influence the decision to enrol in CHI.

At first sight, this observation may appear to contradict the findings from the qualitative research and from previous studies, indicating that people in sub-Saharan Africa resort alternatively to biomedicine and to traditional healing. This apparent inconsistency between the qualitative and the quantitative findings, however, can be explained in relation to the data collection method. While a survey questionnaire forces people to condense their judgement in one single numerical value, qualitative interviews allow people to explain provider choice, balancing provider preferences against considerations on the affordability and the adequacy of a given treatment option. Forcing people to decide on one unique value allowed us to simplify the matter and quantify differences in judgement that would have otherwise escaped a purely qualitative analysis. At the same time, having discussed directly with people the details of treatment preferences, we were able to evaluate critically the quantitative findings and understand that even those having expressed a negative judgement on the adequacy of the healer's treatment, may at times resort to his services if they perceive them to be better suited to treat a given condition. Both our qualitative findings and prior research (Sauerborn 1994; Dong et al. 2004a) in fact, suggested that the preference for a certain provider is not absolute, but rather influenced by considerations on cash availability as well as the typology and severity of the disease.

In addition, one must consider that having judged as adequate the healer's care does not necessarily entail that the individual will systematically choose the healer as his/her preferred provider. The judgement on adequacy can also be made out of the respect which is due to local healers, without necessarily representing health provider preferences, at least not in all instances. The fact that a large portion (over 50%) of non-enrolled individuals judged the care provided by traditional healers not to be adequate is in line with our overall argument against the claim that low enrolment in CHI is purely an expression of a distinct preference for traditional systems of care. Although these people were likely to prefer treatment at modern facilities, they still chose not to enrol in the AMBC. Our findings provide empirical evidence in support of the argument advanced in the literature (Meessen et al. 2002), indicating that prior considerations about the adequacy of treatment by substitute health care providers inevitably influence decision to enrol in CHI, but are by no means a unique determinant of participation in a scheme.

4.2.3 Affordability

4.2.3.1 Socio-economic status

In our conceptual framework, we outline how socio-economic status is likely to affect the decision to enrol in CHI. Evidence from the quantitative analysis supported our theoretical argument and indicated the existence of a strong positive association between enrolment and household socio-economic status. The higher the socio-economic status, the higher the odds that a household had enrolled in the AMBC. In line with the argument postulated in our conceptual framework, both our qualitative and our quantitative findings suggest that poor households may simply be unable to enrol in CHI, even if potentially interested in the benefits of membership. Contrary to what we would have expected, however, we did not observe a decline in the odds of enrolment among the wealthiest households. The theoretical argument that very wealthy households may prefer self-insurance, i.e. coverage through individual savings, to institutional insurance (Shea and Stewart 1995) was contradicted by our findings, indicating that the odds of enrolment were actually the highest among the richest group.

Our findings are in line with most of the evidence emerging from studies conducted both in sub-Saharan Africa (Jütting 2004; Osei-Akoto 2004) and in high income settings (Cameron et al. 1988; Ettner 1997; Harmon and Nolan 2001; Henderson et al. 1995; Hopkins and Kidd 1996; Liu and Chen 2002; Paulin and Dietz 1995; Propper 1989; Propper et al. 1999; Shmueli 1998; Wilcox-Gok and Rubin 1994; Wolfe and Goddeeris 1991). Only three studies on demand for health insurance presented different results with regard to the role of socio-economic status. Two studies identified a non-linear association between socio-economic status and health insurance purchase, indicating that the wealthiest may prefer self-insurance to institutionalised coverage (McCall et al. 1998; Shea and Stewart 1995). In both instances, the result are likely to be influenced by the exclusive focus of the analysis, centred solely on the purchase of additional health insurance coverage among the retired population of the United States. Among studies conducted in sub-Saharan Africa, only Schneider and Diop (2004) found no effect of household socio-economic status on the decision to enrol in CHI. They attributed the lack of association between socio-economic status and enrolment to rather homogenous conditions of generalised poverty. The fact that they did not present mean values for the four income groups included in their analysis, however, induces us to challenge this claim. We find it plausible to attribute their inability to detect an effect of socio-economic status on enrolment to their sampling strategy rather than uniquely to a generalised context of poverty. Schneider and Diop in fact, adopted the same sampling frame as the standard DHS routinely conducted in Rwanda, carrying out their analysis on a sample of 2518 households, of which only 181 enrolled in CHI. Given the low enrolment rate, participation in CHI could have been treated as a rare outcome, requiring the application of differential sampling fractions, which would have probably allowed for greater efficiency and accuracy in the estimation of the model (Cosslett 1981; Beaglehole et al. 1993; Jowett 2003; Propper 1989). This approach might have proved to be more suitable to identify significant relationships between socio-demographic characteristics and enrolment in CHI which are likely to have escaped their analysis.

4.2.3.2 Payment modalities

The qualitative analysis allowed us to decompose the issue of affordability beyond the mere effect of socio-economic status on the decision to enrol. We were able to identify a series of elements, other than socio-economic status itself, that limited the affordability of the new initiative: (1) an erroneous timing of the enrolment campaign; (2) restrictions in payment modalities; and (3) a definition of household which did not suit the reality of everyday decision-making. We identified the existence of a contingent group of households who would have been willing and able to enrol if only the AMBC institutional set up had allowed for greater flexibility of payment. The findings emerging from the qualitative analysis were reflected in the results of the regression model. We noticed in fact that while the odds of enrolment were much higher among the wealthiest group, they were set at very similar values for the two middle income groups. This indicates that the relationship between enrolment and socio-economic status was not linear. In between the very poor and the very rich, there was a large group of people for whom affordability was not only a function of socio-economic status, but also of specific institutional conditions favouring or hampering enrolment. Our findings provide empirical evidence for the theoretical argument advanced by Ahuja and Jütting (2003), which postulates that institutional rigidities constitute a greater barrier to enrolment than poverty *per se.* Our findings are in line with two previous qualitative investigations, exploring the impact on demand for CHI of the timing of the campaign (Atim and Madjiguene 2000) and of the definition of household which guides enrolment (Criel and Waelkens 2003).

Both our study and the study by Criel and Waelkens (2003) recognise that most criticisms against restrictive payment modalities and a constraining enrolment unit emerge from large households. This finding is consistent with the argument outlined in our conceptual framework, claiming that large households may face the highest barriers to enrolment. While it is true that large households are the ones facing the highest total price, it is also true that large households are on average wealthier than others, simply because they are most likely to rely on a larger number of people of productive age. We conducted several interviews with household heads who, while claiming that they could not afford enrolment, watched their large herds leave the house court towards the field. This seems to suggest that large households do not necessarily lack the means to enrol, but that they may be resistant towards investing consistent amount of resources all at once. In line with the argument developed by Criel and Waelkens (2003), we recognise that rural societies in sub-Saharan Africa may simply be unaccustomed to the payment modality imposed by most CHI schemes in the continent, including the AMBC. Other local institutions, such as schools, associations, and micro-credit organisations, allow people to dilute payments over a longer period of time. Although the amount paid may be even higher than what is requested to enrol in CHI, diluted payments are likely to affect the perception of affordability, thus facilitating participation in an organisation.

4.2.3.3 Caring externality

An interesting element which emerged from our analysis is the existence of a caring externality. When presenting the findings, we repeatedly referred to the fact that respondents often criticised features of the scheme which, while suiting their individual needs, hampered enrolment of others in their community. Small households, for example, stated their preference towards paying the whole premium at once, but were aware that both the definition of household applied and the payment modalities prescribed severely limited the capacity of others to participate in the scheme. Thus, they put forward the same suggestions for change advanced by households who were directly affected by the particular limitation. This homogeneity in the criticisms directed against the institutional set-up of schemes pervades all prior qualitative investigations of enrolment behaviour, but so far it has never been appraised critically (Atim and Madjiguene 2000; Criel and Waelkens 2003).

At first sight, homogenous comments on the institutional set-up of a scheme could appear to indicate that, within a region, preferences are homogenous across people. This may be true, but only to a certain extent. Across sub-Saharan Africa in fact, ethnicity and religion, for example, still determine wide differences between groups, which can be expected to be reflected in their preferences. In the case of the Nouna Health District, a deeper reading into people's comments revealed that single households clearly held their own preference, but were also aware of overall community needs. Thus, they were willing to balance individual and collective wishes in such a way as to ensure that the greatest number of people could benefit from the initiative. This willingness may be explained not only in altruistic terms, but also in relation to the fact people were well aware of how the survival of the scheme depends on the extent of risk-pooling and resource mobilisation it achieves. As indicated in the previous chapter, the strongest advocates of change were often individuals who had already enrolled their households in CHI. Those were the same individuals who best understood the concept of risk-sharing and pooling entailed by insurance. Thus, it is plausible to assume that their wish to balance individual and collective preferences served the function of protecting their own households by securing the survival of the scheme through higher enrolment rates.

4.2.3.4 Respect for community preferences

An important lesson which emerged from our findings refers to the importance of systematically exploring community preferences before proceeding with designing and implementing any CHI scheme. It is inevitable to note that although not affordable for all, respondents did not criticise the premium level, which was judged to be fair given the benefits enrolled members are entitled to. The lack of criticism against the level of the premium is most probably attributable to the fact that the scheme premium was set in accordance with the results of a large WTP study which preceded the implementation of the scheme (Dong et al. 2003; Dong et al. 2004b; Dong et al. 2004c; Dong et al. 2005). WTP is widely recognised as one of the most suitable methods to explore preferences and inform subsequent policy decisions (Bridges 2003; Ryan et al. 2001). The values identified through the study informed both the overall level of the premium and the application of differential payments for adults and children. In line with prior research (Sauerborn et al. 1994; Sauerborn et al. 1996b), the WTP study detected a preference towards insuring productive members of the household above children (Dong et al. 2004c; Dong et al. 2005).

The adequacy of exploring people's preferences through WTP methods is reflected not only in the overall appreciation shown for the level of the premium, but also in the specific comments indicating how communities judged as socially and culturally appropriate the choice of setting the child premium at a third of the adult premium. The evidence emerging from the qualitative findings was corroborated by the results of the regression model, indicating that the choice of differential premiums effectively favoured the enrolment of households with larger proportions of children. Given that the ultimate public health goal of CHI is to facilitate access to care for vulnerable populations, among which the very young, the higher enrolment among households with many children obviously constitutes a very positive achievement.

Our findings clearly indicate, however, that while WTP studies can be useful to estimate the value that communities attribute to CHI, they inevitably cannot provide the information necessary to identify adequate strategies that secure the affordability of the new initiative. With their exclusive focus on monetary values, WTP studies are not suitable to explore issues concerning the timing of the campaign, the payment modalities, and the unit of enrolment. Prior to the implementation of the AMBC, community leaders were consulted on all relevant issues, but no systematic research, either qualitative or quantitative, was conducted to explore the preferences of the community at large with regard to those issues. This explains why, following the end of the first enrolment campaign, communities amply criticised some of the institutional choices which were made. In line with previous findings by Criel and Waelkens (2003), our study indicates that scheme initiators may be likely to underestimate the importance of meeting community preferences. The risk is to define a parameter of a scheme, for example household enrolment, in such a way that rather than facilitating the success of the intervention, by controlling adverse selection, it determines its very failure, by severely hampering enrolment.

4.2.4 Product characteristics

As outlined in our conceptual framework, product characteristics are expected to influence considerations regarding the potential costs and benefits of membership and thus influence enrolment. None of the quantitative studies conducted in either high income settings or in sub-Saharan Africa explicitly included product characteristics in their regression model[19]. These studies, however, generally recognise that differences in the demand for health insurance detected across regions may reflect, at least partially, differences in insurance products and health service provision (Hopkins and Kidd 1996; Jütting 2004; Liu and Chen 2002; Osei-Akoto 2004; Paulin and Dietz 1995; Propper et al. 1999; Shmueli 1998; Schneider and Diop 2004). Qualitative investigations

---

[19] As explained in the methods chapter, we did not include product characteristics in our model because the product was constant across the 15 communities included in our study.

carried out in sub-Saharan Africa have limited their investigation of the impact of product characteristics on demand for CHI to issues pertaining to the quality of care available at the contracted health facilities (Atim and Madjiguene 2000; Criel and Waelkens 2003).

In addition to the level of the premium and to the payment modalities, discussed in the section above, our study identified that the product characteristics most likely to influence the decision to enrol in the AMBC were: (1) the scheme managerial structure; (2) the benefit package; and (3) the health service provider network. In high income settings, the offer of competitors is also likely to constitute an important element influencing which insurance plan is purchased. In the case of many remote rural societies in sub-Saharan Africa, not only does CHI constitute the only alternative to out-of-pocket payments, but often the provider contracted by the scheme, is also the unique provider in the region. Thus, given the lack of alternative plans and providers, it becomes superfluous to question whether better offers by competitors are driving demand away from the scheme under study.

4.2.4.1 The scheme managerial structure

In spite of the community poor accurate knowledge regarding the specific function of the single levels of management, our findings identified a generalised appreciation for the scheme administrative structure. The fact that this appreciation was often justified in relation to local socio-cultural norms draws attention to the link that exists between the cultural sensitivity of an intervention and its potential success. In particular, people showed unanimous appreciation for the fact that an AMBC committee had been set up in each community. In spite of their inability to recall the specific responsibility of such committee, people valued its existence in relation to the fact that all other local institutions perform under similar conditions. This allowed people to recognise the AMBC as a socially and culturally sensitive institution, which, although asking to join a risk-sharing arrangement reaching beyond the boundary of kin and ethnicity, is still managed in such a way as not to divert too much from what they are already accustomed to.

In the case of the Nouna Health District, cultural sensitivity was facilitated by the fact that the scheme grew out of a partnership between European and Burkinabè researchers, policy-makers, and communities. This partnership allowed to balance considerations regarding the financial viability and sustainability of the insurance scheme with the respect for the local social and cultural context. In addition, the studies exploring traditional risk-sharing networks allowed the program initiators to gather valuable information to guide the development of a socially and culturally sensitive institutional set-up (Sommerfeld et al. 2002a). To return to the example mentioned above, the choice to establish an AMBC committee in each village/town sector was first advanced by the Burkinabè partners and later supported by the research on risk-sharing arrangements (Sommerfeld et al. 2002a). Such a choice inevitably raises the overhead costs of the scheme (local AMBC representatives receive no compensation for their work, but the AMBC absorbs the cost for their training and for travelling to attend meetings). The project initiators, however, shared the firm belief that the AMBC would be accepted and respected by the community if and only if it kept its institutional set-up as close as possible to that of existing formal risk-sharing arrangements.

Our study confirms and supports the argument put forward by Criel and Waelkens (2003) within the context of their discussion on determinants of enrolment in the Maliando scheme in Guinea-Conakry. We both conclude that integrating socially and culturally sensitive elements, borrowed from existing social institutions such as traditional risk-sharing arrangements, into CHI may determine the acceptability of the new risk-pooling arrangement and thus, positively influence the decision to enrol.

4.2.4.2 The benefit package

Our qualitative findings indicated that, in spite of incomplete and/or inaccurate knowledge on some of its details, communities in the region appreciated the benefit package, understanding that, given the limited premium, not all services could be included. Replicating what already discussed in relation to the WTP study, this lack of criticism against the benefit package reflects the importance of grounding the design of a scheme in the prior exploration of community preferences. The implementation of the AMBC was in fact preceded by an extensive study discussing with the community the inclusion and exclusion of services in the benefit package and the reasons motivating people's preferences (Kouyaté et al. 2001). Our study confirms prior findings by Kouyaté et al. (2001) indicating that, contrary to insurance theory, rural communities in sub-Saharan Africa wish to insure both high-cost low-probability events, such as surgery, and low-cost high-probability events, such as standard treatment for the most common conditions. Given seasonal cash fluctuations in fact, communities recognise that even meeting the cost of a simple malaria treatment can constitute an excessive burden for households in rural Africa. In addition, as described also in the introductory chapter, repeated illness episodes and clustering of illnesses within families further hamper access care and constantly menace households' coping capacity (Sauerborn 1994).

The choice to include both first-line and second-line services in the benefit package differentiates the experience of the AMBC from that of similar insurance arrangements in sub-Saharan Africa. Small schemes are usually centred around a first-line facility, providing exclusive access to first-line care (Fonteneau 2000; La Concertation 2004). On the other end of the spectrum, larger schemes operative at the sub-regional level offer exclusive coverage of second-line care at the district hospital (Atim 1998; Atim and Madjiguene 2000; Criel 1998b; Huber et al. 2002; Jütting 2004; Osei-Akoto 2004). In addition, the AMBC also guarantees ambulance coverage, securing the transport from the first-line to the second-line facility in case of emergency.

The inclusion of both first-line and second-line services among which emergency transport may explain, at least partially, why neither our regression model nor the in-depth interviews identified distance to the health facility as an obstacle to enrolment. This finding clearly contradicted prior evidence (Criel 1998b; Moens 1990; Schneider and Diop 2004), and suggested that the potentially negative effect of distance on enrolment can successfully be counteracted by measures, such as a comprehensive benefit package imposing no co-payments, that encourage participation even among the furthest communities. Households living far from a facility are likely to attribute greater value to the benefits of a scheme because their judgement of the costs and benefits of enrolment is inscribed within a different framework of reference than that of households living close to a facility (Kahneman et al. 1991). When care is needed in fact, households living far from a facility face additional costs, both in terms of time and transport, due to distance. Therefore, when considering enrolment in CHI, they are likely to take into account also these additional costs. Awareness of facing a higher total cost is likely to make these households more willing to engage in an initiative that alleviates at least part of their greater burden. This holds true, however, only as long as households perceive the attributes of the initiative to be attractive and sensitive to their needs. These considerations, emerging primarily from a critical interpretation of the quantitative findings, were confirmed by the fact that during the course of the in-dept interviews, respondents did not identify distance as a primary barrier to enrolment. People in fact, almost unanimously agreed on the fact that distance hampers access to care, but not necessarily enrolment in CHI.

In addition, in line with the theoretical argument developed by Nyman (1999), we also recognise that the inclusion of high-cost procedures in the AMBC benefit package may also explain the higher odds of enrolment among the wealthiest households. In spite of their relative wealth in fact, even rich people may not be able to afford extremely high-cost treatment, such as surgery. Thus, they may choose to enrol in CHI as they recognise insurance to be the only means of accessing care which would otherwise simply be unaffordable for the individual household. Wealthy households can easily cope with the cost of one malaria episode, but may experience severe difficulties if in need for surgery. Evidence in support of this argument also emerged from the qualitative interviews. None of the respondents in fact, referred to the cost of care as trivial. Even relatively wealthy respondents recognised that in case of a severe illness, the cost of care is likely to constitute an excessive burden for the household, which may not be able to cope unless substantially depleting family assets or seeking credit.

Thus, our findings indicate that a comprehensive benefit package, attractive both in the eyes of distant and relatively wealthy households, is instrumental to ensuring that different constituencies within society remain interested in enrolment, securing the large pools necessary for the survival of the scheme.

4.2.4.3 The health provider network

Our findings indicated that the structural characteristics of the referral facility did not significantly influence the decision to enrol in the AMBC. Unlike what expected, our regression model in fact, did not detect an association between enrolment and assignment to either a CSPS or the first-line facility located on the premises of the district hospital in the town of Nouna. This finding can probably be explained in relation to the completeness of the benefit package, ensuring that in case of need patients will be transported to the district facility for more specialised care.

Likewise, the qualitative findings also suggest that the imposition of a gate-keeping system, forcing people to seek care first at a first-line facility, does not necessarily discourage rural communities from enrolling in CHI. Our findings suggest that what may discourage people from enrolling is rather the lack of freedom in the choice of the first-line referral facility. The qualitative findings in fact, suggested that many people held a clear preference for one facility above all others, even if they recognised structural characteristics and the competency of staff to be equivalent across facilities[20]. Direct discussion with the community indicated that their preference was often linked to broader socio-cultural considerations and/or to judgements on the process of care, in particular the perceived quality of the provider-patient encounter. Our findings imply that

---

[20] This is not to say that the competency of staff and the quality of treatment are truly equivalent across facilities. Current research on the quality of malaria treatment indicates that important differences with regard to these two parameters exist between facilities (Somé F, Pfeiffer K, and Sauerborn R – work in progress). However, given their low literacy level and their overall poor knowledge of biomedicine, communities in the District are likely to base their judgement on evaluation criteria that do not capture such differences.

rural households in sub-Saharan Africa may not be willing to trade their preference for one specific first-line facility for the benefits of membership in CHI. Some people rather forgo enrolment than accept to change referral facility.

The lack of criticism against the gate-keeping system represents an encouraging element for the effective implementation of CHI in sub-Saharan Africa. It provides evidence that risk-management measures, such as gate-keeping, can effectively be set in place even in contexts which are new to insurance institutions. The criticism directed against the imposition of one first-line referral facility, however, indicates that such measures can be implemented with success only insofar as they remain sensitive to the preferences of the community and do not impose radical changes in health care seeking choices.

A careful reading of the transcribed text from the interviews indicated that perceptions of the quality of care did influence the decision to enrol. Our study, however, did not identify dissatisfaction with health service provision to be as much of an important element discouraging enrolment as what previously observed by Criel and Waelkens in Guinea-Conakry (2003). The difference between the two studies may be attributed to the dimensions of care which were identified as the source of the dissatisfaction in the two settings (Donabedian 1980). Our study recognized criticism almost exclusively as an expression of discontent with the process component of health care delivery, in particular with the modalities of the provider-patient encounter[21]. The study by Criel and Waelkens, instead, identified criticism as an expression of disappointment with the outcome of treatment, questioning the ability of the providers contracted by the CHI scheme to secure adequate standards of care. The different focus of the criticism among the two communities indicates that the influence on the decision to enrol of the perceived quality of health services may differ considerably across settings. Furthermore, it suggests that the impact on the decision to enrol is largely dependent upon the dimensions of care which constitute the source of dissatisfaction in each specific setting.

In addition, differences in the relationship between enrolment and the perceived quality of care may also be attributable to the timing of the two studies. The study by Criel and Waelkens (2003) focused on the analysis of the decision to

---

[21] At first, we were taken aback by the lack of criticism on structural indicators of the quality of care. Thus, we were curious to verify whether it was true that structural parameters easily observable by patients (equipment and drug supply) were comparable across facilities and met basic national standards. In both instance, we observed that the field conditions were consistent with the respondents' lack of criticism. We found that the equipment was equivalent across first-line facilities and that in 2003, the year preceding the launch of the AMBC, the District suffered almost no drug shortages, ensuring an adequate supply of medications for more than 95% of the year to all first-line facilities in the study area.

enrol two years after the launch of the scheme with considerations on the quality of services pertaining already to a post-implementation period. Similarly to what observed by Atim (2000) in Ghana, Criel and Waelkens encountered the belief that the care on offer for the insured was inferior to the care on offer for the non-insured. Our study refers exclusively to the experience with health service provision prior to the implementation of the scheme and thus, considerations on the quality of care could not yet be affected by comparative judgements on the treatment available for the insured and for the non-insured.

4.2.4.4 Community expectations and empowerment

The different timing of our investigation compared to both the study in Ghana (Atim and Madjiguene 2000) and that in Guinea-Conakry (Criel and Waelkens 2003) may also explain differences in the community discourse describing what expectations have been entrusted upon the insurance scheme. Our findings indicated that communities perceived the insurance as a means of gaining a voice *vis à vis* the providers. Respondents, especially enrolees, were hopeful that the insurance would serve as a means of empowering communities, better protecting their rights as patients, and inducing changes in the provider-patient encounter. In relation to what discussed in the paragraph above, respondents in our study did not ask for better equipped facilities or more efficacious drugs, but simply to be treated with greater respect by the providers. The study in Ghana and the study in Guinea-Conakry, both conducted a few years after the launch of the scheme, identified a link between the decision not to enrol and a generalised sense of disappointment rooted in the comparison between the original expectations the community had entrusted upon the insurance scheme and the reality of service provision which followed implementation. This element of disillusion is particularly evident in the case described by Criel and Waelkens (2003), where enrolment rates rapidly declined as soon as the community perceived the insurance scheme to be unable to meet their original expectations to produce substantial improvements in the quality of health service provision.

Jointly appraising the findings of our own study with those by Criel and Waelkens (2003) and by Atim (2000) allows us to draw broader conclusions on the relationship between the decision to enrol and the quality of health service provision. All three studies indicate that rural communities in sub-Saharan Africa can easily identify the specific problems which pertain to health care provision in their particular setting. Although the origin of the dissatisfaction may differ across regions, communities unanimously recognise CHI as an opportunity to improve health service provision by empowering patients *vis à vis* their providers. The launching of CHI increases people's expectations, inducing communities to trust that CHI will lead to those quality changes they have been unable to demand as individual patients. The common element is the request imposed on the scheme to act as a catalyst for change, although the nature of the change requested may vary substantially across contexts. The experience of the Nouna Health District shows that following the launch of a scheme, the hope for change, measured in terms of raised expectations, motivates enrolment. The experience of Guinea-Conakry and Ghana shows that a few years after the launch of the scheme, these very same raised expectations may hamper enrolment if the hope originally entrusted on CHI turns into disillusion. As illustrated by the experience of the Maliando scheme, it may become impossible to explain to the community that substantial quality improvements cannot be realised only within a two-year period. If communities do not perceive CHI to live up to their expectations, they may withdraw their support to the point of making enrolment fall below minimal requirements.

4.2.5 Household head socio-demographic characteristics

Other than ethnicity, discussed in an earlier section of this chapter, our model identified educational attainment to be the only household head characteristic likely to influence the decision to enrol in CHI. This finding is consistent with previous findings from Rwanda (Schneider and Diop 2004) as well as with findings from studies conducted in high income settings (Ettner 1997; Harmon and Nolan 2001; Liu and Chen 2002; McCall et al. 1998; Paulin and Dietz 1995; Shmueli 1998; Wilcox-Gok and Rubin 1994). Our findings are not consistent with prior findings from Senegal (Jütting 2004) and from Ghana (Osei-Akoto 2004). These two latter studies in fact, identified no association between educational attainment and enrolment in CHI.

Educated people are generally assumed to be more likely to recognise the benefits of improved health and thus, to be more likely to make investments that can produce a direct return on their health (Folland et al. 2001). The underlying assumption is that if investments in health are mediated by one's educational level, the same can be assumed to hold true for investments in health insurance.

Incorporating insights from the discipline of sociology may be useful to further explain the mediating role of education on decisions pertaining to health and health care consumption. Sociologists recognise the existence of non-economic forms of capital, such as cultural capital. The term cultural capital is used to indicate one's stock of knowledge, i.e. the collection of a comprehensive set of information, facts, and principles which influence people's understanding of the world and thus, their behaviour. Sociologists recognise that one's life experience and his/her sources of exposure inevitably influence the content of the cultural capital, i.e. the stock of knowledge, the individual holds[22].

In the African setting, individuals living in rural areas acquire extensive cultural capital mainly concerning elements such as the cycles of nature and their kin customs and traditions. Those who attend school, however, experience continuous exposure also to a different set of information and principles. Thus, they progressively acquire cultural capital which differs from that of the rest of the community. The educational system in fact, still reflects the legacy of colonialism: classes are for the most part held in French and much of the format of teaching replicates the French educational system. Although the curriculum has been gradually adapted to reflect the African life experience, the teaching of Western concepts and principles still prevails.

Therefore, individuals attending school are likely to be exposed to biomedical conceptualisations of illness which differ, at least partially, from traditional aetiological explanatory models. They are also more likely to be brought to believe in the effectiveness of biomedicine above all other healing practices. Thus, *ceteris paribus*, educated individuals are more likely to seek medical care, because they judge the costs and benefits of modern treatment differently from less educated individuals. It follows that, given their greater interest and confidence in modern health services, educated individuals will also attribute different weight to the valuation of the costs and benefits of enrolment in CHI. In addition, education is also likely to shape conceptualisations of risk. Through constant exposure to Western modes of thinking and Western risk-coping strategies, such as health insurance, educated individuals are likely to conceptualise notions of risk and prevention differently from the rest of their community. Last but not least, through education, individuals are also likely to be more frequently exposed to the existence of modern financing arrangements, such as health insurance. Thus, they may be more likely to enrol simply because of their greater acquaintance, and probably their greater confidence in the effectiveness, of such arrangements.

---

[22] The concept of cultural capital was developed by Pierre Bourdieu, who first expanded the notion of capital beyond its economic conception which emphasizes material exchanges, to include "immaterial" and "non-economic" forms of capital. Bourdieu's research focused mainly on the effect of cultural capital on educational attainment, arguing that the acquisition of cultural capital reflects underlying societal structures which grant greater advantages to those individuals who are most integrated in the dominant culture. With time, the notion of cultural capital has been expanded to explain attitudes and behaviours beyond the field of educational research (Richardson 1986; Robbins 2005).

In the light of our discussion, it is plausible to assume that differences between our findings and previous studies detecting no association between educational attainment and the decision to enrol are likely to be due to the adoption of different indicators rather than to represent true differences in the sampled populations. For instance, the indicator adopted by Jütting (2004) measured literacy rather than educational attainment. Measurements of literacy, however, are unlikely to capture the wealth of knowledge, beliefs, and attitudes, which constitute a person's cultural capital, and which are acquired through exposure to institutionalised schooling. At present in fact, many communities across sub-Saharan Africa are the target of intensive alphabetisation programs. People are taught the basics of reading and writing, often in the local language, by their trained peers. Thus, they may end up being able to read and write perfectly, but this does not necessarily mean that they have been exposed to an education comparable to the one delivered through institutionalised schooling. Using literacy as an indicator of educational attainment doubtfully pools together those who have learned to read and write through these peer initiatives with those who have completed some degree of schooling. Unlike Jütting, Osei-Akoto (2004) did measure educational attainment in terms of years of schooling. However, rather than focusing on the experience of the key decision-maker, i.e. the household head, he aggregated information on the educational attainment of all household members into one single variable. This choice might have not allowed him to tease out the effect of the educational attainment of the key decision-maker, confounding information on his/her knowledge, beliefs, and attitudes with those on the rest of the household.

Given that most communication and sensitisation campaigns in the continent do not extensively rely on written materials not to discriminate between literate and illiterate people, the mere ability to read and write is not likely to influence the decision to enrol. In the case of the Nouna Health District for example, given the extremely low literacy level, explicit efforts were made to keep to a minimum the use of written instruments during the communication and sensitisation campaign. Most communication passed through oral channels, either the radio and/or the promotion events organised in each village/town sector. The benefit package, the modalities of health care provision, and the management structure were all illustrated using visual supports, such as drawings and photos, or through the use of theatre and role play.

From the social marketing perspective, our findings appear to be rather discouraging. They indicate that in spite of an explicit effort to privilege the development of marketing tools which are sensitive to the needs of the illiterate population, communication and sensitisation campaigns may still fail to encourage enrolment among the least educated, falling short of compensating for the advantages granted by a higher education. As mentioned earlier in this chapter, however, the comprehensive assessment of the social marketing tools used during the first communication and sensitisation campaign constitutes the object of a separate parallel study. Therefore, our comments to this regard have to be treated with caution.

In line with previous research (Jütting 2004; Schneider and Diop 2004), our findings indicated that the household head's age and sex did not influence his/her decision to enrol in the AMBC. Studies detecting the existence of an association between the decision to purchase insurance and socio-demographic characteristics such as age and sex, all focused on the purchase of individual insurance coverage making it impossible to compare findings with our own (Ettner 1997; Harmon and Nolan 2001; Henderson et al. 1995; Liu and Chen 2002; McCall et al. 1998; Wilcox-Gok and Rubin 1994). In the individual insurance market in fact, the purchaser's age and sex are likely to influence his/her perception of the risk of falling sick and thus his/her decision to invest in insurance coverage for himself/herself. In line with our conceptual framework, however, our findings suggest that the imposition of household enrolment can effectively mediate the effect of age and sex on the decision to enrol in CHI. Through the imposition of household enrolment in fact, the individual is brought to weigh costs and benefits of enrolment in relation to his/her entire family, and not simply in relation to his/her perception of an individual need for future health care. The consistency of our findings with previous studies suggests that in sub-Saharan Africa, the household head's age and sex are not important factors influencing household decisions on enrolment in CHI.

The results of the WTP study suggested that women should have been less likely than men to enrol in CHI (Dong et al. 2004b). Surprisingly, our findings indicated that at least during the first enrolment campaign this was not the case. This apparent inconsistency can easily be explained by the sample adopted in the two studies. While Dong et al. (2003) conducted their study on a random sample of women, we focused exclusively on women who led their own households. It is plausible to assume that out of the need to meet the everyday necessities of their families, these women adopt attitudes and behaviours similar to the ones of men. It is also plausible to assume that their traditional role of care-givers (Sauerborn 1994) compensates for a certain resistance towards joining non-gender-specific institutional arrangements, encouraging them to consider costs and benefits of enrolment in CHI like their male counterparts.

4.3 Conclusions

4.3.1 Implications for policy

The overall goal of our research was to provide more comprehensive evidence for the development of successful policies aimed at enhancing enrolment in CHI in sub-Saharan Africa. Current discussion on CHI focuses in fact, on the need to identify adequate strategies to favour the up-scaling of schemes, progressively moving towards national coverage. The first step towards up-scaling coverage inevitably pertains to expanding enrolment of target populations among already-existing schemes. Unless reaching out to wider strata of the population in fact, CHI risks to remain an initiative exclusively accessible to some groups within society, failing to serve, as its advocates wish, as a step towards national health insurance coverage (Carrin 2003; Carrin et al. 2001), and possibly yielding negative effects on the overall health provision system of a country (Bennett 2004).

Our study highlights that policies aimed at maximising enrolment ought to act at three different levels: individual, household, and community. Exclusively addressing individual and household concerns will prove to be insufficient to secure higher enrolment rates. Some of the interventions we will discuss hereafter are within the reach of local policy-makers, including the Health District and the CHI management structures. Given their local focus, such interventions can potentially be implemented easily and within short time delays. Some of the interventions we will discuss, however, call for shifts in national policies within and beyond the health care sector. Thus, their implementation appears more complex and subject to the political will to promote changes that favour the development of longer term social security policies. Needless to say, in both instances, further research will be needed to evaluate whether the proposed strategies do in fact favour enrolment and lead to substantial increases in membership rates.

The most encouraging element emerging from the experience of the Nouna Health District is that rural communities in sub-Saharan Africa generally recognise CHI as a useful means of facilitating access to care and of protecting household financial assets, through the reduction of burdensome health spending. The appreciation for CHI is linked to the underlying appreciation for the effectiveness of biomedicine. This generalised appreciation for biomedicine and for the principle of health insurance indicates that there is major potential for the implementation of CHI in the continent. Therefore, policy-makers should not be discouraged by low enrolment rates and abandon altogether any hope that CHI will ever constitute an important element of health sector reform in sub-Saharan Africa. Learning from the experience of several European countries (Barnighausen and Sauerborn 2002; Criel and Van Dormael 1999), policy-makers engaged in CHI should rather focus on identifying concrete measures to progressively expand coverage over time, by building on this initial appreciation for the principle of insurance. Several lessons on how to maximise enrolment can be drawn from our analysis of the experience of the AMBC in the Nouna Health District.

The first important lesson is that the implementation of CHI schemes ought always to be tied to prior systematic explorations of community preferences. In addition, our findings indicate that research can be extremely helpful to guide policy as it allows for such systematic exploration. A clear illustration of our argument comes from observing how in the Nouna Health District, we identified an almost unanimous appreciation for those elements of the insurance scheme which had been the object of extensive preliminary research (the level of the premium, the benefit package, and the management structure), but an almost unanimous criticism for those elements which had not been the object of research and as such, had not been discussed with the community extensively (the payment modalities, the timing of the enrolment campaign, and the definition of the unit of enrolment).

Our study further highlights that there should be no fear to implement relatively complex risk management tools, such as group enrolment and gate-keeping mechanisms, insofar as the implementation details of such tools are discussed *a priori* with the community. While the scheme initiators may think exclusively of standard measures coherent with the theory and practice of insurance, communities have proved to be very creative in identifying solutions that allow risk management concerns to be harmonised with their needs and their customs. In the case of the Nouna Health District for example, communities have shown to be willing to accept the imposition of gate-keeping insofar as they are allowed to retain their autonomy in choosing their referral first-line facility. Similarly, communities have shown to understand and accept the rationale behind group enrolment, but they have asked that the definition of household applied is relaxed to suit their everyday habits and needs. In addition, our findings highlight how prior to the implementation of any scheme, it is important to discuss with the community not only the premium level, but also the specificities of the payment modalities. Allowing for greater flexibility in payment modalities, for example by opening enrolment throughout the year and/or by allowing to dilute payment over several months, may increase the complexity of a scheme management, but is likely to facilitate enrolment considerably.

The experience of the Nouna Health District shows that a comprehensive benefit package, including both first and second-line services, reflects community preferences and represents a key-success factor, potentially counteracting the negative effect of other elements, e.g. distance to the referral facility, on the decision to enrol. In line with the argument put forward by Macintyre (1999), we further advise policy-makers to follow the example of the Nouna Health District and consider the inclusion of emergency transport and emergency care in the benefit package as an essential element encouraging enrolment. We also recognise, however, the difficulty of balancing the need to keep the premium affordable with the wish to provide coverage for both first and second-line services. Interestingly, discussion with the project initiators revealed that prior to the study exploring community preferences for the benefit package (Kouyaté et al. 2001), they had thought of offering coverage exclusively for high-cost low-probability events. However, the results of the study induced the project initiators to reconsider their position and expand coverage also to first-line services, inevitably increasing the level of the premium. Our study indicates that this decision has later proved to constitute a major element of strength for the AMBC, encouraging enrolment in the scheme.

The community's clear wish to preserve their freedom in choosing providers indicates that in the Nouna Health District, as elsewhere in sub-Saharan Africa, policy makers should pay close attention to community preferences also when establishing contractual arrangements with health care facilities. In settings where several health care providers co-habit within a region, communities need to be consulted in the preparatory phase and their preference for a given provider taken into account when establishing contracting arrangements. In settings with an exclusive health care provider, government or private, individual households can be left free to choose their first-line referral facility. Allowing patients to freely choose their preferred provider may not only encourage enrolment, but also induce competition among providers, potentially inducing quality improvements across facilities. Our study indicates in fact, that people are willing to travel beyond their closest referral facility if they perceive the benefit of seeking care in one specific setting to outweigh the costs associated with increased distance.

The second lesson pertains to the central role of knowledge in favouring enrolment. In the light of our findings, we advise policy-makers to channel systematic efforts towards ensuring that communities have access to the complete set of information necessary to adequately judge costs and benefits of membership in CHI. As mentioned above, we cannot comment on the specific effectiveness of the different tools and procedures applied during the first communication and sensitisation campaign. Thus, we cannot offer any specific policy recommendation to this regard. In principle, however, given the low knowledge level we observed in the community, we deduce that, in spite of the efforts done, the tools and procedures applied during the first campaign fell short of reaching effectively all community members. Therefore, we would urge policy-makers in the Nouna Health District to reconsider the content and the form of the first sensitisation campaign to identify, also on the basis of the *ad hoc* study currently under way, strengths and weaknesses of the work done in 2004. We feel that, in the Nouna Health District as elsewhere in sub-Saharan Africa, much attention should be paid to the development of tools and procedures that allow communities to retain precise information not only on the principle of insurance, but also on the specific details of the scheme. The different enrolment rate observed among certain groups, e.g. the Bwaba and the higher educated, also induces us to recommend that marketing messages be developed in such a way as to be sensitive to the socio-cultural peculiarities of each sub-group within society. This appears to be the only means to balance enrolment across ethnic/religious groups and/or to overcome the comparative advantage due to higher education. Increased investments in education in fact, although desirable on their own because of the long-term impact on the development of a nation, are unlikely to produce an immediate effect on enrolment.

The experience of some villages in the Nouna Health District also indicates that securing the support of key community leaders may greatly facilitate the task of CHI promotion teams. Local leaders in fact, better than any CHI manager travelling from a district capital, are familiar with the social norms and the cultural values shaping attitudes and regulating behaviour among their own community. Thus, they can more easily frame the insurance discourse in such a way as to capture, through the development of culturally sensitive messages, the attention of that specific community at that specific moment in time. It may be helpful, in the Nouna Health District as elsewhere in the continent, to delegate to community leaders much of the active promotion of the scheme. This approach would then allow CHI communication specialists to sustain the campaign with target interventions, for example by focusing on traditionally marginalised groups and/or on those groups who have been identified to be the least likely to enrol. In order to inform future communication and sensitisation campaigns, it may be worthwhile for the AMBC management team to reflect on their previous experience and understand what circumstances have shaped the different reactions to the new initiative which were observed among the different community leaders. Such a reflection on their part may allow to identify the circumstances necessary for the establishment of a fruitful collaboration, informing policy-making both within and beyond the Nouna Health District.

The third lesson sheds light on the important influence of cultural beliefs and practices on the decision to enrol in CHI. Given a certain resistance towards making advanced investments in health out of fear of attracting bad fate, communication and sensitisation campaigns should reinforce that health insurance does not constitute a means of preventing illness, but more simply a means of protecting one's assets from future shocks through active sharing of risks and resources across a community. In addition, given a certain resistance towards earmarking savings, in contexts where this is possible, policy-makers may wish to consider the feasibility of linking health insurance coverage to systems of protection from other types of risk. Looking outside the African continent, important lessons could be learned from models developed in Asia which have successfully combined health insurance either with harvest and asset insurance or with micro-credit institutions (Desmet et al. 1999; Devadasan 2005; Ranson 2004). In the case of the Nouna Health District, the AMBC management may wish to consider establishing a partnership with the local micro-credit institution, ATN. This may allow both organisations to become more attractive, combining into one broader entity the range of support services on offer to the community.

The fourth lesson relates to the finding that poor knowledge of the scheme management, combined with previous negative experiences in other formal or semi-formal risk-sharing arrangements, may nurture feelings of scepticisms and distrust. In the Nouna Health District as elsewhere in sub-Saharan Africa, optimising enrolment inevitably entails that such sentiments of scepticism and distrust are defeated. In order to do so, policy-makers are advised first and foremost to increase knowledge of the scheme management and to ensure transparency of all operations. In line with the argument developed by Criel and Waelkens (2003), we recognise that scepticism and distrust are likely to accompany novel initiatives, but may disappear when management structures prove to carry out their work professionally and ethically. Thus, the scepticism and mistrust observed in our study may disappear in the following years if the AMBC management team meets the community expectation of facilitating access to health services and is not involved in any case of fraud. Given that communities are more likely to trust newly emerging schemes if they can identify an affiliation between the CHI scheme and some well-established institution, we would also advise policy-makers to seek out such affiliations and acknowledge them explicitly. As far as the specific experience of the AMBC is concerned, we would strongly recommend that the Management Unit openly discusses with the community the role of the CRSN, bridging the link between the research focus and the scheme implementation. In other settings, newly emerging CHI schemes can actively seek the collaboration of well-established local NGOs, charity organisations, or missions.

The fifth lesson leads us back to a theme discussed extensively in the health system literature on sub-Saharan Africa, i.e. quality of care. All studies on decision to enrol agree on the fact that, to one extent or another, dissatisfaction with the care on offer may discourage enrolment. Thus, we would advise policy-makers to accompany the implementation of CHI with active investments in quality improvement. In doing so, however, policy-makers ought to pay special attention to discern what components of the care currently on offer do not meet the expectations of the community. Otherwise, the risk is to invest substantial amounts of resources to improve aspects of the quality, e.g. infrastructures, which are not perceived by the community to constitute the priority. In the case of the Nouna Health District, for example, improving the behavioural component of the provider-patient encounter would be sufficient to guarantee a much higher appreciation for the services on offer. However, the lack of criticism we recorded against the structural components of the quality of care, i.e. infrastructures, equipment, and drug supply, may be attributed to the fact that starting in the late 1990s, substantial efforts were channelled towards securing that facilities may meet basic standards of care. Thus, by the time the AMBC was launched, communities had no longer a reason to complain about the structural component of care, but continued to have reasons to complain about the process of care, mainly accusing lack of respect on the part of providers.

The experience of the Nouna Health District invites us to reflect upon the need to invest in adequate infrastructures and reliable drug supplies before proceeding with the implementation of more complex health sector reforms, such as CHI. Unless communities perceive that basic standards of care can be met, they are unlikely to show any interest in CHI. Our study indicates than when simply dissatisfied with the behavioural component of the provider-patient encounter, communities may still enrol, counting on the fact that the CHI will act as a catalyst for change and help patients gain a voice *vis á vis* the providers.

In the light of the joint appraisal of our study and of those by Atim (2000) and by Criel and Waelkens (2003), we would also advise policy-makers to explicitly acknowledge from the very beginning the limitations of any CHI scheme to produce immediate quality improvements. Likewise, communication and sensitisation campaigns should be careful not to overestimate the effectiveness of biomedicine. Open discussion regarding both the extent of reasonable quality improvements and the effectiveness of biomedicine, given the infrastructures available, is necessary to ensure that the expectations of the community do not rise to a level where they can no longer be met. Experiences outside the Nouna Health District, such as the one in Guinea-Conakry (Criel and Waelkens 2003), have shown in fact that sentiments of disappointment are one of the leading factors discouraging re-enrolment in subsequent years.

Producing quality improvements entails that the communication between the CHI scheme and the providers is fluent and that the two share a common objective, that of providing good quality services at an affordable price to the community. The experience of the Nouna Health District, however, suggests that in certain instances, prior to investing in quality improvements, the scheme management has to focus on overcoming providers' resistance, turning nurses and physicians from the scheme opponents to its best allies. As addressed in detail in the following and last section of this chapter, winning the resistance of providers entails in the very first place understanding its causes and rationale.

The experience of the Nouna Health District is also indicative that policy-makers should pay more attention to the concerns of providers prior to the implementation of any scheme. By keeping into account the preferences of all community constituencies, including health care providers, in the original design of the scheme, policy-makers may be able to avoid much of the conflict observed in the Nouna Health District. Prior to the implementation of any CHI, it may be useful to invest in conducting a comprehensive stakeholder analysis, considering what opportunities and threats await the new scheme and how the interests of the different constituencies may come into conflict with one another. While waiting for more research to be completed on the specific reasons underlying providers' resistance in sub-Saharan Africa, policy-makers could turn to the literature discussing the implementation of health maintenance organisations (HMOs) in the United States. Given the radical shift in service provision and reimbursement policies which they entailed, HMOs also experienced at first similar problems in regulating the relationship between insurers and providers.

The sixth and last lesson pertains to the importance of subsidising the premium for the very poor. In line with previous research, our study clearly identifies a group of people who, in spite of any other intervention aimed at increasing trust or improving the quality of services, will not be able to afford enrolment in CHI. The obvious policy recommendation here, is to mobilise government and/or donor resources to be channelled in targeted subsidies to compensate for the disadvantage due to a low socio-economic status. As mentioned earlier in this section, CHI schemes should actively strive to secure the enrolment of all strata in society. Otherwise, instead of offering protection to the most vulnerable groups in society, among which the very poor, they run the risk of ending up favouring already privileged groups, i.e. the wealthy. The experience of user fees, however, has shown that the identification of the poorest for targeted subsidies remains a challenging task. Thus, we do recognise that the distribution of targeted subsidies should be preceded by research exploring effective means of identifying the poorest. This constitutes an essential step to ensure that the scarce resources available to subsidise programs actually reach those most in need.

Linked to such recommendation is the observation that in the Nouna Health District, enrolment was higher in communities where levels of socio-economic inequality were lower. This is a clear indication that prior efforts towards equalising the distribution of economic resources within a community pay off by favouring subsequent efforts channelled towards the same direction. We have already commented on how the level of socio-economic inequality we observed across communities in the Nouna Health District is more likely to be linked to village-specific dynamics than to institutionalised policies defined at the national level. In the light of our finding, however, policy-makers at the national level may be interested to consider how investments in other social security policies are likely to generate a positive externality beyond their most immediate effect of reducing gaps in socio-economic status. Thus, they may have an additional incentive to promote social security programmes, such as micro-level financial support, income subsidies for needy households, and/or disability pensions. Our findings seem to suggest that the reduction of socio-economic inequality which may result from the implementation of such programmes is likely to encourage enrolment in CHI, by altering for the better attitudes towards social cohesion and perceptions of fairness within a community. In turn, higher enrolment in CHI is expected to reduce the poverty gap, lowering levels of socio-economic inequality, and potentially supporting the implementation of such social security programmes. This argument emerges from our direct observation on the field. We recognise, however, that it appears to be in line with the currently prevailing international movement towards promoting complementary social security interventions in parallel (Jütting 1999; Devereux 2002; van Ginneken 2003).

4.3.2 Implications for future research

The discussion of our findings highlights that several questions pertinent to understanding the decision to enrol in CHI remain to be explored by further research.

First, our discussion recognises an immediate need to study health providers' perceptions of CHI to explain their resistance and identify possible means to overcome it. Like all previous research on the decision to enrol in CHI in fact, we focused exclusively on understanding community attitudes and behaviours. At different points in our analysis, however, it became clear that the decision to enrol is also severely constrained by the attitudes and behaviours of other stakeholders, first among all the health care providers. Thus, understanding providers' perceptions of CHI, their wishes and their fears, and their reasons for resisting the implementation of a scheme is essential to secure the success of the new initiative. Without first understanding what causes health providers to resist the implementation of CHI, it is simply impossible to design policy measures that can adequately address their concerns. Understanding providers' resistance to the implementation of CHI would most probably require the joint application of qualitative and quantitative methods of analysis, replicating, to a certain extent, the approach we adopted in our study. At first, qualitative methods could be used to identify providers' broad areas of concern. Later, conjoint analysis could be applied to explore the extent to which health providers are willing to trade the potential costs and benefits arising for them from the new initiative.

Second, we recognise the need to critically appraise the tools and procedures used during the communication and sensitisation campaigns that accompany the implementation of any CHI scheme in sub-Saharan Africa. To the present day, little attention has been paid to understanding how different marketing tools may favour or disfavour the acquisition of adequate knowledge on CHI and actively promote enrolment. As mentioned earlier in this chapter, the first comprehensive attempt to appraise systematically all the tools and procedures of a CHI communication campaign is the one currently under-way in the Nouna Health District. Prior research on CHI has most often not even acknowledged the potential influence of different marketing strategies on the decision to enrol. This lack of interest in assessing CHI communication and sensitisation campaigns appears rather surprising when considering how much attention is usually paid to the field of marketing, in high and in low-income countries alike. For example, across sub-Saharan Africa, the effectiveness of different communication and sensitisation tools used in the field of health promotion, e.g. in the fields of road safety and HIV prevention, has been extensively evaluated (Blantari et al. 2005; Eloundou-Enyegue et al. 2005; Meekers and Rahaim 2005).

Following the example of what is being done in the Nouna Health District, research on the effectiveness of different marketing tools can easily be conducted by "piggy-backing" the implementation of a CHI scheme. Again through the application of a mixed-methodology approach, research could focus on assessing knowledge of a scheme components, attitudes towards health insurance, and ultimately enrolment rates, across comparable regions where the promotion of CHI has relied on different marketing tools. Given that research has consistently identified the least educated to be the least likely to enrol, research should especially focus on identifying which marketing tools can most effectively compensate for the comparative advantage due to schooling.

Third, further research efforts should be channelled towards unravelling why important differences in enrolment behaviour exist across religious and ethnic groups. Further qualitative analysis is needed to unravel how socio-cultural elements likely to influence the decision to enrol, such as conceptualisations of illness and perceptions of risk and vulnerability, may differ across African societies. Understanding differences represents in fact, the first step towards adequately addressing socio-cultural concerns through the development of promotion tools and policies which are sensitive to the specificities of each community. The incredible ethnic and cultural diversity of the African continent inevitably represents a challenge to the large-scale implementation of CHI because it does not allow for the development of "one fit all" model. This ethnic and cultural diversity also represents, however, the most valuable asset of the continent since it constitutes a continuous source of creative thinking.

Understanding how the experience of each group may enrich that of others may prove to be beneficial to promote the large-scale implementation of CHI in the continent.

Fourth, we would like to stress the need to replicate our study in other regions of the continent as well as in Asian and Latin American settings. Although we have framed most of our discussion within the context of sub-Saharan Africa, we recognise that CHI has been identified as a probable solution to the problem of health financing in low and middle income settings across all continents. Therefore, we acknowledge not only that much of the wisdom emerging from our study may apply beyond the African borders, but also that studies similar to our own are equally needed to inform policy-making across all low and middle income settings. We hope to have effectively proved that the adoption of a mixed-methodology and a joint focus on individual, household, and community characteristics can provide a powerful insight into the decision to enrol in CHI. Given the paucity of prior research, we still think that more studies similar to our own need to be conducted before the scientific community can confidently assume to fully understand reasons motivating or discouraging enrolment in CHI. Further evidence is in fact needed to confirm our findings and/or to highlight how certain elements may play out differently under different circumstances in different settings.

Given the ability to jointly capture household and community level characteristics, we would advise researchers to adopt our same statistical technique, i.e. multilevel modelling. We would also advise researchers to develop data collection instruments that adequately capture all dimensions relevant to measure the possible effect of prior health status and prior health service utilisation on the decision to enrol. As discussed in an earlier section of this chapter in fact, we were unable to include in our model an adequate measurement of prior health care spending as well as a measurement of health status which included both chronic and acute illness reporting. It would also be desirable to replicate our study on a larger sample of households and communities. The sample selection problem linked to low enrolment rates and to limited resources could potentially be bypassed by pooling together information from different regions, conducting a sort of meta-analysis of decision to enrol in CHI in sub-Saharan Africa. Next to the need to replicate our study, we also recognise the need to keep monitoring enrolment and determinants of enrolment over time. As addressed earlier in this chapter in fact, reasons motivating and/or discouraging enrolment are likely to change over time as a result of wider social, economic, and political processes.

Fifth, we would like to draw attention to the implications of our findings for future research on themes other than decision to enrol in CHI. As discussed earlier, our findings suggest that community characteristics, such as socio-economic inequality, may play an important role in shaping decisions concerning health and health care consumption. Still, most quantitative analyses have largely ignored the potential impact of community characteristics on the decision of the single household to seek care. In the light of our findings, we trust that neglecting to include community characteristics, such as socio-economic inequality, in the regression model causes the estimates to be incomplete. Thus, we advise researchers to include community characteristics in future analyses exploring decision-making processes concerning health and health care consumption, e.g. studies exploring determinants of health service utilisation.

Last but not least, we would like to remind the reader that this study was inscribed within the framework of a wider research project, aimed at monitoring the implementation of CHI in the Nouna Health District to identify problems and possible solutions and to assess scientifically the impact of CHI on health service utilisation, quality of care, and poverty. As the author concludes her writing, the work of the research team continues both in Nouna and Heidelberg. The design of policies which can secure the successful implementation of CHI rests in fact, on the ability of research to provide an answer to different sets of issues. At present, the AMBC management unit has just completed its second enrolment campaign. A new wave of the household survey is currently under way and will be analysed in the coming months. The data will be used both to continue and expand the analysis on enrolment and to investigate whether enrolment in CHI has in fact facilitated access to care. At the same time, one colleague, Patience Kofie, is completing an evaluation of the first communication and sensitisation campaign, while another colleague, Irina Soloveitchik, is just starting to develop a tool to measure the impact of CHI on poverty reduction. Two more colleagues, Karolin Pfeiffer and Florent Somé, are engaged in a study to assess differences in quality of care at the various District facilities. One of the people who accompanied the author throughout her work, Mamadou Sanon, is conducting a study exploring providers' perception and attitudes towards CHI. In October 2005, we will all meet the AMBC team in Nouna to discuss with them, in the light of the research results, how we can best inform policies for the future of the scheme.

5. Bibliography

Abel-Smith B (1992). Health insurance in developing countries: lessons from experience. Health Policy and Planning. 7: 215-226.

Ahuja R and Jütting J (2003). Design of incentives in community based health insurance schemes. Discussion Paper on Development Policy No. 63. Bonn: Centre for Development Research.

Ahuja R and Jütting J (2004). Are the poor too poor to demand health insurance? Journal of Microfinance 6:1-20.

Arhin D (1995). Health insurance in rural Africa. Lancet 345: 44-45.

Arhin-Tenkorang D (2004). Experience of community health financing in the African region. In Preker AS and Carrin G (Eds.): Health financing for poor people - Resource mobilization and risk sharing (pp. 157-198). Washington: The World Bank.

Arrow KJ (1963). Uncertainty and the welfare economics of medical care. The American Economic Review LIII: 941-973.

Asenso-Okyere WK, Anum A, Osei-Akoto I, and Adukonu A (1998). Cost recovery in Ghana: are there any changes in health care seeking behaviour? Health Policy and Planning 13: 181-188.

Atim C (1998). The contribution of mutual health organizations to financing, delivery, and access to health care: synthesis of research in nine West and Central African countries. Bethesda, MD: Partnerships for Health Reform Project, Abt Associates Inc.

Atim C (1999). Social movements and health insurance: a critical evaluation of voluntary, non-profit insurance schemes with case studies from Ghana and Cameroon. Social Science and Medicine 48: 881-896.

Atim C and Madjiguene S (2000). An external evaluation of the Nkoranza Community Financing Health Insurance Scheme, Ghana. Bethesda, MD: Partnerships for Health Reform Project, Abt Associates Inc.

Balkenhol B and Churchill C (2002). From microfinance to micro health insurance. In Dror DM and Preker AS (Eds.): Social Re Insurance (pp. 75-102). Washington: The World Bank.

Baltussen RM, Ye Y, Haddad S, and Sauerborn RS (2002). Perceived quality of care of primary health care services in Burkina Faso. Health Policy and Planning 17: 42-48.

Barnighausen T and Sauerborn R (2002). One hundred and eighteen years of the German health insurance system: are there any lessons for middle- and low-income countries? Social Science and Medicine 54: 1559-1587.

Beaglehole R, Bonita R, and Kjellstrom T (1993). Basic Epidemiology. Geneva: The World Health Organisation.

Bennett S, Creese A, and Monasch R (1998). Health insurance schemes for people outside formal sector employment. Geneva: World Health Organisation.

Bennett S (2004). The role of community-based health insurance within the health care financing system: a framework for analysis. Health Policy and Planning 19: 147-158.

Bernard HR (1990). Research methods in cultural anthropology. Newbury Park: Sage Publications.

Besley T (1991). The demand for health care and health insurance. In McGuire A, Fenn P, and Mayhew K (Eds.): Providing health care: the economics of alternative systems of finance and delivery (pp. 46-64). Oxford and New York: Oxford University Press.

Besley T (1995). Nonmarket institutions for credit and risk sharing in low-income countries. The Journal of Economic Perspectives 9: 115-127.

Bitran R and Giedion U (2003). Waivers and Exemptions for health services in developing countries. Social Protection Discussion Paper No. 0308. Washington: The World Bank.

Blantari J, Asiamah G, Appiah N, and Mock C (2005). An evaluation of the effectiveness of televised road safety messages in Ghana. International Journal of Injury Control and Safety Promotion 12: 23-29.

Boeing H, Frentzel-Beyme R, Berger M, Berndt V, Gores W, Korner M, Lohmeier R, Menarcher A, Mannl HF, and Meinhardt, M (1991). Case-control study on stomach cancer in Germany. International Journal of Cancer 47: 858-864.

Bridges JFP (2003). Stated preference methods in health care evaluation: an emerging methodological paradigm in health economics. Applied Health Economics and Health Policy 2: 213-224.

Brown W and Churchill CF (2000). Insurance provision in low income communities. Bethesda, MD: Microenterprise Best Practices.

Browne MJ (1992). Evidence of adverse selection in the individual health insurance market. The Journal of Risk and Insurance 59: 13-33.

Burnard P (1991). A method of analysing interview transcripts in qualitative research. Nurse Education Today 11: 461-466.

Cameron AC, Trivedi PK, Milne F, and Piggott J (1988). A microeconometric model for the demand for health care and health insurance in Australia. The Review of Economic Studies 55: 85-106.

Carrin G (1987). Community financing of drugs in Sub-Saharan Africa. International Journal of Health Planning and Management 2: 125-145.

Carrin G (1988). Community financing of health care. World Health Forum 9: 601-606.

Carrin G and Vereecke M (1992). Strategies for health care finance in developing countries. London: MacMillan Press.

Carrin G, Desmet M, and Basaza R (2001). Social health insurance development in low-income developing countries: new roles for government and nonprofit health insurance organizations in Africa and Asia. In Scheil-Adlung X (Ed.): Building Social Security: The Challenge of Privatization (pp. 125-150). New Brunswick, New Jersey: Transaction Publishers.

Carrin G (2002). Social health insurance in developing countries: a continuing challenge. International Social Security Review 55: 57-69.

Carrin G (2003). Community based health insurance schemes in developing countries: facts, problems and perspectives. Geneva: WHO/EIP Department of Health Financing and Stewardship.

Central Intelligence Agency (2005). The World Factbook - Burkina Faso. Washington: The Central Intelligence Agency of the United States of America. Available at URL: http://www.cia.gov/cia/publications/factbook/geos/uv.html (accessed on May 1st, 2005).

Chang FR and Trivedi PK (2003). Economics of self-medication: theory and evidence. Health Economics 12: 721-739.

Chawla M and Ellis RP (2000). The impact of financing and quality changes on health care demand in Niger. Health Policy and Planning 15: 76-84.

Chee G, Smith K, and Kapinga A (2002). Assessment of the community health fund in Hanang District, Tanzania. Bethesda, MD: Partners for Health Reform Plus Project, Abt Associates Inc.

Chernick MR and Friis RH (2003). Introductory biostatistics for the health sciences - Modern applications including bootstrap. Hoboken, New Jersey: John Wiley and Sons, Inc.

Coast J (1999). The appropriate uses of qualitative methods in health economics. Health Economics 8: 345-353.

Coast J (2001). Citizens, their agents and health care rationing: an exploratory study using qualitative methods. Health Economics 10: 159-174.

Coast J, Donovan J, Litva A, Eyles J, Morgan K, Shepherd M, and Tacchi J (2002). "If there were a war tomorrow, we'd find the money": contrasting perspectives on the rationing of health care. Social Science and Medicine 54: 1839-1851.

Collins D, Quick JD, Musau SN, Kraushaar K, and Hussein IM (1996). The fall and rise of cost sharing in Kenya: the impact of phased implementation. Health Policy and Planning 11: 52-63.

Cosslett SR (1981). Efficient estimation of discrete-choice models. In Manski CF and McFadden D (Eds.): Structural analysis of discrete data with econometrics applications (pp. 51-111). Cambridge, MA: MIT Press.

Creese AL (1991). User charges for health care: a review of recent experience. Health Policy and Planning 6: 309-319.

Criel B, De Vos P, Van Lerberghe W, and Van der Stuyft P (1996). Community financing or cost recovery: empowerment or social dumping? Tropical Medicine and International Health 1: 281-282.

Criel B and Kegels G (1997). A health insurance scheme for hospital care in Bwamanda District, Zaire: lessons and questions after 10 years of functioning. Tropical Medicine and International Health 2: 654-672.

Criel B (1998a). District-based health insurance in sub-Saharan Africa. Part I: From Theory to Practice. Antwerp: ITG Press.

Criel B. (1998b). District-based health insurance in sub-Saharan Africa. Part II: Case Studies. Antwerp: ITG Press.

Criel B, van Dormael M, Lefevre P, Menase U, and Van Lerberghe W (1998). Voluntary health insurance in Bwamanda, Democratic Republic of Congo. An exploration of its meanings to the community. Tropical Medicine and International Health 3: 640-653.

Criel B, Van der Stuyft P, and Van Lerberghe W (1999). The Bwamanda hospital insurance scheme: effective for whom? A study of its impact on hospital utilization patterns. Social Science and Medicine 48: 897-911.

Criel B, Barry AN, and von Roenne F (2002). Le Projet PRIMA en Guinée Conakry. Une expérience d'organisation de mutuelles de santé en Afrique rurale. Brussels: Medicus Mundi.

Criel B and Waelkens MP (2003). Declining subscriptions to the Maliando Mutual Health Organisation in Guinea-Conakry (West Africa): what is going wrong? Social Science and Medicine 57: 1205-1219.

Criel B, Atim C, Basaza R, Blaise P, and Waelkens MP (2004). Community health insurance in sub-Saharan Africa: researching the context. Tropical Medicine and International Health 9: 1041-1043.

Cutler DM and Zeckhauser RJ (1999). The anatomy of health insurance. Working Paper 7176. Cambridge, MA: National Bureau of Economic Research.

Daly MC, Duncan GJ, Kaplan GA, and Lynch JW (1998). Macro-to-micro links in the relation between income inequality and mortality. The Milbank Quarterly 76: 315-339.

De Béthune X (1989). The influence of an abrupt price increase on health service utilisation: evidence from Zaire. Health Policy and Planning 4: 76-81.

Dercon S (2002). Income risk, coping strategies, and safety nets. The World Bank Research Observer 17: 141-166.

Derriennic Y, Wolf K, and Kiwanuka-Mukiibi P (2005). An assessment of community-based health financing activities in Uganda. Bethesda, MD: The Partners for Health Reform Plus Project, Abt Associates Inc.

Desmet M, Chowdhury AQ, and Islam MK (1999). The potential for social mobilisation in Bangladesh: the organisation and functioning of two health insurance schemes. Social Science and Medicine 48: 925-938.

Devadasan N (2005). Community health insurance in India - A compilation of case studies. Ahmedabad, India: Friends of Women's World Banking.

Devereux S (2002). Social protection for the poor: lessons from recent international experience. IDS Working Paper 142. Brighton: Institute of Development Studies.

Diop F, Yazbeck A, and Bitran R (1995). The impact of alternative cost recovery schemes on access and equity in Niger. Health Policy and Planning 10: 223-240.

DiPrete Brown L, Miller Franco L, Rafeh N, and Hatzell T (2004). Quality Assurance of Health Care in Developing Countries. Bethesda, MD: USAID.

Donabedian A (1980). Methods for deriving criteria for assessing the quality of medical care. Medical Care Review 37: 653-698.

Dong H, Kouyaté B, Cairns J, Mugisha F, and Sauerborn R (2003). Willingness-to-pay for community-based insurance in Burkina Faso. Health Economics 12: 849-862.

Dong H, Gbangou A, De Allegri M, and Sauerborn R (2004a). The difference in characteristics between health-care users and non-users - implications for introducing community-based health insurance in Burkina Faso. Submitted.

Dong H, Kouyaté B, Snow R, Mugisha F, and Sauerborn R (2004b). Gender's effect on willingness-to-pay for community-based insurance in Burkina Faso. Health Policy 64: 153-162.

Dong H, Kouyaté B, Cairns J, and Sauerborn R (2004c). Differential willingness of household heads to pay community-based health insurance premia for themselves and other household members. Health Policy and Planning 19: 120-126.

Dong H, Mugisha F, Gbangou A, Kouyaté B, and Sauerborn R (2004d). The feasibility of community-based health insurance in Burkina Faso. Health Policy 69: 45-53.

Dong H, Kouyaté B, Cairns J, and Sauerborn R (2005) Inequality in willingness to pay for community-based health insurance. Health Policy 72: 149-156.

Dror DM (2002). Health insurance and reinsurance at the community level. In Dror DM and Preker AS (Eds.): Social Re Insurance (pp. 103-123). Washington: The World Bank.

Edmond J, Comfort A, and Leighton C (2002). Maternal health financing profile: Burkina Faso. Bethesda, MD: Partnerships for Health Reform Project, Abt Associates Inc.

Ekman B (2004). Community-based health insurance in low-income countries: a systematic review of the evidence. Health Policy and Planning 19: 249-270.

Eloundou-Enyegue PM, Meekers D, and Calves AE (2005). From awareness to adoption: the effect of AIDS education and condom social marketing on condom use in Tanzania (1993-1996). Journal Biosocial Science 37: 257-268.

Ensor T and Cooper S (2004). Overcoming barriers to health service access: influencing the demand side. Health Policy and Planning 19: 69-79.

Ettner SL (1997). Adverse selection and the purchase of Medigap insurance by the elderly. Journal of Health Economics 16: 543-562.

Fabricant SJ, Kamara CW, and Mills A (1999). Why the poor pay more: household curative expenditures in rural Sierra Leone. International Journal of Health Planning and Management 14: 179-199.

Farley PJ and Monheit AC (1985). Selectivity in the demand for health insurance and health care. Advances in Health Economics and Health Services Research 6: 231-248.

Flessa S. (2005). Simulation of revenue and costs under insurance. In Sauerborn R, Kouyaté B, and Dong H (Eds.): Financing health care for the poor: the scientific basis for community-based health insurance in Burkina Faso (forthcoming). Frankfurt: Peter Lang.

Folland S, Goodman AC, and Stano M (2001). The economics of health and health care (third edition) Upper Saddle River, New Jersey: Prentice-Hall, Inc.

Fonteneau R (2000). L'emergence des pratiques d'economie sociale en matière de financement de la santé au Burkina Faso. Economie et Solidarieté, 31.

Foster AD and Rosenzweig MR (2001). Imperfect commitment, altruism, and the family: evidence from transfer behaviour in low-income rural areas. The Review of Economics and Statistics 83: 389-407.

Frank RH (2002). Microeconomics and behavior. (fifth edition) New York: McGraw-Hill.

Gbangou A, Dong H, van der Pol M, Cairns J, and Sauerborn R (2005). Individual and social time preferences in a rural and semi-urban area in Burkina Faso. Submitted.

Gertler P, Locay L, and Sanderson W (1987). Are user fees regressive? Journal of Econometrics 36: 67-88.

Gertler P and Gruber J (2002). Insuring consumption against illness. The American Economic Review XCII: 51-70.

Gilbert PB (2000). Large sample theory of maximum likelihood estimates in semi-parametric biased sampling modelling. Annals of Statistics 28: 151-194.

Gilson L and Mills A (1995). Health sector reforms in sub-Saharan Africa: lessons of the last 10 years. Health Policy 32: 215-243.

Gilson L (1997). The lessons of user fee experience in Africa. Health Policy and Planning 12: 273-285.

Gilson L, Kalyalya D, Kuchler F, Lake S, Oranga H, and Ouendo M (2000). The equity impacts of community financing activities in three African countries. International Journal of Health Planning and Management 15: 291-317.

Gilson L, Kalyalya D, Kuchler F, Lake S, Oranga H, and Ouendo M (2001). Strategies for promoting equity: experience with community financing in three African countries. Health Policy 58: 37-67.

Glaser B and Strauss AL (1967). The discovery of Grounded Theory. Chicago: Aldine Press.

Glesne C and Peshkin A (1992). Becoming qualitative researchers - An introduction. London: Longman.

Goldstein H (2003). Multilevel statistical models. London: Arnold Press.

Goldstein H (2005). Personal communication.

Goldstein M, de Janvry A, and Sadoulet E (2005). Is a friend in need a friend indeed? Inclusion and exclusion in mutual health insurance networks in southern Ghana. In Dercon S (Ed.): Insurance Against Poverty (forthcoming). Oxford and New York: Oxford University Press.

Greene WH (1997). Econometric analysis. (third edition) Upper Saddle River, New Jersey: Prentice-Hall, Inc.

Griffin C and Shaw RP (1996). Health insurance in sub-Saharan Africa: aims, findings, policy implications. In Shaw RP and Ainsworth M (Eds.): Financing Health Services Through User Fees and Insurance - Case Studies from sub-Saharan Africa (pp. 143-167). Washington: The World Bank.

Grossman M (1972). On the concept of health capital and the demand for health. The Journal of Political Economy 80: 233-255.

Haddad S and Fournier P (1995). Quality, costs and utilisation of health services in developing countries. Social Science and Medicine 40: 743-753.

Hammer GP, Somé F, Mueller O, Kynast-Wolf G, Kouyaté B, and Becher H (2005). Pattern of cause-specific childhood mortality in North Western Burkina Faso: analysis of DSS data from 1999-2003. Submitted.

Harmon C and Nolan B (2001). Health insurance and health services utilization in Ireland. Health Economics 10: 135-145.

Hills M and De Stavola BL (2003). A short introduction to Stata 8 for Biostatistics. London: Timberlake Consultants Ltd.

Hjortsberg C (2003). Why do the sick not utilise health care? The case of Zambia. Health Economics 12: 755-770.

Hopkins S and Kidd MP (1996). The determinants of the demand for private health insurance under Medicare. Applied Economics 28: 1623-1638.

Huber G, Hohmann J, and Reinhard K (2002). Mutual health insurance (MHO) - Five years experience in West Africa. Eschborn: GTZ GmbH Division 4320 - Health and Population.

Hutton G (2004). Is the jury still out on the impact of user fees in Africa? A review of the evidence from selected countries on user fees and determinants of health service utilisation. East African Medical Journal 81: S45-S60.

International Labour Organisation (2001). La micro-assurance santé en Afrique - Guide en gestion administrative et financière des mutuelles de santé. Geneva: International Labour Organisation.

International Labour Organisation (2002). Extending social protection in health through community based health organizations. Geneva: International Labour Organisation.

Jakab M and Krishnan C (2004). Review of the strengths and weaknesses of community financing. In Preker AS and Carrin G (Eds.): Health financing for poor people - Resource mobilization and risk sharing (pp. 53-118). Washington: The World Bank.

Jakab M, Preker AS, Krishnan C, Schneider P, Diop F, Jütting J, Gumber A, Ranson MK, Supakankunti S (2004). Analysis of community financing using household surveys. In Preker AS and Carrin G (Eds.): Health financing for poor people - Resource mobilization and risk sharing (pp. 199-230). Washington: The World Bank.

Jowett M (2003). Do Informal risk sharing networks crowd out public voluntary health insurance? Evidence from Vietnam. Applied Economics 35: 1153-1161.

Jütting J (1999). Strengthening Social Security Systems in Rural Areas of Developing Countries. Bonn: Centre for Development Research.

Jütting J (2004). Do community-based health insurance scheme improve poor people's access to health care? Evidence from rural Senegal. World Development 32: 273-288.

Kahneman D and Tversky A (1979). Prospect theory: an analysis of decision under risk. Econometrica 47: 263-291.

Kahneman D, Knetsch JL, and Thaler RH (1991). Anomalies: the endowment effect, loss aversion, and status quo bias. The Journal of Economic Perspectives 5: 193-206.

Kevane M and Wydick B (2001). Social norms and the time allocation of women's labor in Burkina Faso. Review of Development Economics 5: 119-129.

Kleinbaum DG and Klein M (2002). Logistic regression - A self-learning text. (second edition) New York: Springer.

Kivumbi GW and Kintu F (2002). Exemptions and waivers from cost sharing: ineffective safety nets in decentralized districts in Uganda. Health Policy and Planning 17 (supplement 1): 64-71.

Korte R, Richter H, Merkle F, and Gorgen H (1992). Financing health services in Sub-Saharan Africa: options for decision makers during adjustment. Social Science and Medicine 34: 1-9.

Kouyaté B, Sanon M, and Mugisha F (2001). Community preference for a benefit package under community-based insurance. SFB Discussion Papers. Heidelberg: University of Heidelberg.

Krause G and Sauerborn R (2000). Comprehensive community effectiveness of health care. A study of malaria treatment in children and adults in rural Burkina Faso. Annals of Tropical Paediatrics 20: 273-282.

Kynast-Wolf G, Sankoh OA, Stieglbauer G, Kouyaté B, Yé Y, Gbangou A, Sanou A, Würthwein R, Sauerborn R, and Becher H (2001). Mortality in a rural region in sub-Saharan Africa - Results from a Demographic Surveillance System in Nouna, Burkina Faso. SFB Discussion Paper. Heidelberg: University of Heidelberg.

La Concertation (2004). Inventaire des mutuelles de santé en Afrique - Synthèse des travaux de recherche dans les 11 Pays. Dakar, Senegal: La Concertation.

Lawrance, EC (1991). Poverty and the rate of time preference: evidence from panel data. Journal of Political Economy 99: 54-77.

Leighton C (1995). Overview: health financing reforms in Africa. Health Policy and Planning 10: 213-222.

Leighton C and Diop F (1995). Protecting the poor in Africa: impact of means testing on equity in the health sector in Burkina Faso, Niger, and Senegal. Technical Note No. 40. Bethesda, MD: Abt Associates, Inc.

Litvack JI and Bodart C (1993). User fees plus quality equals improved access to health care: results of a field experiment in Cameroon. Social Science and Medicine 37: 369-383.

Litva A, Coast J, Donovan J, Eyles J, Shepherd M, Tacchi J, Abelson J, and Morgan K (2002). 'The public is too subjective': public involvement at different levels of health-care decision making. Social Science and Medicine 54: 1825-1837.

Liu TC and Chen CS (2002). An analysis of private health insurance purchasing decisions with national health insurance in Taiwan. Social Science and Medicine 55: 755-774.

Magadi MA, Madise NJ, and Rodrigues RN (2000). Frequency and timing of antenatal care in Kenya: explaining the variations between women of different communities. Social Science and Medicine 51: 551-561.

Makinen M, Waters H, Rauch M, Almagambetova N, Bitran R, Gilson L, McIntyre D, Pannarunothai S, Prieto AL, Ubilla G, and Ram S (2000). Inequalities in health care use and expenditures: empirical data from eight developing countries and countries in transition. Bulletin of the World Health Organisation 78: 55-65.

Maier B, Görgen R, Kielmann AA, Diesfeld HJ, and Korte R (1994). Assessment of the district health system using qualitative methods. London: The MacMillan Press Ltd.

Mariko M and Cisse B (2000). Equité dans l'accès aux soins de santé: cas de 5 capitales ouest africaines. Project Santé Urbaine financed by the French Cooperation and by UNICEF. Abidjan, Cote d'Ivoire: UNICEF.

Marquis MS and Long SH (1995). Worker demand for health insurance in the non-group market. Journal of Health Economics 14: 47-63.

Marquis MS and Holmer MR (1996). Alternative models of choice under uncertainty and demand for health insurance. The Review of Economics and Statistics 78: 421-427.

Martinez C, Rietbrock S, Wise L, Ashby D, Chick J, Moseley J, Evans S, and Gunnell D (2005). Antidepressant treatment and the risk of fatal and non-fatal self harm in first episode depression: nested case-control study. British Medical Journal 330: 389-393.

Mauny F, Viel JF, Handschumacher P, and Sellin B (2004). Multilevel modelling and malaria: a new method for an old disease. International Journal of Epidemiology 33: 1337-1344.

McCall N, Driver S, Bauer E, and Knickman J (1997). The partnership for long-term care: who are the partnership policy purchasers? Medical Care Research Review 54: 472-489.

McCall N, Mangle S, Bauer E, and Knickman J (1998). Factors important in the purchase of partnership long-term care insurance. Health Service Research 33: 187-203.

McPake B (1993). User charges for health services in developing countries: a review of the economic literature. Social Science and Medicine 36: 1397-1405.

McPake B, Hanson K, and Mills A (1993). Community financing of health care in Africa: an evaluation of the Bamako initiative. Social Science and Medicine 36: 1383-1395.

Mechanic D (1998). The functions and limitations of trust in the provision of medical care. Journal of Health Politics, Policy and Law 23: 661-686.

Meekers D and Rahaim S (2005). The importance of socio-economic context for social marketing models for improving reproductive health: evidence from 555 years of program experience. BMC Public Health 5: 10. Available from URL: http://www.biomedcentral.com/content/pdf/1471-2458-5-10.pdf (accessed on June 1st, 2005).

Meessen B, Criel B, and Kegels G (2002). Formal pooling of health risks in sub-Saharan Africa: reflections on the obstacles encountered. International Social Security Review 55: 71-93.

Meessen B, Zhenzhong Z, Van Damme W, Devadasan N, Criel B, and Bloom G (2003). Iatrogenic poverty. Tropical Medicine and International Health 8: 581-584.

Microsoft Corporation (2002). Microsoft Access Software. Microsoft Corporation.

Ministry of Health of Ghana (2003). The proposed national health insurance programme. Ghana: Annual Health Sector Review 2002.

Moens F (1990). Design, implementation, and evaluation of a community financing scheme for hospital care in developing countries: a pre-paid health plan in the Bwamanda health zone, Zaire. Social Science and Medicine 30: 1319-1327.

Morduch J (1995). Income smoothing and consumption smoothing. The Journal of Economic Perspectives 9: 103-114.

Mugisha F, Kouyaté B, Dong H, and Sauerborn R (2002a). Costing health care interventions at primary health facilities in Nouna, Burkina Faso. African Journal of Health Sciences 9: 63-73.

Mugisha F, Kouyaté B, Gbangou A, and Sauerborn R (2002b). Examining out-of-pocket expenditure on health care in Nouna, Burkina Faso: implications for health policy. Tropical Medicine and International Health 7: 187-196.

Musau SN (1999). Community-based health insurance: experiences and lessons learned from East and Southern Africa. Bethesda, MD: Partnerships for Health Reform Project, Abt Associates Inc.

Nabyonga J, Desmet M, Karamagi H, Kadama P, Omaswa F, and Walker O (2005). Abolition of cost-sharing is pro-poor: evidence from Uganda. Health Policy and Planning 20: 100-108.

Nyman JA (1999). The value of health insurance: the access motive. Journal of Health Economics 18: 141-152.

Oberlander L and Elverdan B (2000). Malaria in the United Republic of Tanzania: cultural considerations and health-seeking behaviour. Bulletin of the World Health Organisation 78: 1352-1357.

Osei-Akoto, I. (2004). Demand for voluntary health insurance by the poor in developing countries: evidence from rural Ghana Center for Development Research (ZEF), University of Bonn.

Palmer N, Mueller DH, Gilson L, Mills A, and Haines A (2004). Health financing to promote access in low income settings-how much do we know? Lancet 364: 1365-1370.

Patton MQ (1990). Qualitative evaluation and research methods (second edition). Newbury Park: Sage Publications, Inc.

Paulin GD and Dietz EM (1995). Health insurance coverage for families with children. Monthly Labor Review 8: 13-23.

Peters DH, Elmendorf AE, Kandola K, and Chellaraj G (2000). Benchmarks for health expenditures, services and outcomes in Africa during the 1990s. Bulletin of the World Health Organisation 78: 761-769.

Phelps CE (1973). Demand for health insurance: a theoretical and empirical investigation. Santa Monica, CA: RAND Corporation.

Platteau JP (1997). Mutual Insurance as an elusive concept in traditional rural communities. The Journal of Development Studies 33: 764-796.

Pokhrel S (2004). Role of price, income, and gender on the demand for child health care in Nepal. Doctoral thesis. Faculty of Medicine. University of Heidelberg.

Pokhrel S, Snow R, Dong H, Hidayat B, Flessa S, and Sauerborn R (2005). Gender role and child health care utilisation in Nepal. Health Policy. In press.

Preker AS, Carrin G, Dror D, Jakab M, Hsiao W, and Arhin-Tenkorang D (2002a). Effectiveness of community health financing in meeting the cost of illness. Bulletin of the World Health Organisation 80: 143-150.

Preker AS, Langenbrunner J, and Jakab M (2002b). Rich-poor differences in health care financing. In Dror DM and Preker AS (Eds.): Social Re Insurance (pp. 21-36). Washington: The World Bank.

Preker AS, Carrin G, Dror DM, Jakab M, Hsiao W, and Arhin-Tenkorang D. (2004). Rich-poor differences in health care financing. In Preker AS and Carrin G (Eds.): Health financing for poor people - Resource mobilization and risk sharing (pp. 3-52). Washington: The World Bank.

Propper C (1989). An econometric analysis of the demand for private health insurance in England and Wales. Applied Economics 21: 777-792.

Propper C (1993). Constrained choice sets in the UK demand for private medical insurance. Journal of Public Economics 51: 287-307.

Propper C, Rees H, and Green K (1999). The demand for private medical insurance in the UK: a cohort analysis. Bristol: CMPO - University of Bristol.

Raberg M and Jeene H (2002). Selling out rights. How policy affects access to health services in East and Central Africa. London: Save the Children Fund.

Ranson MK (2004). The SEWA Medical Insurance Fund in India. In Preker AS and Carrin G (Eds.): Health financing for poor people - Resource mobilization and risk sharing (pp. 275-292). Washington: The World Bank.

Rashid SF, Hadi A, Afsana K, and Begum SA (2001). Acute respiratory infections in rural Bangladesh: cultural understandings, practices and the role of mothers and community health workers. Tropical Medicine and International Health 6: 249-255.

Reerink IH and Sauerborn R (1996). Quality of primary health care in developing countries: recent experiences and future directions. International Journal of Quality in Health Care 8: 131-139.

Rhine SL and Ng YC (1998). The effect of employment status on private health insurance coverage: 1977 and 1987. Health Economics 7: 63-79.

Richardson JG (1986). Handbook of theory and research for the sociology of education (first edition). New York: Greenwood Press.

Ridde V (2003). Fees-for-services, cost-recovery, and equity in a district of Burkina Faso operating the Bamako Initiative. Bulletin of the World Health Organisation 81: 532-538.

Robbins D (2005). The origins, early development and status of Bordieu's concept of "cultural capital". The British Journal of Sociology 56: 13-30.

Ron A (1999). NGOs in community health insurance schemes: examples from Guatemala and the Philippines. Social Science and Medicine 48: 939-950.

Rosner B (2000). Fundamentals of Biostatistics (fifth edition). Pacific Grove, CA: Duxbury Press.

Ross NA, Wolfson MC, Dunn JR, Berthelot J, Kaplan GA, and Lynch JW (2000). Relation between income inequality and mortality in Canada and in the United States: cross sectional assessment using census data and virtual statistics. British Medical Journal 320: 898-902.

Rothman KJ and Greenland S (1998). Modern Epidemiology. Second edition. Philadelphia: Lippincott - Raven.

Russell S (1996). Ability to pay for health care: concepts and evidence. Health Policy and Planning 11: 219-237.

Russell S (2004). The economic burden of illness for households in developing countries: a review of studies focusing on malaria, tuberculosis, and human immunodeficiency virus/acquired immunodeficiency syndrome. American Journal of Tropical Medicine and Hygiene 71: 147-155.

Ryan M, Scott DA, Reeves C, Bate A, van Teijlingen ER, Russell EM, Napper M, and Robb CM (2001). Eliciting public preferences for healthcare: a systematic review of techniques. Health Technology Assessment 5: 1-186.

Sachs J (2001). Macroeconomics and health: investing in health for economic development Geneva: World Health Organisation.

Sachs J and Malaney P (2002). The economic and social burden of malaria. Nature 415: 680-685.

Salkeld G, Ryan M, and Short L (2000). The veil of experience: do consumers prefer what they know best? Health Economics 9: 267-270.

Samuelsen H (2004). Illness transmission and proximity: local theories of causation among the Bissa in Burkina Faso. Medical Anthropology 23: 89-112.

Samuelson W and Zeckhauser R (1998). Status quo bias in decision making. Journal of Risk and Uncertainty 1: 7-59.

Sarker M, Milkowski A, Slanger T, Gondos A, Sanou A, Kouyaté B, and Snow R (2005). The role of HIV related knowledge and ethnicity in determining HIV risk perception and willingness to undergo HIV testing among rural women in Burkina Faso. AIDS and Behavior. In press.

Sauerborn R (1994). Household strategies to cope with the economic cost of illness - a community based study in Burkina Faso. Doctoral Dissertation. School of Public Health, University of Harvard.

Sauerborn R, Nougtara A, and Latimer E (1994). The elasticity of demand for health care in Burkina Faso: differences across age and income groups. Health Policy and Planning 9: 185-192.

Sauerborn, R., Ibrango, I., Nougtara, A., Borchert, M., Hien, M., Benzler, J. et al. (1995). The economic costs of illness for rural households in Burkina Faso. Tropical Medicine and Parasitology 46: 54-60.

Sauerborn R, Adams A, and Hien M (1996a). Household strategies to cope with the economic costs of illness. Social Science and Medicine 43: 291-301.

Sauerborn R, Berman P, and Nougtara A (1996b). Age bias, but no gender bias, in the intra-household resource allocation for health care in rural Burkina Faso. Health Transition Review 6: 131-145.

Sauerborn R, Nougtara A, Hien M, and Diesfeld HJ (1996c). Seasonal variations of household costs of illness in Burkina Faso. Social Science and Medicine 43: 281-290.

Schneider P (2004). Why should the poor insure? Theories of decision-making in the context of health insurance. Health Policy and Planning 19: 349-355.

Schneider P and Diop F (2004). Community-based health insurance in Rwanda. In Preker AS and Carrin G (Eds.): Health financing for poor people - Resource mobilization and risk sharing (pp. 251-274). Washington: The World Bank.

Schoemaker PJH (1982). The expected utility model: its variants, purposes, evidence and limitations. Journal of Economic Literature 20: 529-563.

Secretariat General du Ministère de la Santé du Burkina Faso (2000a). Plan Triennal 2001-2003. Ouagadougou: Ministry of Health of Burkina Faso.

Secretariat General du Ministère de la Santé du Burkina Faso (2000b). Projet de Document de Politique Sanitaire National. Ouagadougou: Ministry of Health of Burkina Faso.

Secretariat General du Ministère de la Santé du Burkina Faso. (2002). Annuaire statistique de la santé. Ouagadougou: Ministry of Health of Burkina Faso.

Sekhri N and Savedoff W (2005). Private health insurance: implications for developing countries. Bulletin of the World Health Organisation 83: 127-134.

Sekwat A. (2003). Health financing reform in sub-Saharan Africa: major constraints, goals, and strategies. Journal of Health Care Finance 29: 67-78.

Sepehri A, Chernomas R, and Akram-Lodhi H (2005). Penalizing patients and rewarding providers: user charges and health care utilization in Vietnam. Health Policy and Planning 20: 90-99.

Shea DG and Stewart RP (1995). Demand for insurance by elderly persons: private purchases and employer provision. Health Economics 4: 315-326.

Shepard DS and Benjamin ER (1988). User fees and health financing in developing countries: mobilizing financial resources for health. In Bell DE and Reich MR (Eds.): Health, nutrition, and economic crises: approaches to policy in the third world (pp. 401-424). Dover, Massachusetts: Auburn House.

Shmueli A (1998). Supplemental health insurance ownership in Israel: an empirical analysis and some implications. Social Science and Medicine 46: 821-829.

Smith RD (1996). Is regret theory an alternative basis for estimating the value of healthcare interventions? Health Policy 37: 105-115.

Sommerfeld J, Sanon M, Kouyaté B, and Sauerborn R (2002a). Informal risk-sharing arrangements (IRSAs) in rural Burkina Faso: lessons for the development of community-based insurance (CBI). International Journal of Health Planning and Management 17: 147-163.

Sommerfeld J, Sanon M, Kouyaté B, and Sauerborn R (2002b). Perceptions of risk, vulnerability, and disease prevention in rural Burkina Faso: implications for community-based care and insurance. Human Organization 61: 139-146.

Soucat A, Levy-Bruhl D, Gbedonou P, Drame K, Lamarque JP, Diallo S, Osseni R, Adovohekpe P, Ortiz C, Debeugny C, and Knippenberg R (1997). Local cost sharing in Bamako Initiative systems in Benin and Guinea: assuring the financial viability of primary health care. International Journal of Health Planning and Management 12 (Supplement 1):S109-35.

StataCorp (2003). Stata Statistical Software (version 8.1). College Station Texas: Stata Corporation.

Steindorf K, Schmidt M, Kropp S, and Chang-Claude J (2003). Case-control study of physical activity and breast cancer risk among pre-menopausal women in Germany. American Journal of Epidemiology 157: 121-130.

Stierle F, Kaddar M, Tchicaya A, and Schmidt-Ehry B (1999). Indigence and access to health care in sub-Saharan Africa. International Journal of Health Planning and Management 14: 81-105.

Strauss AL (1987). Qualitative analysis for social scientists. Cambridge: Cambridge University Press.

Su T and Flessa S (2005a). Annual household cost-of-illness and its determinants in Nouna Health District, Burkina Faso. Submitted.

Su T, Kouyaté B, and Flessa S (2005b). Catastrophic household expenditure for health care in a low-income society: a study from Nouna Health District, Burkina Faso. Bulletin of the World Health Organisation. In press.

Tabor SR (2005). Community-based health insurance and social protection policy. Washington: The World Bank.

Task Force on Establishment of Mandatory National Social Health Insurance (2005). National social health insurance strategy. Nairobi: Ministry of Health of Kenya.

The Health Insurance Association of America (2001). Health insurance nuts and bolts - An introduction to health insurance operations. Washington: The Health Insurance Association of America.

The Scientific Software Development (2003). ATLAS.ti - Visual qualitative data analysis software (version 5.0). Berlin: The Scientific Software Development.

The World Bank (2001). World Development Report 2000-2001 - Attacking poverty. Washington: The Word Bank.

Townsend RM (1995). Consumption insurance: an evaluation of risk-bearing systems in low income economies. The Journal of Economic Perspectives 9: 83-102.

Tversky A and Kahneman D (1992). Advances in prospect theory: cumulative representation of uncertainty. Journal of Risk and Uncertainty 5: 297-323.

United Nations Development Program (2005). Human Development Report. United Nations Development Program. Available from URL:

http://hdr.undp.org/statistics/data/cty/cty_f_BFA.htm (accessed on May 1st, 2005).

van Ginneken W (1996). Social security for the informal sector: issues, options, and tasks ahead. Geneva: International Labour Organisation.

Veenstra G (2005). Location, location, location: contextual and compositional health effects of social capital in British Columbia, Canada. Social Science and Medicine 60: 2059-2071.

Vogel RJ (1993). Financing health care in sub-Saharan Africa. Westport: Greenwood Press.

Waddington C and Enyimayew K (1989). A price to pay. Part 1: the impact of user charges in Ashanti-Akim district, Ghana. International Journal of Health Planning and Management 4: 17-47.

Waddington C and Enyimayew K (1990). A price to pay. Part 2: the impact of user charges in the Volta region of Ghana. International Journal of Health Planning and Management 5: 287 - 312.

Waelkens MP and Criel B (2004). Les mutuelles de santé en Afrique sub-Saharienne - Etat des lieux et reflexions sur un agenda de recherche. Health, nutrition and population discussion paper. Washington: The World Bank.

Wagstaff A, Paci P, and Joshi H (2001). Causes of inequality in health: who you are? Where you live? Or who your parents are? Washington: The World Bank.

Wagstaff A (2002). Poverty and health sector inequalities. Bulletin of the World Health Organisation 80: 97-105.

Wagstaff A and van Doorslaer E (2003). Catastrophe and impoverishment in paying for health care: with applications to Vietnam 1993-1998. Health Economics 12: 921-934.

Weinberger K (2000). Women's participation: an economic analysis in rural Chad and Pakistan. Frankfurt am Main: Peter Lang GmbH.

Wiesmann D and Jütting J (2000). The emerging movement of community based health insurance in sub-Saharan Africa: experiences and lessons learned. Afrika Spectrum 35.

Wiesmann D and Jütting J (2001). Determinants of viable health insurance schemes in sub-Saharan Africa. Quarterly Journal of International Agriculture 40: 361-378.

Wilcox-Gok V and Rubin, J (1994). Health insurance coverage among the elderly. Social Science and Medicine 38: 1521-1529.

Williams P (1994). The use of community-based household data for improved health planning in the Gambia. Banjul: Ministry of Health and Social Welfare of the Gambia.

Willis CY and Leighton C (1995). Protecting the poor under cost recovery: the role of means testing. Health Policy and Planning 10: 241-256.

Wladarsch E (2003). "Patience is the Future". Cultural conceptions of time and their manifestation in health-related time preferences in Rural Burkina Faso. An Interdisciplinary Approach Between Anthropology and Public Health. Doctoral Dissertation. Faculty of Ethnography, University of Heidelberg.

Wolfe JR and Goddeeris JH (1991). Adverse selection, moral hazard, and wealth effects in the Medigap insurance market. Journal of Health Economics 10: 433-459.

World Health Organisation (2000a). World Health Report 2000 - Health systems: improving performance. Geneva: World Health Organisation.

World Health Organization. (2000b). WHO Health System Profiles Database - Country Burkina Faso. Geneva: World Health Organisation.

World Health Organisation (2001). World Health Report 2001 - Mental health: new understanding, new hope. Geneva: World Health Organisation.

Würthwein R, Gbangou A, Kouyaté B, Mugisha F, Yé Y, Becher H, Schmidt CM, and Sauerborn R (2001). The Nouna Health District Household Survey - Design and Implementation. SFB Discussion Papers. Heidelberg: University of Heidelberg.

Xu K, Evans DB, Kawabata K, Zeramdini R, Klavus J, and Murray CJ (2003). Household catastrophic health expenditure: a multicountry analysis. Lancet 362: 111-117.

Xu B, Fochsen G, Xiu Y, Thorson A, Kemp JR, and Jiang, QW (2004). Perceptions and experiences of health care seeking and access to TB care - a qualitative study in Rural Jiangsu Province, China. Health Policy 69: 139-149.

Zio B (2001). Rapport sur l'étude de faisabilité institutionnelle d'une assurance maladie a base communautaire (AMBC) dans l'aire du District Sanitaire de Nouna (DSN). Nouna, Burkina Faso: Centre de Recherche en Santé de Nouna.

6. Appendices

Appendix A: The Nouna Health District Household Survey

Appendix B: Interview guide (in-depth interviews)

Appendix C: Additional data collection tool (in-depth interviews)

Appendix D: Complete list of codes used for qualitative analysis

Appendix E: Test for sensitivity of quadrature estimator

Appendix F: Basic socio-demographic characteristics of the 32 respondents (in-depth interviews)

MODULE 1: SOCIO-ECONOMIE DES MÉNAGES

Village |__|__| **Nom et Prénoms du Chef du Ménage** ____________________ **IDM** |__|__| |__|__|__| |__|

Date de visite |__|__| |__|__| |__|__|__|__|**Nom et prénoms de l'enquêteur** ____________________ **Code** |__|__|__|

Section 1 : Animaux et biens et du ménage

1.1 Animaux

Combien de têtes d'animaux et de volaille chaque membre de votre ménage possède-t-il actuellement ?

Rang	Nom et Prénom	Membre possède animaux ou volaille ? OUI/NON	Volaille	Moutons	Chèvres	Bœufs	Anes	Porcs	Cheval
1	2	3	4	5	6	7	8	9	10
|__|__|		|__|__||__|	|__|__|	|__|__|	|__|__|	|__|__|	|__|	|__|__|	|__|
|__|__|		|__|__||__|	|__|__|	|__|__|	|__|__|	|__|__|	|__|	|__|__|	|__|
|__|__|		|__|__||__|	|__|__|	|__|__|	|__|__|	|__|__|	|__|	|__|__|	|__|
|__|__|		|__|__||__|	|__|__|	|__|__|	|__|__|	|__|__|	|__|	|__|__|	|__|
|__|__|		|__|__||__|	|__|__|	|__|__|	|__|__|	|__|__|	|__|	|__|__|	|__|

1.2 Biens du ménage

Demandez à **chaque** membre du ménage s'il possède des biens comme donné dans la grille donnée ci-dessous

Rang	Nom et Prénom	Membre possède quelque chose Oui / Non	Charrettes	Charrues	Vélos	Mobylettes	Motos	Voitures	Radios	TV	Téléphone	Frigo	Cuisinière moderne	Autre
1	2	3	4	5	6	7	8	9	10	11	12	13	14	15

Section 2 : Revenues du ménage

2.1 Production agricole pendant la campagne passée (2003/2004)

Posez la question suivante à chaque membre actif de 10 ans et plus du ménage: au cours de la campagne agricole passée avez-vous cultivé les produits agricoles que je vous lis maintenant ? (Voir le manuel pour la liste des codes)

Rang	Nom et Prénom	Cultivé quelque chose ? Oui / Non	Produit agricole	Quantités	Unité de mesure
1	2	3	4	5	6
|_|_|		|_|_|_|	|_|_|_|	|_|_|_|	|_|_|_|
|_|_|		|_|_|_|	|_|_|_|	|_|_|_|	|_|_|_|
|_|_|		|_|_|_|	|_|_|_|	|_|_|_|	|_|_|_|
|_|_|		|_|_|_|	|_|_|_|	|_|_|_|	|_|_|_|
|_|_|		|_|_|_|	|_|_|_|	|_|_|_|	|_|_|_|
|_|_|		|_|_|_|	|_|_|_|	|_|_|_|	|_|_|_|
|_|_|		|_|_|_|	|_|_|_|	|_|_|_|	|_|_|_|
|_|_|		|_|_|_|	|_|_|_|	|_|_|_|	|_|_|_|
|_|_|		|_|_|_|	|_|_|_|	|_|_|_|	|_|_|_|
|_|_|		|_|_|_|	|_|_|_|	|_|_|_|	|_|_|_|

2.2 Revenues monétaires par vente des produits agro-pastoraux

Enquêteurs attention: Le montant de la colonne 6 n'est pas le produit de la colonne 5 par 5. Il s'agit des montants réels perçus par chaque membre pour chacun des 5 derniers mois, qui ont précédé le mois passé (d'octobre 2003 à mai 2004). Expliquez-le très bien à chaque répondant. (Voir le manuel pour la liste des codes)

Rang	Nom et Prénom	Avez-vous vendu des produits agro-pastoraux?	Lesquels?	Montant du mois passé	Montant des 5 mois précédents le mois passés
1	2	3	4	5	6

2.3 Transferts et versements

Demandez à chaque membre du ménage: avez-vous reçu de l'argent de l'une des sources et destiné à des utilisations que je vous lis maintenant? (Voir le manuel pour la liste des codes)

Rang	Nom et Prénom	Reçu de l'argent ? Oui / Non	Montant du mois passé	Montant des 5 mois précédents le mois passé	Source	Utilisation
1	2	3	4	5	6	7

2.4 Revenues monétaires

Posez la question suivante à chaque membre du ménage de 10 ans et plus: Avez-vous des revenues monétaires telles que je vous lis maintenant? A l'exclusion de ce que nous venons de voir ci-dessus: revenues agricoles, transferts, et versements. (Voir le manuel pour la liste des codes)

Rang	Nom et Prénom	Revenue monétaire? Oui / Non	Montant du mois passé	Montant des 5 mois précédents le mois passé	Source
1	2	3	4	5	6

Section 3: Dépenses du ménage

Demandez à chaque membre du ménage: avez-vous dépensé de l'argent pour l'une des raisons que je vous lis maintenant ? (Voir le manuel pour la liste des codes)

Rang	Nom et Prénom	Dépenses ?	Mois passé		5 mois précédents le mois passé	
			Motif de la dépense	Montant	Motif de la dépense	Montant
1	2	3	4	5	6	7

MODULE 2: MORBIDITE ET DEMANDE DE SOINS

Village |__|__| **Nom et Prénoms du Chef du Ménage** ____________________ **IDM** |__|__||__|__|__||__|

Date de visite |__|__||__|__||__|__|__|__|**Nom et prénom de l'enquêteur** ____________________ **Code** |__|__|__|

Section 1: Inventaire des handicaps

Demandez aux membres du ménage qui ont déclaré avoir un handicap (Col.25 questionnaire mère) la nature du handicap qu'ils ont s'il n'est pas visible (Voir le manuel pour la liste des codes)

Rang	Nom et Prénom	N° handicap	Quel handicap avez-vous?	Quelle était la cause du handicap?	Qui vous l'a dit?	Date de début du handicap	Limitations
1	2	3	4	5	6	7	8
|__|__|		|__|	|__|__|__|	|__|__|__|	|__|__|__|	|__|__||__|__||__|__|	|__|
|__|__|		|__|	|__|__|__|	|__|__|__|	|__|__|__|	|__|__||__|__||__|__|	|__|
|__|__|		|__|	|__|__|__|	|__|__|__|	|__|__|__|	|__|__||__|__||__|__|	|__|
|__|__|		|__|	|__|__|__|	|__|__|__|	|__|__|__|	|__|__||__|__||__|__|	|__|
|__|__|		|__|	|__|__|__|	|__|__|__|	|__|__|__|	|__|__||__|__||__|__|	|__|

Section 2: Inventaire des maladies chroniques (maladies qu'on a au mois depuis plus de 3 mois)

Demandez aux membres du ménage à propos de leurs maladies chroniques (Voir le manuel pour la liste des codes)

Rang	Nom et prénom	Avez vous une maladie chronique?	De quelle maladie chronique s'agit-il ?	Code maladie	Qui vous l'a dit?	Date de début de la maladie	Date de fin de la maladie	Limita -tion	Prenez vous des médicam ents pour éviter des crises ?	Qualité traite -ment	Dépense médicament
1	2	3	4	5	6	7	8	9	10	11	12

Section 2: Crises / épisodes des maladies chroniques (Voir le manuel pour la liste des codes)

Rang	Nom et Prénom	Questions sur les crises / épisodes des maladies chroniques						
		Code de la maladie	S'est-elle manifesté au cours des 30 derniers jours	N° épisode de la maladie chronique	Symptoms	Date de début	Episode terminé	Date de fin
1	2	13	14	15	16	17	18	19

Section 3: Inventaire des maladies aiguës dans les 30 derniers jours

A part les maladies dont on vient de parler, avez-vous eu des maladies de courte durée le mois passé ? (Voir le manuel pour la liste des codes)

Rang	Nom et Prénom	N° épisode de la maladie	Quelle maladie avez-vous?	Code maladie	Qui vous l'a dit?	Symptômes	Date de début	Episode terminé	Date de fin	Limi -tations
1	2	3	4	5	6	7	8	9	10	11

Section 4: Sévérité du problème de santé et ce qu'on a fait face au problème (Voir le manuel pour la liste des codes)

Rang	Nom et Prénoms	Type de maladie	Code de la maladie/ handicap	N^{o} épisode/ problème de santé	Ce problème de santé a menacé votre vie ?	Quel est son degré de sévérité?	Constitué un problème sociale?	Empêché de travailler?	Empêché d'aller à l'école ?	Combien de temps? (J,S,M,A)
1	2	3	4	5	6	7	8	9	10	11

Section 4: Sévérité du problème de santé et ce qu'on a fait face au problème (suite)

Rang	Nom et Prénoms	Pendant votre maladie, quelqu'un de votre ménage s'est occupé de vous ?	Cela lui a t-il empêché de travailler ?	Arrangement de travail	Avez-vous eu des dépenses pour des traitements, des médicaments, le transport etc.?	Comment vous êtes vous arrangés pour faire face à ces dépenses?	Est-ce que quelqu'un n'a pas du tout pu aller à l'école à cause de votre maladie?	Pendant combien de temps est-ce qu'il n'est pas allé à l'école? (H,J)	Pourquoi il n'a pas pu aller à l'école?
1	2	12	13	14	15	16	17	18	19
				1e 2e 3e		1e 2e 3e			
				1e 2e 3e		1e 2e 3e			
				1e 2e 3e		1e 2e 3e			
				1e 2e 3e		1e 2e 3e			
				1e 2e 3e		1e 2e 3e			
				1e 2e 3e		1e 2e 3e			

Section 5: Demande de soins (Voir le manuel pour la liste de codes)

Rang	Nom et Prénoms	Type de maladie	Code de la maladie	N° épisode / problème de santé	Avez-vous traité la maladie d'une manière ou d'une autre ?	Durée entre le début de la maladie et la 1ère recherche des soins ?
1	2	3	4	5	6	7
└─┴─┘		└─┘	└─┴─┴─┘	└─┘	└─┴─┴─┘	└─┴─┘└─┘
└─┴─┘		└─┘	└─┴─┴─┘	└─┘	└─┴─┴─┘	└─┴─┘└─┘
└─┴─┘		└─┘	└─┴─┴─┘	└─┘	└─┴─┴─┘	└─┴─┘└─┘
└─┴─┘		└─┘	└─┴─┴─┘	└─┘	└─┴─┴─┘	└─┴─┘└─┘
└─┴─┘		└─┘	└─┴─┴─┘	└─┘	└─┴─┴─┘	└─┴─┘└─┘
└─┴─┘		└─┘	└─┴─┴─┘	└─┘	└─┴─┴─┘	└─┴─┘└─┘
└─┴─┘		└─┘	└─┴─┴─┘	└─┘	└─┴─┴─┘	└─┴─┘└─┘
└─┴─┘		└─┘	└─┴─┴─┘	└─┘	└─┴─┴─┘	└─┴─┘└─┘
└─┴─┘		└─┘	└─┴─┴─┘	└─┘	└─┴─┴─┘	└─┴─┘└─┘

Section 5: Demande de soins (suite)

Rang	Nom et Prénoms	Qui a soigné votre maladie?			C'était ou?			Pourquoi ce choix ?			Pourquoi n'avez-vous pas traité la maladie ?
		1ère fois	2ème fois	3ème fois	1ère fois	2ème fois	3ème fois	1ère fois	2ème fois	3ème fois	
1	2	8	9	10	11	12	13	14	15	16	17

Section 5: Demande de soins (suite)

Rang	Nom et Prénom	Qualité du traitement			Dépenses pour le transport			Durée du voyage		
		1ère fois	2ème fois	3ème fois	1ère fois	2ème fois	3ème fois	1ère fois	2ème fois	3ème fois
1	2	18	19	20	21	22	23	24	25	26

Section 5: Demande de soins (suite)

Rang	Nom et Prénom	Dépenses frais de séjour			Dépenses services rendus			Dépenses médicaments/ matériels		
		1ère fois	2ème fois	3ème fois	1ère fois	2ème fois	3ème fois	1ère fois	2ème fois	3ème fois
1	2	27	28	29	30	31	32	33	34	35

Section 5: Demande de soins (suite)

Rang	Nom et Prénom	Autres dépenses			Succès du traitement			Avez-vous été hospitalisé pour cette maladie ? Si oui, combien de temps ? (J,S,M)	Où avez-vous été hospitalisé?	Combien avez-vous payé pour cette hospitalisation?
		1ère fois	2ème fois	3ème fois	1ère fois	2ème fois	3ème fois			
1	2	36	37	38	39	40	41	42	43	44

Section 6: Assistants du malade

Durant la maladie du répondant, est-ce que quelqu'un du ménage l'a assisté ? Si oui, remplissez la grille ci-après (voir le manuel pour la liste des codes)

<table>
<tr><td>Rang

|__|__|</td><td>Nom et prénoms du malade
____
Type maladie |__|
Code maladie |__|__|__|</td><td>N° épisode

|__|__|</td><td></td><td>Rang

|__|__|</td><td>Nom et prénoms du malade
____
Type maladie |__|
Code maladie |__|__|__|</td><td>N° épisode

|__|__|</td></tr>
<tr><td>Rang</td><td>Nom et prénoms de l'assistant</td><td>Temps perdus (H,J,S)</td><td></td><td>Rang</td><td>Nom et prénoms de l'assistant</td><td>Temps perdus (H,J,S)</td></tr>
<tr><td>|__|__|</td><td></td><td>|__|__| |__|</td><td></td><td>|__|__|</td><td></td><td>|__|__| |__|</td></tr>
<tr><td>|__|__|</td><td></td><td>|__|__| |__|</td><td></td><td>|__|__|</td><td></td><td>|__|__| |__|</td></tr>
<tr><td>|__|__|</td><td></td><td>|__|__| |__|</td><td></td><td>|__|__|</td><td></td><td>|__|__| |__|</td></tr>
<tr><td>|__|__|</td><td></td><td>|__|__| |__|</td><td></td><td>|__|__|</td><td></td><td>|__|__| |__|</td></tr>
<tr><td>|__|__|</td><td></td><td>|__|__| |__|</td><td></td><td>|__|__|</td><td></td><td>|__|__| |__|</td></tr>
<tr><td>|__|__|</td><td></td><td>|__|__| |__|</td><td></td><td>|__|__|</td><td></td><td>|__|__| |__|</td></tr>
</table>

MODULE 3 : SOINS PRÉVENTIFS –MODULE REDUIT

Village |__|__| **Nom et Prénoms du Chef du Ménage** ______________________ **IDM** |__|__| |__|__|__| |__|

Date de visite |__|__| |__|__| |__|__|__|__| **Nom et prénom de l'enquêteur** ______________________ **Code** |__|__|__|

Section 1 : Utilisation des soins à appliquer à tous les membres du ménage (Voir le manuel pour la liste des codes)

Rang	Nom et Prénom	Durant les 12 derniers mois avez-vous visité un ou plusieurs centres de santé ?	Quel centre de santé avez-vous visité ?	C'était pour quelle raison?	Avez-vous eu des dépenses pour ces soins?	Si vous avez eu des dépenses, comment vous vous êtes arrangés pour y faire face?	Est-ce que vous utilisez des méthodes de planification familiale?	Si oui, quelle méthode utilisez-vous?
1	2	3	4	5	6	7	8	9
|__|__|		|__|__|__|	|__|__|__|	|__| |__|	|__|__|__|	|__|	|__|__|__|	|__|__|__|
|__|__|		|__|__|__|	|__|__|__|	|__| |__|	|__|__|__|	|__|	|__|__|__|	|__|__|__|
|__|__|		|__|__|__|	|__|__|__|	|__| |__|	|__|__|__|	|__|	|__|__|__|	|__|__|__|
|__|__|		|__|__|__|	|__|__|__|	|__| |__|	|__|__|__|	|__|	|__|__|__|	|__|__|__|
|__|__|		|__|__|__|	|__|__|__|	|__| |__|	|__|__|__|	|__|	|__|__|__|	|__|__|__|

MODULE 4: PARTAGE DE RISQUE, CONNAISSANCE DE L'ASSURANCE, PERCEPTION DE LA QUALITE' DE SOINS

Village |__|__| **Nom et Prénoms du Chef du Ménage** ______________________ **IDM** |__|__| |__|__|__| |__|

Date de visite |__|__| |__|__| |__|__|__|__| **Nom et prénom de l'enquêteur** ______________________ **Code** |__|__|__|

Section 1 : Inventaire de participation aux réseaux de solidarité – toute le module est à être administré seulement aux membre du ménage de 20 à 70 ans (Voir le manuel pour la liste des codes)

Rang	Nom et Prénom	Etes-vous membre d'un réseau de solidarité?	Si oui, nombre de réseaux de solidarité auxquels vous êtes membre	Quelle est l'activité la plus courante du réseau de solidarité ?	Code activité	Typologie du réseau de solidarité	Depuis quand êtes- vous membre du réseau de solidarité? (M,A)	Quelle est sa taille?	Quel est son rayon d'action?
1	2	3	4	5	6	7	8	9	10

Section 1 : Inventaire de participation aux réseaux de solidarité (suite)

Rang	Nom et Prénom	Y a t-il une prime d'adhésion au réseau?	Indiquez le montant de la prime	Indiquez la nature et le nombre		Y a t-il des cotisations fixés?	Indiquez le montant de la cotisation	Indiquez la nature et le nombre	
				Nature	Nombre			Nature	Nombre
1	2	11	12	13	14	15	16	17	18

Section 1 : Inventaire de participation aux réseaux de solidarité (suite)

Rang	Nom, prénom et ID	Fréquence de paiement de la cotisation	Si la cotisation est annuelle, indiquez la période de paiement des cotisations	Position occupée au sein du réseau de solidarité	Etes-vous encore membre du réseau de solidarité?	Si non, depuis quand n'êtes-vous plus membre du réseau (M,J)	Pour quelle raison n'êtes-plus membre du réseau?
1	2	19	20	21	22	23	24

Section 2: Connaissance de l'assurance et perceptions de la qualité des soins (Voir le manuel pour la liste des codes)

Rang	Nom et Prénom	Avez-vous déjà entendu parler d'assurance?	Si oui par quel canal?	Avez-vous déjà entendu parler d'une mutuelle de santé?	Si oui par quel canal?	Si un mutualiste ne tombe pas malade au cour de l'année, peut-il reprendre sa cotisation?	Si une telle mutuelle de santé est crée dans votre zone, allez-vous y adhérer?
1	2	3	4	5	6	7	8
|__|__|		|__|__|__|	|__|__|__|	|__|__|__|	|__|__|__|	|__|__|__|	|__|__|__|
|__|__|		|__|__|__|	|__|__|__|	|__|__|__|	|__|__|__|	|__|__|__|	|__|__|__|
|__|__|		|__|__|__|	|__|__|__|	|__|__|__|	|__|__|__|	|__|__|__|	|__|__|__|
|__|__|		|__|__|__|	|__|__|__|	|__|__|__|	|__|__|__|	|__|__|__|	|__|__|__|
|__|__|		|__|__|__|	|__|__|__|	|__|__|__|	|__|__|__|	|__|__|__|	|__|__|__|
|__|__|		|__|__|__|	|__|__|__|	|__|__|__|	|__|__|__|	|__|__|__|	|__|__|__|
|__|__|		|__|__|__|	|__|__|__|	|__|__|__|	|__|__|__|	|__|__|__|	|__|__|__|

Section 2: Connaissance de l'assurance et perceptions de la qualité des soins (suite)

Rang	Nom et Prénom	Sur une échelle de 1 à 6, évaluez la qualité de soin qu'une personne peut recevoir dans votre zone						
		Hopital de Nouna	CSPS de votre localité	Agents de santé villageois	Pharmacie privée	Clinique privée	Accoucheuse villageoise	Guérisseur traditionnel
1	2	9	10	11	12	13	14	15
□□		□	□	□	□	□	□	□
□□		□	□	□	□	□	□	□
□□		□	□	□	□	□	□	□
□□		□	□	□	□	□	□	□
□□		□	□	□	□	□	□	□
□□		□	□	□	□	□	□	□
□□		□	□	□	□	□	□	□
□□		□	□	□	□	□	□	□
□□		□	□	□	□	□	□	□

MODULE 5: ADHÉSION À L'ASSURANCE

Village |__|__| **Nom et Prénoms du Chef du Ménage** ____________________ **IDM** |__|__| |__|__|__| |__|

Date de visite |__|__| |__|__| |__|__|__|__| **Nom et prénom de l'enquêteur** ____________________ **Code** |__|__|__|

Module adhésion à l'assurance – ce module doit être administré uniquement au chef du ménage (Voir le manuel pour la liste des codes)

Rang	Nom et Prénom	Avez-vous déjà entendu parlé de l'AMBC dans le district sanitaire de Nouna	Si oui, par quel canal			Avez-vous adhéré à l'AMBC?
1	2	3	4			5
			1er	2eme	3eme	
|__|__|		|__|__|__|	|__|__|	|__|__|	|__|__|	|__|__|__|
|__|__|		|__|__|__|	|__|__|	|__|__|	|__|__|	|__|__|__|
|__|__|		|__|__|__|	|__|__|	|__|__|	|__|__|	|__|__|__|
|__|__|		|__|__|__|	|__|__|	|__|__|	|__|__|	|__|__|__|
|__|__|		|__|__|__|	|__|__|	|__|__|	|__|__|	|__|__|__|

Module adhésion à l'assurance (suite)

Rang	Nom et Prénom, ID	Si oui, comment avez-vous obtenu l'argent?	Si oui, pourquoi avez-vous choisie d'adhérer à l'AMBC?	Si oui, comment la décision a t-elle été prise?	Si non, pourquoi avez-vous choisie de ne pas adhérer à l'AMBC?	Si non, comment la décision de ne pas adhérer a t-elle été prise?
1	2	6 1er 2eme 3eme	7 1er 2eme	8 1er 2eme	9 1er 2eme	10 1er 2eme
└─┴─┘		└─┴─┘ └─┴─┘ └─┴─┘	└─┴─┘ └─┴─┘	└─┴─┘ └─┴─┘	└─┴─┘ └─┴─┘	└─┴─┘ └─┴─┘
└─┴─┘		└─┴─┘ └─┴─┘ └─┴─┘	└─┴─┘ └─┴─┘	└─┴─┘ └─┴─┘	└─┴─┘ └─┴─┘	└─┴─┘ └─┴─┘
└─┴─┘		└─┴─┘ └─┴─┘ └─┴─┘	└─┴─┘ └─┴─┘	└─┴─┘ └─┴─┘	└─┴─┘ └─┴─┘	└─┴─┘ └─┴─┘
└─┴─┘		└─┴─┘ └─┴─┘ └─┴─┘	└─┴─┘ └─┴─┘	└─┴─┘ └─┴─┘	└─┴─┘ └─┴─┘	└─┴─┘ └─┴─┘
└─┴─┘		└─┴─┘ └─┴─┘ └─┴─┘	└─┴─┘ └─┴─┘	└─┴─┘ └─┴─┘	└─┴─┘ └─┴─┘	└─┴─┘ └─┴─┘
└─┴─┘		└─┴─┘ └─┴─┘ └─┴─┘	└─┴─┘ └─┴─┘	└─┴─┘ └─┴─┘	└─┴─┘ └─┴─┘	└─┴─┘ └─┴─┘
└─┴─┘		└─┴─┘ └─┴─┘ └─┴─┘	└─┴─┘ └─┴─┘	└─┴─┘ └─┴─┘	└─┴─┘ └─┴─┘	└─┴─┘ └─┴─┘
└─┴─┘		└─┴─┘ └─┴─┘ └─┴─┘	└─┴─┘ └─┴─┘	└─┴─┘ └─┴─┘	└─┴─┘ └─┴─┘	└─┴─┘ └─┴─┘
└─┴─┘		└─┴─┘ └─┴─┘ └─┴─┘	└─┴─┘ └─┴─┘	└─┴─┘ └─┴─┘	└─┴─┘ └─┴─┘	└─┴─┘ └─┴─┘

Appendix B: Interview guide (in-depth interviews)

Introduction

Présentation :

Bonjour, nous nous appelons Manuela et Aline et nous sommes de gens du Centre de Recherche en Santé de Nouna. Comme vous savez, nous travaillons dans le cadre de projets de santé pour comprendre les stratégies que les ménages utilisent pour se soigner.

Explication du but de l'entrevue :

Notre recherche fait partie intégrante du travail que le Centre de Recherche en Santé fait dans la région. Présentement, nous sommes intéressés à est votre opinion à propos du projet d'assurance maladie à base communautaire. Le but est de savoir ce que les gens pensent à propos de ce projet, pour comprendre s'il peut vraiment être quelque chose d'utile et pour comprendre comment on peut améliorer sa mise en place. Nous sommes bien intéressés à votre opinion quoi que vous avez choisi de vous enregistrer ou pas dans l'AMBC. Il ne faut pas avoir peur d'exprimer votre opinion très librement. Nous ne jugeons pas ce que vous avez choisi de faire ou ce que vous nous dites.

Possibilité de refus :

On voudrait souligner que si vous préférez ne pas être interviewé, nous respectons votre choix parfaitement. Le ménage n'aurait aucun désavantage de votre refus.

Confidentialité

Tout ce que nous apprenons pendant cette interview est confidentiel. Nous n'en allons parler à personne dans le village ou ailleurs. Si on va parler du cas du ménage au niveau du service, nous n'allons pas utiliser votre nom ou le nombre d'identité de votre ménage.

Si vous acceptez, nous allons enregistrer nos paroles. Ceci nous évite de prendre des notes pendant la causerie pour ne pas oublier ce qui a été dit et pour pouvoir écouter ce que vous nous dites plusieurs fois. Retourné à Nouna, nous allons écrire toutes nos paroles dans un cahier.

Interview

Informations socio-démographiques et enregistrement dans l'AMBC :

On ouvre l'interview en demandant à la personne de nous décrire son ménage, sa taille et sa composition. On demande aussi à la personne si le ménage est enregistré dans l'AMBC et quand on a fait l'enregistrement. Dans le cas où le ménage soit dans l'AMBC, on demande à la personne de nous décrire où on a trouvé l'argent pour payer la prime.

Perception de la campagne de sensibilisation :

On invite la personne à décrire comment il/elle est venue à connaissance de l'AMBC. Si la personne a participé aux séances de sensibilisation dans le village, on lui demande de décrire et critiquer ces séances. On demande aussi à la personne si les représentants villageois et les leaders du village ont parlé de l'AMBC.

Quels sont les aspects de la campagne que les gens on bien aimé ? Quoi est-ce qu'il faudrait changer dans la prochaine campagne pour améliorer la connaissance de l'AMBC ?

Connaissance de l'AMBC :

On demande à la personne de nous décrire avec ses propre mots l'AMBC. On demande aussi de décrire le but et les modalités de fonctionnement de l'AMBC. On invite la personne à identifier les bénéficiers de la nouvelle initiative. Qui va profiter de l'AMBC ?

En particulier, on explore la compréhension du principe de « partage de risque ». Est-ce que la personne comprend que l'AMBC constitue un système de partage de risque ? Dans le cadre de cette discussion, on explore la perception de propriété de l'AMBC. A qui appartient l'AMBC ? On pose aussi des questions directes pour voir si la personne connaît et comprendre les différents éléments de l'AMBC (paquet de soins, système de gestion, unité d'enregistrement, etc.).

Dans le cadre de cette discussion, on invite la personne à exprimer son opinion à propos de la structure de gestion de l'AMBC. Est-ce que la personne aime le système de gestion qui a été mis en place ?

Participation à des autres systèmes de partage de risque :

On veut savoir si la personne fait partie d'autres réseaux de partage de risque. On veut aussi comprendre quelles différences et quelles similarités la personne voit entre l'AMBC et les autres systèmes de partage de risque dans sa communauté.

Dans le cadre de cette discussion, on invite la personne a décrire soit sa propre expérience au sein d'autres systèmes de partage de risque soit l'expérience collective dans le village.

On invite aussi la personne à décrire l'esprit de solidarité dans sa communauté. Est-ce que les gens s'aident les uns avec les autres ? Quoi est-ce qu'on fait quand il y a une nécessité de toute la communauté ? Est-ce que les gens travaillent ensemble souvent ?

Décision de s'enregistrer :

On veut comprendre comment on a pris la décision de s'enregistrer ou de ne pas s'enregistrer. Explorer le processus de décision à l'intérieur de la famille et de la communauté.

Il faut sonder les motivations qui ont encouragé la personne à s'enregistrer ou à ne pas s'enregistrer. Pourquoi est-ce que la personne a choix d'enregistrer ou de ne pas enregistrer son ménage ? D'abord, il faut laisser la personne libre d'exprimer ses opinions primaires. Après, il faut la solliciter à discuter ses opinions par rapport à chaque élément qui pourrait avoir encouragé ou découragé l'enregistrement (niveau de la prime, paquet de soins, unité d'enregistrement, modalité de payement, etc.). Quel est le rôle que chaque élément a joué pour encourager ou décourager l'enregistrement ? Quelle est l'opinion de la personne à propos de chaque élément de l'AMBC ?

On invite aussi la personne à discuter le problème d'enregistrement au niveau communautaire. Pourquoi est-ce que des autres ménages dans la communauté ont choisi de s'enregistrer ou de ne pas s'enregistrer ? Quoi est-ce qu'il faudrait faire pour faciliter l'enregistrement des gens ? Dans le cadre de cette discussion, on invite la personne à critiquer activement n'importe-quel élément de l'AMBC (niveau de la prime, paquet de soins, unité d'enregistrement, modalité de payement, etc.)

Confiance dans le système de gestion de l'AMBC :

On explore le niveau de confiance de la personne par rapport au système de gestion de l'AMBC. On invite la personne à exprimer soit sa propre opinion soit à discuter l'opinion des autres dans la communauté. On veut aussi explorer pourquoi les gens ont confiance ou ils n'ont pas confiance dans la nouvelle initiative.

Etat de santé et accès aux soins de santé :

On invite la personne à décrire l'expérience de maladie au sein de sa famille. On explore le comportement qu'on a tenu dans les cas de maladie et le comportement qu'on va tenir la prochaine fois qu'on tombe malade. On invite aussi les gens à motiver leurs choix. Pourquoi est-ce qu'on a choisi le traitement qu'on a choisi ?

Dans le cadre de cette discussion, on invite aussi la personne à exprimer ses opinions à propos de la qualité de soins de santé. On discute soit les soins des guérisseurs traditionnels soit les soins dans les structures du district sanitaire.

Croyances culturelles :

Il faut explorer avec la personne les croyances culturelles autour de l'épargne et de la maladie. On explore soit les croyances au niveau de toute la communauté soit l'expérience et les croyances individuelles. Est-ce qu'on a l'habite à épargner dans la communauté ? Comment on épargne ? Est-ce qu'il est acceptable dans la communauté d'épargner pour les soins de santé ?

Conclusion

On conclut l'interview en faisant un petit résumé de ce qu'a été dit. Ca est le moment pour clarifier tout ce que n'est pas encore claire. Si la personne n'a pas bien expliqué quelque chose, on peut retourner sur le sujet. Il faut aussi demander à la personne si elle veut exprimer une opinion qui n'a pas été touché pendant l'interview. A la fin, on remercie la personne et on lui souligne l'importance de son contribue. On lui demande aussi d'exprimer ses impressions à propos de l'interview. En concluant, on lui donne aussi l'opportunité de nous poser des questions libres.

Appendix C: Additional data collection tool (in-depth interviews)

Village:

Age :

Ethnie :

Religion :

Taille et composition du ménage : Adultes : Enfants :

Niveau d'instruction :

Date de enregistrement à l'AMBC:

Date interview :

Impressions générales à propos de l'interview.

1. Est-ce que la personne a été ouverte à répondre à toutes les questions ?

____

____

____

____

____

2. Quelles questions ont posé plus de difficulté ? Pourquoi ?

____

____

____

____

____

3. Décrivez l'environnent de l'interview. Est-ce qu'on a eu des interruptions ? Des distractions ?

____

____

____

____

____

4. Est-ce que la personne interviewée a été satisfaite de l'interview ? Quels comments est-ce qu'elle a donnés ?

___

___

___

___

___

5. Est-ce que la personne a dit quelque chose d'important dehors de l'interview ? Quoi est-ce que la personne a dit?

___

___

___

___

___

Appendix D: Complete list of codes used for qualitative analysis

The software Atlas.ti stores codes, as they are progressively created, in alphabetical order. In order to ease reading and comprehension, however, we have preferred to re-organise codes in meaningful broad categories. We provide a brief description of the codes which may not be self-explanatory.

Age:
- below 40 years
- 41 to 60 years
- above 61 years

Sex
- Female
- Male

Ethnicity:
- Bwaba
- Dafing
- Mossi
- Peulh
- Samo

Religion:
- Animist
- Catholic
- Muslim

Marital status:
- monogamous
- polygamous
- single
- widow

Educational attainment:
- literate - can read and write in local language
- illiterate - cannot read and write at all
- secondary school
- post-secondary school
- Koranic school

Occupation:
- farmer/livestock keeper
- revenue generating activity
- salaried person

Socio-economic status:
- poor – below median income value
- rich – above median income value

Special role of respondent:
- rep of AMBC committee – representative of the local AMBC committee
- village *délégué*
- village elder/leader

Household characteristics:
- small household - household up to 6 people
- average household - household between 7 and 10 people
- above average household - household between 11 and 15 people
- extremely large household - households with 16 and more people
- even adult child ratio - at least one adult for every 2 children in the household
- uneven adult child ratio - less than one adult for every two children in household

Assigned health facility:
- Dara
- Lékuy
- Koro
- Toni
- Sono
- Nouna

Distance to facility:
- near facility – within 5 km from health facility
- far from facility - more than 5 km from health facility

Overall enrolment behaviour in village:
- low enrolment - village with enrolment rate below 4%
- average enrolment - village with enrolment rate between 4 and 10%
- high enrolment - village with enrolment rate above 10%
- délégué enrolled
- délégué not enrolled

- community leaders enrolled
- community leaders not enrolled

Enrolment status & behaviour:
- in AMBC
- not in AMBC
- premium payment - how was money for the payment of the premium obtained
- early registration - registration in AMBC before March 5th
- late registration – registration in AMBC after March 5th

Decision-making process:
- decision sharing - how was decision to enrol reached within the household
- family consensus - no household consensus on enrolment could be found
- peer pressure – the individual was pressured to enrol by his/her peers
- self peer pressure – the individual pressured his peers to enrol

Source of knowledge on AMBC:
- *animateur villageois*
- CRSN staff (outside the feasibility study)
- family/neighbours
- feasibility study
- radio
- AMBC staff/sensitisation campaign
- health providers
- local AMBC representatives

Knowledge of AMBC and its elements:
- knowledge level - statements on overall knowledge of AMBC
- knowledge of benefit package
- knowledge of care modalities
- knowledge of enrolment unit
- knowledge of management structures
- knowledge of money keeping
- knowledge of ownership
- knowledge of P & MF – statements on knowledge of premium & fees
- knowledge of payment modalities
- knowledge of risk sharing & pre-payment

Social constructions of AMBC:
- AMBC & other risk sharing – comparison between AMBC and other risk-sharing arrangements

- AMBC as aid - statements framing AMBC as an aid
- AMBC as Ton - statements framing AMBC as a *tontine*, a *groupement*, an association
- AMBC benefit - statements expressing the perceived benefits of AMBC
- AMBC drugs - statements expressing AMBC benefit in relation to drugs
- AMBC *wariko* – statements expressing AMBC benefit as "burden alleviation"
- AMBC return on investment - statements expressing AMBC benefit as the relationship between the premium paid and the return on such premium
- disease vs. service discourse - statements framing benefit package as the inclusion/exclusion of diseases rather than services
- link AMBC to CRSN – statements identifying a link between AMBC and the CRSN
- link AMBC to providers – statements identifying a link between AMBC and the providers
- old taxes – comparison between AMBC and old French taxes
- other insurance – comparison between AMBC and other insurance schemes
- risk sharing – statements conceptualising risk-sharing
- pooling – statements conceptualising pooling

Immediate reasons motivating non-enrolment:
- education discourse - statements framing the lack of education/cultural capital
- lack of access to credit
- lack of means
- large household
- lack of understanding
- "sit and wait" attitude

Preferences for AMBC elements (statements indicating how attractive people judged the single components of the AMBC & their suggestions for change):
- comments on benefit package
- comments on sensitisation campaign
- comments on care modalities – statements on gate-keeping & assigned facility
- comments on AMBC: general
- comments on distance
- comments on enrolment unit
- comments on management structure
- comments on money keeping
- comments on P & MF - statements on premium and membership fee
- comments on payment modalities
- comments on quality of care

Health status and health care seeking behaviour:
- disease experience - statements describing household health status & disease experience
- healthcare seeking behaviour - statements describing what people do when sick
- cost of illness - statements on how much is spent for care
- illness coping – statements describing how money for care is gathered
- future health seeking behaviour - statements on care seeking behaviour after enrolment

Solidarity & integration:
- individual integration - statements describing individual integration in community
- social conditions - statements describing village/town sector solidarity attitudes

Saving practices:
- saving - statements describing saving habits and how is saving spent
- saving for illness - statements looking at the relationship between saving and illness

Trust & scepticism:
- scepticism - statements describing or hinting at scepticism
- trust - statements describing trust in AMBC and its management
- providers' talk – statements describing providers counter-sensitisation

Appendix E: Test for sensitivity of the quadrature estimation

Variables	Fitted quadrature[1]		
	12 points	*8 points*	*16 points*
Sex			
Male	-0.02042168	-0.02042168	-0.02042168
Ethnicity			
Bwaba	0.72362282	0.72362282	0.72362282
Education			
Primary school	1.3519015	1.3519015	1.3519015
Secondary school	2.0084501	2.0084501	2.0084501
Age in years			
41 to 60	0.18916592	0.18916592	0.18916592
61+	0.16929864	0.16929864	0.16929864
Occupation			
Non-farmer	-0.13431121	-0.13431121	-0.13431121
Rating of healer's care			
"non-adequate"	2.5917259	2.5917259	2.5917259
Socio-economic status			
2nd quartile	1.2355731	1.2355731	1.2355731
3rd quartile	1.2436349	1.2436349	1.2436349
4th quartile	2.0371403	2.0371403	2.0371403
Kids/adults ratio			
> 1	0.56799032	0.56799032	0.56799032
Chronic diseases			
At least one	0.02532794	0.02532794	0.02532794
Use of curative care			
At least one contact	0.24692221	0.24692221	0.24692221
Use of preventive care			
At least one contact	0.32213516	0.32213516	0.32213516
Distance to health facility			
Far (> 5 km)	1.5073437	1.5073437	1.5073437
Referral facility			
Any CSPS	-0.97022953	-0.97022953	-0.97022953
Wealth equality			
Middle level of equality	0.21925022	0.21925022	0.21925022
High level of equality	2.0200089	2.0200089	2.0200089
Participation in other risk-sharing			
Middle level of participation	-0.20710082	-0.20710082	-0.20710082
High level of participation	0.43730402	0.43730402	0.43730402
Log-likelihood	-193.33686	-193.33686	-193.33686
constant	-5.9409702	-5.9409702	-5.9409702

[1] Numbers indicate coefficients

Appendix F: Basic socio-demographic characteristics of the 32 interviewees

Interview	AMBC status	Distance to facility	Socio-economic status	Sex	Age	Marital status	Ethnicity	Education	Occupation	Household size
1	not enrolled	> 5 km	above median income	M	52	polygamous	Peulh	no schooling	farmer	16
2	enrolled	> 5 km	above median income	M	64	monogamous	Peulh	no schooling	farmer	7
3	enrolled	< 5 km	below median income	M	37	monogamous	Dafing	primary school	farmer	10
4	not enrolled	< 5 km	above median income	M	41	polygamous	Dafing	primary school	farmer	12
5	enrolled	< 5 km	below median income	F	54	widow	Bwaba	no schooling	dolo maker	4
6	not enrolled	< 5 km	below median income	F	56	widow	Bwaba	no schooling	farmer	3
7	not enrolled	> 5 km	above median income	M	41	monogamous	Dafing	no schooling	farmer	5
8	enrolled	> 5 km	below median income	M	44	monogamous	Dafing	no schooling	farmer	5
9	not enrolled	> 5 km	below median income	M	39	monogamous	Dafing	no schooling	farmer	8
10	enrolled	> 5 km	above median income	M	69	polygamous	Dafing	no schooling	farmer	13

11	not enrolled	> 5 km	above median income	M	49	polygamous	Dafing	no schooling	farmer	12
12	enrolled	> 5 km	above median income	M	40	polygamous	Dafing	no schooling	farmer	17
13	not enrolled	> 5 km	above median income	F	42	single	Dafing	no schooling	dolo maker	8
14	not enrolled	> 5 km	below median income	M	36	monogamous	Dafing	no schooling	farmer	12
15	not enrolled	> 5 km	below median income	F	49	widow	Bwaba	no schooling	hair dresser	1
16	enrolled	> 5 km	below median income	M	42	polygamous	Dafing	primary school	farmer	10
17	not enrolled	< 5 km	above median income	M	39	polygamous	Dafing	no schooling	farmer	9
18	enrolled	< 5km	above median income	M	53	polygamous	Dafing	primary school	farmer	10
19	not enrolled	< 5 km	above median income	M	72	polygamous	Mossi	no schooling	farmer	31
20	enrolled	< 5 km	above median income	M	41	polygamous	Samo	primary school	trader	14
21	enrolled	< 5 km	below median income	M	61	monogamous	Mossi	no schooling	farmer	4
22	not enrolled	< 5 km	below median income	M	43	monogamous	Samo	primary school	farmer	8

23	enrolled	< 5 km	below median income	M	42	monogamous	Bwaba	secondary school	civil servant	6
24	not enrolled	< 5 km	below median income	M	31	monogamous	Samo	no schooling	farmer	10
25	not enrolled	< 5 km	above median income	M	70	monogamous	Samo	no schooling	farmer	11
26	enrolled	< 5 km	above median income	F	40	monogamous	Samo	secondary school	civil servant	5
27	not enrolled	< 5 km	below median income	F	54	widow	Samo	no schooling	cook	8
28	enrolled	< 5 km	above median income	M	33	monogamous	Dafing	secondary school	civil servant	15
29	enrolled	> 5 km	above median income	F	32	single	Bwaba	primary school	farmer	7
30	not enrolled	> 5 km	below median income	M	49	monogamous	Bwaba	no schooling	farmer	7
31	enrolled	> 5 km	below median income	M	30	monogamous	Bwaba	no schooling	farmer	4
32	enrolled	> 5 km	below median income	F	23	single	Bwaba	no schooling	cook	3

Medizin in Entwicklungsländern

Editor: Prof. Hans Jochen Diesfeld

Band 1 Wolfgang Bichmann: Die Problematik der Gesundheitsplanung in Entwicklungsländern. Ein Beitrag zur Geschichte, der Situation und den Perspektiven der Planung des nationalen Gesundheitswesens in den > Least Developed Countries < Afrikas. 1979.

Band 2 Jens Herrmann: Ambition and Reality - Planning for Health and Basic Health Services in the Yemen Arab Republic. 1979.

Band 3 J.M. Pönninghaus: The Cost Benefit of Measles Immunisation. A Study from Southern Zambia. 1979.

Band 4 Hilde Wander (Hrsg.): Bedingungen und Möglichkeiten der Integrierung bevölkerungspolitischer Programme in die nationale und die internationale Entwicklungspolitik. 1980.

Band 5 M. Heidegger/H.J. Diesfeld/A. Selheim: Demographische und soziale Wirkungen von Familienplanung. 1980.

Band 6 H.J. Diesfeld (Hrsg.): Importierte Krankheiten und ärztliche Untersuchungen vor und nach Tropenaufenthalt. Kongreßbericht über die X. Tagung der Deutschen Tropenmedizinischen Gesellschaft vom 22.-24. März 1979 in Heidelberg. 1980.

Band 7 Alexander Boroffka: Benedict Nta Tanka's Commentary and Dramatized Ideas on "Disease and Witchcraft in our Society". A Schreber Case from Cameroon Annotated Autobiographical Notes by an African on his Mental Illness. 1980.

Band 8 Hartmut Brandt: Work Capacity Restraints in Tropical Agricultural Development. 1980.

Band 9 nicht erschienen

Band 10 Tilman Nitzschke / Donata von Lüttwitz: Annehmbarkeit präventiver und promotiver Maßnahmen eines Health Centre für die Bevölkerung. Dargestellt am Beispiel der ländlichen Gesundheitsversorgung der Vereinigten Republik Kamerun. 1981.

Band 11 H.J. Diesfeld (Ed.): Health Research in Developing Countries. Proceedings of the Joint Meeting of the Belgische Vereniging voor Tropische Geneeskunde, Societé Belge de Medecine Tropicale, the Nederlandse Vereniging voor Tropische Geneeskunde and the Deutsche Tropenmedizinische Gesellschaft. 1982.

Band 12 Axel Kroeger/Francoise Barbira-Freedman: Cultural Change and Health: The Case of Southamerican Rainforest Indians. With special reference to the Shuar/Achuar of Ecuador. 1982.

Band 13 Dorothea Sich: Mutterschaft und Geburt im Kulturwandel. Ein Beitrag zur transkulturellen Gesundheitsforschung aus Korea. 1982.

Band 14 Uwe K. Brinkmann: Onchozerkose in Westafrika. 1982.

Band 15 Peter Oberender/Hans Jochen Diesfeld/Wolfgang Gitter (Hrsg.): Health and Development in Africa. International, Interdisciplinary Symposium, 2-4 June 1982, University of Bayreuth. 1983.

Band 16 Josef Boch (Hrsg.): Tropenmedizin, Parasitologie, Trypanosomiasis, Malaria, Bilharziose, Onchozerkose, Importierte Virusinfektionen, Lepra, Intermediate Technology, Zecken und durch sie übertragene Krankheiten, Immundiagnostik. 1984.

Band 17 Abdin Hamid Shaddad: Anforderungen an Gesundheitseinrichtungen der Basisversorgung im Sudan. Ein Beitrag zur Gesundheitsversorgung und zu baulichen Maßnahmen für die Gesundheitseinrichtungen unter besonderer Berücksichtigung der vorhandenen Ressourcen, der sozialen Verhältnisse und der klimatischen Bedingungen. 1984.

Band 18 Gerhard Heller: Krankheitskonzepte und Krankheitssymptome. Eine empirische Untersuchung bei den Tamang von Cautara/Nepal zur Frage der kulturspezifischen Prägung von Krankheitserleben. 1985.

Band 19 Hans-Jochen Diesfeld / Sigrid Wolter (Hrsg.): Medizin in Entwicklungsländern. Handbuch zur praxisorientierten Vorbereitung für medizinische Entwicklungshelfer. 5. neubearbeitete Auflage. 1989.

Band 20 Verena Kücholl: Soziokulturelle Wege des Heilens. Eine ethnomedizinische Analyse und Interpretation des Samkhya und der Heiltradition der Navajo. 1985.

Band 21 Frank-Peter Schelp (Ed.): Health Problems in Asia and in the Federal Republic of Germany. How to solve them? Proceedings of a seminar on "Techniques and Problems of Intervention Trials in Developing and Developed Countries". 1985.

Band 22 Rolf Heinmüller, Winfried Kern: Primäre Gesundheitsversorgung im südwestlichen Sudan. Eine Feldforschung bei den südsudanesischen Azande zur Evaluierung der Einflüsse des 'Primary Health Care'-Programms auf gesundheitliche Lage und allgemeine Lebensbedingungen. Detailed English Summary. 1987.

Band 23 Andreas Hahold/Axel Kroeger: Krankheitsbewältigung im Andenhochland Perus. Ergebnisse einer Bevölkerungsbefragung. 1986.

Band 24 Georg Kamm / Peter Witton / Hatibu Lweno: Anaesthesia Notebook for Medical Auxilaries. With special Reference to Anaesthesia Practice in Developing Countries. 1989.

Band 25 Alice S. Kuhn: Heiler und ihre Patienten auf dem Dach der Welt. Ladakh aus ethnomedizinischer Sicht. 1988.

Band 26 Wolfgang Bichmann: Community Involvement in Nepal's Health System. A case study of district health services management and the Community Health Leader scheme in Kaski district. 1989.

Band 27 M. Luisa Vázquez / Renate Lipowsky / Axel Kroeger: Malaria und kutane Leishmaniase in Kolumbien. Vorkommen, Volkskonzepte und traditionelle Behandlungsformen. 1989.

Band 28 Heinrich Berg / Axel Kroeger / Carmen Perez-Samaniego / Fernando Malo: Kranke Menschen – krankes Gesundheitswesen? Eine epidemiologische Untersuchung in Nord-Mexiko. 1989.

Band 29 Emmie Ho-Tsui / Margit Urhahn: Medizin und Gesundheitsforschung in Entwicklungsländern. Bibliographie des Instituts für Tropenhygiene 1984-1988. 1991.

Band 30 Thomas Lux: Gespräche mit afrikanischen Krankenpflegern und Heilern. Bilder von Krankheit im Mikrokosmos von Malanville(Benin), 1991.

Band 31 Christopher Knauth: Arzneimittelgebrauch armer Bevölkerungsschichten in städtischen Elendsvierteln Perus. Möglichkeiten und Grenzen der Gesundheitserziehung zum rationalen Arzneimittelgebrauch. 1991.

Band 32 Erhard Hinz: Geomedizinische und biogeographische Aspekte der Krankheitsverbreitung und Gesundheitsversorgung in Industrie- und Entwicklungsländern. 1991.

Band 33 Klaus Hoffmann: Psychiatrie in Afrika. Eine Einführung für Entwicklungshelfer. 1992.

Band 34 Dorothea Sich / Hans Jochen Diesfeld / Angelika Deigner / Monika Habermann (Hrsg.): Medizin und Kultur. Eine Propädeutik für Studierende der Medizin und der Ethnologie mit 4 Seminaren in Kulturvergleichender Medizinischer Anthropologie (KMA). 1993. 2., unveränd. Aufl. 1995.

Band 35 Annette Wiemann-Michaels: Die verhexte Speise. Eine ethnopsychosomatische Studie über das Depressive Syndrom in Nepal. 1994.

Band 36 Christine Loytved: Hebammen in Ozeanien zwischen traditioneller und westlicher Medizin. Weiterbildung traditioneller Hebammen in Westsamoa und Tonga. 1994.

Band 37 Andrea Materlik: Medizinisch-anthropologische Aspekte von Lepra im Amazonas und ihre Bedeutung für die Gesundheitserziehung. 1994.

Band 38 Oliver Razum: Improving Service Quality through Action Research, as applied in the Expanded Programme on Immunization (EPI). 1994.

Band 39 Ulrich Schramm: Einflußfaktoren auf die Akzeptanz von baulichen Anlagen der ländlichen Gesundheitseinheiten in Ägypten. Fallstudie am Beispiel der staatlichen Einheit in Zebeda unter Verwendung der Post-Occupancy Evaluation. 1995.

Band 40 Rainer Sauerborn / Adrien Nougtara / Hans Jochen Diesfeld (Eds.): Recherche sur les systèmes de santé: Le cas de la zone médicale de Solenzo, Burkina Faso. Auteurs: Rainer Sauerborn, Adrien Nougtara, Hans Jochen Diesfeld, Gaston Sorgho, Joseph Bidiga, Lougousse Tiébélessé, Eric Latimer, Roberto Sallier de La Tour, Uwe Brinkmann, Don Shepard. 1995.

Band 41 Rainer Sauerborn / Adrien Nougtara / Hans Jochen Diesfeld (Eds.): Les Côuts Economiques de la Maladie pour les Ménages au Milieu Rural du Burkina Faso. Avec des contributions de Rainer Sauerborn, Adrien Nougtara, Maurice Hien, Issouf Ibrango, Matthias Borchert, Justus Benzler, Eberhard Koob, Hans Jochen Diesfeld. 1996.

Band 42 Erhard Hinz: Helminthiasen des Menschen in Thailand. 1996.

Band 43 Matthias Perleth: Historical Aspects of American Trypanosomiasis (Chagas' Disease). 1997.

Band 44 Christiane Fischer: Über die Effektivität der Dorfgesundheitsarbeiterinnen innerhalb der Nichtregierungsorganisation ACCORD in Tamil Nadu/Südindien. Aktionsforschung im Rahmen der Gesundheitssystemforschung. 1998.

Band 45 Maureen Dar lang: Assessment of antenatal and obstetric care services in a rural district of Nepal. 1999.

Band 46 Julia Katzan: *sòi mendan* – Die Sache mit dem Wasser... Eine medizinethnologische Untersuchung zum Zusammenhang von Wasser und Krankheit aus indigener Sicht. 2001.

Band 47 Catharina Will: Malaria-Selbstmedikation mit Chloroquin in einem hyperendemischen Gebiet (Mali). 2001.

Band 48 Ansgar Gerhardus: Entscheidungsprozesse im Gesundheitssektor. Der Beitrag der Theorie der politischen Ökonomie. 2001.

Band 49 Sylvie Schuster: Der Schwangerschaftsabbruch im Grasland Kameruns. Medizin, Kultur und Praxis. 2004.

Band 50 Sascha Klotzbücher: Das ländliche Gesundheitswesen der VR China. Strukturen – Akteure – Dynamik. 2006.

Challenges in Public Health

Herausgegeben von Prof. Dr. Oliver Razum

Band 51 Ulrich Ronellenfitsch: Cardiovascular Mortality among Ethnic German Immigrants from the Former Soviet Union. 2007.

Band 52 Manuela De Allegri: To Enrol or not to Enrol in Community Health Insurance. Case Study from Burkina Faso. 2007.

www.peterlang.de

Kolibri 360 GmbH
Ferdinand-Jühlke-Straße 7
99095 Erfurt, Deutschland
produktsicherheit@kolibri360.de

Druck:
CPI Druckdienstleistungen GmbH
im Auftrag der
Kolibri 360 GmbH
Ferdinand-Jühlke-Str. 7
99095 Erfurt